LIVING LIFE UNDAUNTED

D1056059

Also by Christine Caine

Undaunted

Undaunted video curriculum

LIVING LIFE UNDAUNTED

365 Readings
and Reflections
from Christine Caine

ZONDERVAN

Living Life Undaunted
Copyright © 2014 by Christine Caine

This title is also available as a Zondervan ebook. Visit www.zondervan.com/ebooks.

Requests for information should be addressed to:

Zondervan, *3900 Sparks Drive SE, Grand Rapids, Michigan 49546*

Library of Congress Cataloging-in-Publication Data

Caine, Christine.
Living life undaunted : 365 readings and reflections from Christine Caine. — First edition.
pages cm
ISBN 978-0-310-34141-3 (softcover)
1. Devotional calendars. I. Title.
BV4811.C335 2013
242'.2—dc23 2013041229

All Scripture quotations, unless otherwise indicated, are taken from The Holy Bible, *New International Version®, NIV®*. Copyright © 1973, 1978, 1984, 2011 by Biblica, Inc.® Used by permission. All rights reserved worldwide. Scripture quotations marked ASV are taken from the American Standard Version, copyright © 1901. Public domain. Scripture quotations marked ESV are taken from *The Holy Bible, English Standard Version*, copyright © 2001 by Crossway Bibles, a division of Good News Publishers. Used by permission. All rights reserved. Scripture quotations marked KJV are taken from the King James Version of the Bible. Scripture quotations marked MSG are taken from *The Message*. Copyright © 1993, 1994, 1995, 1996, 2000, 2001, 2002. Used by permission of NavPress Publishing Group. Scripture quotations marked NASB are taken from the *New American Standard Bible*. Copyright © 1960, 1962, 1963, 1968, 1971, 1972, 1973, 1975, 1977, 1995 by The Lockman Foundation. Used by permission. Scripture quotations marked NKJV are taken from the New King James Version. Copyright © 1982 by Thomas Nelson, Inc. Used by permission. All rights reserved. Scripture quotations marked NLT are taken from the *Holy Bible, New Living Translation*, copyright © 1996, 2004. Used by permission of Tyndale House Publishers, Inc., Wheaton, Illinois. All rights reserved.

Any Internet addresses (websites, blogs, etc.) and telephone numbers in this book are offered as a resource. They are not intended in any way to be or imply an endorsement by Zondervan, nor does Zondervan vouch for the content of these sites and numbers for the life of this book.

All rights reserved. No part of this publication may be reproduced, stored in a retrieval system, or transmitted in any form or by any means—electronic, mechanical, photocopy, recording, or any other—except for brief quotations in printed reviews, without the prior permission of the publisher.

Cover design: Studio Gearbox
Cover and interior photography: Thinkstock®
Interior design: Beth Shagene

Printed in the United States of America

---

14 15 16 17 18 19 20 /DCI/ 23 22 21 20 19 18 17 16 15 14 13 12 11 10 9 8 7 6 5 4 3 2 1

To The A21 Campaign Team:

You're truly living life UNDAUNTED,
and you inspire me to keep following Jesus
passionately into the future.

☼

Contents

I kneel before the Father, from whom every family in heaven and on earth derives its name. I pray that out of his glorious riches he may strengthen you with power through his Spirit in your inner being, so that Christ may dwell in your hearts through faith. And I pray that you, being rooted and established in love, may have power, together with all the Lord's holy people, to grasp how wide and long and high and deep is the love of Christ, and to know this love that surpasses knowledge—that you may be filled to the measure of all the fullness of God.

EPHESIANS 3:14–19

Introduction

☼

It's been said that we are shaped by our thoughts. If this is true, can you imagine where one healthy thought can lead each day?

Life is hectic and busy at times, but I've learned that one simple thought can center and align my heart for the day. I've used devotional readings to reset and recalibrate my mind each morning, and I believe they can do the same for you. As the Word of God has brought health, wholeness, healing, and life to this once very broken woman, I want you to know the same freedom that I have found.

If I were still broken, wounded, and rejected, I would have no power to preach goodness to the poor. If I had not found freedom, how could I shine a light for others to find theirs? If I were still brokenhearted because of my past, how could I help to heal someone else's broken heart? And if I were still in captivity, how could I possibly proclaim liberty to others? The same is true for you. No one is immune to the attacks of the enemy, but we all can be more than conquerors through Christ Jesus!

Living Life Undaunted is strategically laid out to walk through the four quarters of the year and can be started at any time. The first quarter lovingly confronts our own brokenness while trusting God in the process of healing. The second reveals God's unconditional love for us and helps us learn to become more like Christ. The third challenges us to seek wholeness as well as to reap a harvest in our own lives as we grow in faith. And the fourth calls us to minister to others, seek the lost, and make a difference in the world. We have been loved, rescued, healed, and restored so that we may live powerful, fruit-bearing lives.

I believe one year of healthy daily thoughts can reap a great spiritual harvest in our lives. So my prayer, as you read this book, is that you'll begin to live in the fullness for which you were created . . . that you'll live life UNDAUNTED!

With so much love,
Christine

BROKEN

January

WE ALL HAVE WOUNDS

January 1

It All Starts with a Choice

Choose life, so that you and your children may live and that you may love the LORD your God, listen to his voice, and hold fast to him. For the LORD is your life, and he will give you many years in the land.

DEUTERONOMY 30:19 – 20

None of us can change what we did or did not do in the year gone by, but we can put the past behind us and press forward. We can lay hold of the purpose of God in the year ahead.

In the coming year, we get to make all new choices. We get to make up our minds if we will live in:

- Regret land
- Wishful thinking land
- Fantasy land
- Shame land
- Guilt land
- Defeat land
- Negativity land
- Bitterness land
- Unforgiveness land
- Jealousy land
- Anger land
- Self-pity land

Or, we can deal with those thoughts, attitudes, habits, and behaviors that have been holding us back so that we can step into the promises of God and the purpose for which we were created. We can live full of faith, hope, love, joy, peace, and purpose by making a simple decision to choose life.

Believe me, it all starts with a choice.

The good news is that with Jesus we can have a fresh start today. We do not need to focus on what we have lost, what we have not done, what we are not. We can embrace all we are and can be in him. Nothing is irredeemable. It's never too late. We cannot change the past, but the choices we make today can change the future.

Make a decision to make this year count; God has something very special for each of us to do.

MOMENT OF REFLECTION

What land will you live in this coming year?

January 2

Completely Whole

"I will restore you to health and heal your wounds," declares the LORD, *"because you are called an outcast."*

JEREMIAH 30:17

Most of us have experienced hurt in one form or another. An overbearing boss crushes our spirit. An unfaithful spouse betrays our trust. Cruel friends trample our heart with spiteful words. Insensitive parents strip our confidence. Unthinking teachers call us stupid and tell us that we will never amount to anything, squashing our self-worth. Rebellious children stomp all over us. An abuser tries to take our soul. Whatever the source of attack, the hurt stings and the damage goes deep.

And, of course, we usually remember the exact moment of the damage—how the earth seemed to stop spinning, how the world came to a halt. We can't forget the sights, the smells, the song that was playing, what we wore, who else was there. These things freeze in memory, and a part of us freezes with them, forever stuck in that place, unable to move on. We may have been delivered from our situation, but we still aren't free.

That was true for me. For more than twelve years, I had been wounded by abuse. All that pain made me seal away a part of my heart and soul in what I thought was a safe, protected place. I desperately craved close relationships, but feared them too—because I never wanted to be hurt again. Though I was no longer in bondage to my abusers, I had shuttered my heart. I didn't trust anyone, not even God. I kept him at a distance by giving him my time, but not all of myself. I didn't trust him to take care of me. Nor could I forgive the men who hurt me, not even myself for being abused. Worse, I realized that I hadn't forgiven God. Where was he, after all, when I was a helpless child and those men laid hands on me? How could I compel others to love God with their whole hearts when I kept a part of my own from him?

Although I was shocked by this revelation, God was not. Since he knows everything, he knew that if I were to be truly free, I needed to deal with my wounds. He was able to heal me—but I had to choose that healing. I had to accept that I needed help. I had to reach out to God and others as part of the healing exercise of a whole heart.

MOMENT OF REFLECTION

What are the hurts in your life?
Have you dealt with them?

January 3

For Our Good

You intended to harm me, but God intended it for good to accomplish what is now being done, the saving of many lives.

GENESIS 50:20

The Bible tells us that Joseph was abused by his brothers, sold by them into slavery, and then repeatedly scarred and neglected by his enemies. But Joseph made an amazing discovery: anything meant in this world for evil, God can use for good. This is no less true for us today. God is able to take the messes of our past—our trials and our tests—and turn them into a testimony.

God's Word does not say that all things that happen to us *are* good, but it does say that God is able to work all things together *for* the good of those who love him and are called according to his purpose.

Very often, the thing the enemy uses to try to destroy our lives is the very thing God uses to help others. God can heal every hurt and turn our scars into signs of strength for his glory. Our past mistakes, hurts, and pain can help give someone else a future if we allow God to redeem them.

Joseph could have held on to anger, bitterness, unforgiveness, or resentment because of the way he was mistreated by his brothers. Instead, he chose to love and forgive them. This was the higher road, albeit the more difficult one. When he saw his brothers many years later, instead of taking revenge, he was able to save their lives and show that the very thing that was designed to destroy him and his destiny was actually the thing that God used to catapult him into it.

Joseph could have allowed his wounds and scars to stop him from fulfilling his purpose. Instead he allowed God to heal his hurts. Healing brings wholeness and wholeness unleashes destiny. It is healed people whom God can use to heal people.

MOMENT OF REFLECTION

Have you ever had anything happen to you that was unfair? Have you allowed God to heal you or are you limping through life with an open wound?

January 4

Spiritual Heart Attacks

Beloved, I pray that in all respects you may prosper and be in good health, just as your soul prospers.

3 JOHN 2 NASB

Unhealthy habits can often account for the breakdown of our physical bodies. For example, the most common causes of a physical heart attack are stress, a high-fat diet, smoking, high blood pressure, and lack of exercise. By eliminating these potentially harmful behavior patterns that lead to blockages in our arteries, we can prevent a heart attack from ever happening. The best cure is prevention.

The same is true in our spiritual lives. We cannot ignore those things that can create a blockage in our spiritual heart muscle, for eventually we will leave our first love and suffer a spiritual heart attack. Once that happens, we find our hearts no longer beat passionately for God or his purposes. Instead, we substitute formalism for faith and empty ritual for the life of the Spirit. In essence, by just going through the religious motions, we plug ourselves into an artificial life-support system. We mistakenly think we are alive when, in reality, we are only existing.

We were never created to settle for mere religion. Jesus did not die so that we could have a religious belief system—but rather a life-giving relationship with our Father.

I believe that as Christians we all possess a sincere desire to love God with all our hearts, yet we often unknowingly allow subtle deterrents to build up inside us. Slowly, these small obstructions form larger blockages, which over a period of time clog our spiritual arteries and harden our hearts by depriving them of access to their life source. We must do whatever it takes to ensure that these have no place in our lives as followers of Jesus.

MOMENT OF REFLECTION

Can you identify two thoughts or behaviors in your life that jeopardize your spiritual core? Why should these be given no place in your life?

January 5

Who Am I?

Give thanks to the God of heaven. His love endures forever.

PSALM 136:26

Some years ago, my mum disclosed that my brother and I were adopted. At first, I was shaken, but I wasn't shaken loose. Even as the underpinnings of my world were shifting radically, they were resettling in a more secure place. The truth of God's love was holding me together.

I knew God loved me, unquestionably, unconditionally, whether I was adopted or not. His love is relentless, unyielding, passionate, unfailing, perfect. A feeling of peace—supernatural peace—engulfed me. Everything was going to be okay. That may seem like an odd conclusion, in light of the fact that my life, or at least everything I'd thought I knew about my life, was unraveling before my eyes. Nevertheless, I felt undaunted because of an unchanging, never-failing truth: God was in control of my life.

I had memorized countless verses about God's love for me. I

desperately needed his love now more than ever, and when I read how he loved me, I soaked it up. I meditated upon those words, pondered and prayed over them. I found life in them. The words contained promises that excited me. Now those promises were holding me.

The truth we store up in silence comes back to us in the storm and lifts us away as on a life raft from the fears and disappointments that would otherwise pull us under. When we abide in his Word, he abides in us.

MOMENT OF REFLECTION

Do you know that you know that you know that God loves you?
How easily can your foundations crumble?

January 6

Sticks and Stones

The unfolding of your words gives light; it gives understanding to the simple.

PSALM 119:130

We can allow the names we call ourselves to define us. We can let the labels that others give us define us. After all, from the time we're born, and then throughout life, we're put in a box. We're defined by our family of origin, address, education, experience, bank account, credit rating, employer, friends, race, and ethnicity. We're called one thing after another: *poor, spoiled, uneducated, inexperienced, young, old, troublemaker, shy.* We can allow those words and labels to limit us. A teacher, parent, colleague, or ex can call us *loser, fat, ugly,* and *hopeless* —and those labels can stick, hurt, and damage us because we start to believe them.

Remember that old saying, "Sticks and stones can break my bones, but names can never hurt me"? That thought may help us keep a resilient will, but it's not true about the heart. We can be hurt plenty by labels like *stupid, ignorant, alcoholic, addict, criminal, weak, pitiful.* Names like these can break our spirits as much as physical sticks and stones can whack our bodies—especially if we believe them and begin to use them on ourselves. We can be brought to our knees, stopped in life before we even get started. Even when those names reveal something true about us, they are at best a partial truth —as well as a misleading one. If we allow those labels to loom larger in our hearts and minds than the promises of God, they can fool us into missing God's truth about who we are, into not pursuing the purpose God has had in mind for us from the beginning of time.

Our heads can insist that God created us and loves us, but our hearts and emotions may keep punching away at that knowledge with such thoughts as: "What's wrong with me? I never seem to do anything right!" Eventually, we feel an overwhelming sense of worthlessness and rejection, because that is what untruth does. It beats us down and knocks us out.

When there is a fight between my heart and my head, experience has taught me that the best thing to do is pick up my Bible and remind myself of what God says.

MOMENT OF REFLECTION

What are some of the labels that have been used to describe you? Scratch through all those labels and replace each one with something that God would use to describe you, such as loyal, kind, generous, caring, and devoted.

January 7

The Highest Value

But God demonstrates his own love for us in this: While we were still sinners, Christ died for us.

ROMANS 5:8

For many years I struggled with my worth and value primarily because I had been the victim of abuse from a very young age. I thought that there must have been something inherently wrong with me because people did unthinkable things to me. I must have been worthless because I was often treated like a worthless object instead of a valuable person.

Then I viewed a sermon illustration that profoundly affected me.

The speaker held up a brand-new, crisp $100 bill and asked the congregation if anyone wanted it. Of course, we all shouted that we did. The speaker then scrunched up the bill and jumped on it. He held it up again and asked who wanted it. Again, we shouted that we wanted it.

He then told us that the $100 bill had been stolen, used to buy drugs, and used to pay for sex with a prostitute. Then he asked if anyone still wanted it. Undaunted, the entire congregation immediately raised their hands. We all understood that the value of money was not determined by what it had experienced or even how it looked. Its value was determined by the Treasury Department that had printed the bill. The speaker then drew the parallel between our view of the $100 bill and God's view of a lost person.

That day, I truly began to understand that our value in God's eyes is not determined by our past, our achievements, our failures, or our circumstances. Rather, our value is determined by the love that God has for us. That value is expressed in the fact that Jesus died for every single one of us, in spite of our shortcomings. Jesus did not wait for us to get cleaned up before rescuing us. Even on our worst day, we are worth the blood of Jesus—and nothing is more valuable than that.

MOMENT OF REFLECTION

Take the general down to the specific by asking yourself, "How do I see value in other people?"

January 8

Where Were You?

The LORD is close to the brokenhearted and saves those who are crushed in spirit.

PSALM 34:18

I will never forget the day that my husband Nick and I spent with a dozen female victims of sex trafficking. Several of the women had told their stories and another, Sonia, had asked us a probing question: "Why are you here?"

I started to tell her about the amazing God who had sent me. "He is the one who made us, each of us, for a unique purpose and a magnificent destiny. He makes right what the world makes wrong. His plans are for good, not for evil. His ways are straight and merciful. He came to give me a hope and a future—and to give you one too. His promises are true. His love is full of forgiveness and peace, joy and kindness, grace. He saves us from any prison, whether physical or emotional or spiritual, the ones we're forced into and the ones we fall into on our own. He chooses us. He can make all things new. He loves us without condition, unrelentingly, forever. He loves us broken, and he loves making us whole again. And he asks those of us who love him to love others the same way. To be agents of his hope, his forgiveness, his grace.

"That's why I'm here," I said.

Sonia's eyes filled with tears. I could see her grappling with the concept of unconditional love, the meaning of grace, of all things being made new. All the "whys" and "hows" of what I'd said furrowed her brow. All the "what ifs" and possibilities had died in her long ago. Yet here I was, resurrecting them. "What if there are good people and true promises and a merciful God who loves me and chooses me and can lift me from the impoverishment, the betrayal and fear, the hurt and horror? What if . . ."

No! Sonia could not believe all this. It was too good to be true. The risk of allowing hope to reenter her life, only to see that hope dashed again, was too much. Her anguish returned to anger, and she pushed back from the table. "If what you are telling me is true," she yelled, "if what you say about your God is true—then where were you? Where have you been? Why didn't you come sooner?"

MOMENT OF REFLECTION

Have you ever asked why God had waited
so long to rescue you from a crisis situation in your life?
What did you learn from that situation?

January 9

It's All about Vision

Where there is no vision, the people perish.

PROVERBS 29:18 KJV

Experienced marathon runners will visualize their whole race—the entire 26.3 miles. Long-distance runners connect with the race internally, in their hearts, before ever setting foot on the course. While it is not possible for them to visualize every inch of the course in detail, they can mentally prepare for bends and curves, uphill and downhill stretches, times when they will want to slack off, and times of extreme fatigue when every inch of their bodies will want to stop. Runners prepare themselves mentally so these changes in the landscape and in their perspective will not catch them by surprise. The visualization process empowers them for what lies ahead.

We need to have that same overall sense of vision for every area of our lives. Having a clear picture of what the race of life is all about, where we are heading, and what we are likely to encounter along the way will sustain us for the duration. Keeping the end in sight will help us keep going when things get tough—when we are struggling over rough terrain or laboring up hills. Many people do not finish their race simply because they lack a long-term vision. At the first sign of opposition, difficulty, or adversity, they simply give up.

While having a vision for our lives is critical, it does not immunize us against the obstacles and pitfalls that will inevitably crop up. In life, things happen that we don't like. It's just a fact and there is nothing we can do about it. Jesus said, "I have told you these things, so that in me you may have peace. In this world you will have trouble. But take heart! I have overcome the world" (John 16:33).

Yes, trials will come in life, but we do not have to drop out of the race because of them. By maintaining our vision, we can stay on track. I have encountered many trials and challenges in my race thus far, and I'm sure there are many more ahead.

MOMENT OF REFLECTION

Are there areas in your life where you feel you have given up?
Try to identify the point when you gave up
so that you can renew your vision.

January 10

Heart Pain

He heals the brokenhearted and binds up their wounds.

PSALM 147:3

I had to tackle many challenges from my past in order to step into my God-given destiny. I was left in a hospital unnamed and unwanted when I was born and am living proof that no matter how you start in life, you can take charge of your life and run to win. We do not need to live like victims; rather we can appropriate the truth of the Word of God in every area of our lives and experience complete healing and wholeness.

If I had not allowed God's Word to bring healing into my life, I would not be fulfilling my destiny now. Despite having the God-given gifts and talents that I needed, I was so weak emotionally that my soul would not allow me to go where my gifts could take me. It was crucial that I dealt with all the areas of brokenness in my heart.

Our inner world totally affects our outer world. If there is a disparity between what's going on inside our hearts and what's happening in our external world, we will eventually implode; our lives will break down or blow up. The Bible is full of examples of people who did not run their race and finish their course because they did not deal with issues of their soul.

Ensure that you allow God to work deeply *in* you so that he is able to work powerfully *through* you.

MOMENT OF REFLECTION

Is your inner world affecting your outer world
in positive or negative ways?

January 11

The Heart of the King

Kish had a son named Saul, as handsome a young man as could be found anywhere in Israel, and he was a head taller than anyone else.

1 SAMUEL 9:2

Saul's outer world was in conflict with his inner world. His life held much promise that went wasted and unfulfilled and eventually ended in suicide.

When the people of Israel insisted that they wanted a king, God had the prophet Samuel anoint Saul, who was at that time a young, faithful man with an obedient heart. He had a good background and a striking appearance.

At first, Saul was humble and conscientious about his God-given role—but pride soon set in. Saul's pride turned to envy when a talented young man named David came on the scene. Saul feared David would steal his crown, and that fear soon deteriorated into anger and jealousy, which caused a deficit in his soul.

Saul could easily have cheered David on and rejoiced in his exploits—they were, after all, fighting for the same cause. But his longing for power and affirmation turned him bitter and led him to make many wrong decisions.

As we can see from the life of Saul, it is imperative that we deal with the broken, wounded, or undeveloped areas in our soul realm if we are going to run to win. We must also realize that this is an ongoing process—one that lasts a lifetime.

Some people say, "The past is the past. I dealt with that stuff years ago." But I would challenge everyone to consider this: Are we so healed that we don't need Jesus anymore? There are always areas that God wants to work on in our lives. Admitting that we need help doesn't imply a lack of faith. Some say, "By faith I am whole." I would agree, but I know that we must daily walk out the fullness of the healing that Jesus died to give us. The key is a constant and ongoing submission to the Holy Spirit as he ministers in our lives.

MOMENT OF REFLECTION

Are you ready to address the weaknesses in your soul and let God heal you? How will you begin?

January 12

Every Weight

Let us lay aside every weight, and the sin which so easily ensnares us, and let us run with endurance the race that is set before us.

HEBREWS 12:1 NKJV

The fact that the writer to the Hebrews tells us to lay aside "every weight" and "the sin which so easily ensnares" suggests to me that there is a difference between a "weight" and a "sin." In other words, if you are not running to your optimum capacity, it may not be because of some gross sin you are committing but because of an unnecessary "weight" that is holding you back.

For example, a "weight" in this context could be the fact that you consistently hang out with the wrong people. They may or may not be Christians, but for whatever reason, they are holding you back from aspiring to greater things in Christ. Perhaps they are feeding you with negativity and dragging you down to their level instead of encouraging you and building you up. It may sound a little harsh, but you need to shed some of that weight!

Maybe your "weight" is the fact that you have reached a plateau in your Christian life and don't know how to break through to the next level. For instance, you may be looking to God for a financial breakthrough. It could be that God is challenging you to actually give more and be stretched in your faith. If you know that God has spoken to you about this but you are holding back from doing it, this is a weight that is preventing you from progressing. It's not a sin, but it *is* a weight!

We need to continually look at our lives and see where we can shed weight, casting off any excess layers that are adding nothing to our racing gear and slowing us down. We need to keep ourselves streamlined and flexible in order to do what God calls us to do.

MOMENT OF REFLECTION

What weight is keeping you from moving forward in God's plan for your life?

January 13

First Be Healed

He was despised and rejected by mankind, a man of suffering, and familiar with pain. Like one from whom people hide their faces he was despised, and we held him in low esteem.

ISAIAH 53:3

It is unwise for runners to compete while suffering a stress fracture or a bad muscle sprain. But many Christians attempt to "run injured" in their spiritual lives. Many are carrying emotional and spiritual injuries from their past—unforgiveness, hurt, guilt, anger, shame, bitterness, pain, abuse, injustice—that they have not addressed.

We can never move on if we refuse to admit we are wounded. Some people in church can't submit to authority because of a flawed understanding of the true nature of fatherhood. Others won't fully commit to God because of abandonment issues. Still others won't give financially because they have a poverty mentality, perhaps from a poor background, and fear not having enough. Still others don't build healthy emotional attachments because of past abuse. And the list goes on.

As a young Christian, I had many emotional scars. Although they weren't immediately apparent from the outside, I knew these "fault lines" in my personality, left unaddressed, would eventually hinder me. I had to allow God to deal with those broken areas in my soul or there would be no way I could finish my course in life. Somewhere along the line, one of those injuries would have flared up and taken me out of the race.

We have to allow the Holy Spirit to do a deep work of healing and restoration in us. We must allow him to go into those wounded, broken places in our souls and mend them so we can run our race unhampered by injury.

MOMENT OF REFLECTION

Can you identify any wounds that you need to allow Jesus to heal?

January 14

Grace for the Past

In all these things we are more than conquerors through him who loved us.

ROMANS 8:37

By God's grace, I have not only conquered my past, but God is now using it to give hope to others who have been abused, marginalized, and oppressed. It would have been so easy for me to look at my life and become bitter, disillusioned, and crippled by emotional pain, which is what happens when we stay focused on yesterday.

I could have easily taken on the role of a victim and blamed everyone else for my condition. But Jesus came into my life and helped me see that I had a life beyond my past. It was this hope of a better future that gave me the strength and courage to work through the pain and hurt. Jesus did not want me to simply survive my past but to conquer it. Being more than a conqueror is about being victorious and helping others to win as well.

Sometimes in life, we have to look back to look forward. Addressing issues from our past that we would rather forget can be painful, but it is essential that we address such issues if we don't want them to trip us up in the future.

MOMENT OF REFLECTION

Are you struggling to forgive yourself for a past sin? What is it about this sin that makes you think it's unforgivable?

January 15

Second Chances

If we confess our sins, he is faithful and just and will forgive us our sins and purify us from all unrighteousness.

1 JOHN 1:9

One of the most important things to remember about running our race and finishing our course is that we all fail at times. Everyone stumbles and falls (unless of course we are perfect!). Some of us, however, make the mistake of not getting back up and continuing to run.

If we trip and fall in a race, we are not disqualified. We are only out of the race if we don't get back up and carry on! One of the greatest schemes of the enemy is to fool us into thinking that because we've fallen, we are no longer fit to run in God's race. That's just wrong! I've discovered that God's grace is a lot more expansive than most of us realize. God never gives up on us. He is the God of second chances, third chances, fourth chances, and so on. There is always another chance with God—at least on this side of eternity!

It would be foolish to think that there are no consequences for our actions in life; of course there are. But no matter what mistakes we have made, we can still finish our race. We may feel guilty and ashamed about things that we have done in the past, but that guilt and shame can be overcome if we bring our sins to Jesus and repent.

MOMENT OF REFLECTION

Do you feel that something you've done has taken you out of the race? What do you intend to do about it?

January 16

Forgiven

David said to Nathan, "I have sinned against the LORD." Nathan replied, "The LORD has taken away your sin."

2 SAMUEL 12:13

The story of King David shows us how even the godliest, most passionate believer in God can make a terrible mistake. And it also shows us that, though our actions have consequences, God's grace is sufficient to restore us and bring us to wholeness.

David is known in Scripture as "a man after God's own heart," but he got sloppy. It started with a lustful look and ended up with a national scandal. He committed adultery with a woman named Bathsheba and had her husband sent to the front lines of battle where he would surely be killed (and indeed he was)—all that so no one would stand in the way of their affair.

David was about fifty years old at the time. He had been ruling the nation successfully for almost twenty years and had distinguished himself as a man of God, a great musician, a poet, a writer, and a warrior. But David became complacent. The nation of Israel was at war, but instead of being where a king should be—out leading his troops and urging them to victory—he was kicking back instead. This sometimes happens to us. We are running our race, doing well, and then we begin to relax. We let down our spiritual guard and before we know it, we fall flat on our face.

David's adultery had terrible consequences. It led to murder and then God's judgment, which resulted in the death of David's baby son. At last David came to his senses and repented of his sin, asking God for forgiveness. In similar circumstances, many people would have thought to themselves, "It's all over for me now. I knew better, but I've destroyed my destiny in God." David didn't do that. He got back up, repented, accepted God's forgiveness, and finished his race. He suffered the consequences of his actions, but got back on course.

MOMENT OF REFLECTION

How does it make you feel to know that God is ready to forgive you and make you whole once again?

January 17

Beautiful and Smart

Yet to all who did receive him, to those who believed in his name, he gave the right to become children of God.

JOHN 1:12

My daughter Catherine knows who she is and has no problem displaying it! Soon after she started school at age five, she had an argument with a boy from her class. I think it was over a global issue, like who was going to take the teddy bear home that night! At one point in the argument, the boy grabbed the teddy bear from Catherine's arms and said to her, "Catherine Bobbie, you are dumb and ugly."

Later that day, Catherine's teacher relayed the story to me because she was stunned by Catherine's response to the situation. She watched as Catherine looked the boy squarely in the eyes and confidently asserted, "No I'm not. My daddy says that I am beautiful and smart." She then proceeded to take back the teddy bear and walk away.

I absolutely love this story, not only because my daughter ended up with the teddy bear, but because of her confidence in knowing what her daddy says about her—which is exactly what your Father in heaven thinks about you! Empowered by knowing what God's Word says about you, you can refute the lies of the enemy when they come.

Just like this little boy, the enemy comes to tell us we are unworthy, unlovable, and unable. He throws insults and doubts at our minds, trying to make us believe we are far less than we really are. But if we can learn to possess the bold, childlike faith of Catherine and simply (and deeply) believe we are who God says we are, then we'll be able to confidently grab that teddy bear right back and walk away with our heads held high. To win the race, we must undoubtedly believe we really are who God says we are, and we can only achieve this through the Word of God ... and nothing else!

MOMENT OF REFLECTION

Do you know what God says about you?
Who he says you are?

January 18

Identity Theft

The thief comes only to steal and kill and destroy; I have come that they may have life, and have it to the full.

JOHN 10:10

Knowing our true identity is only half the battle; once we know it, we have to guard it. I recently received a distraught call from a friend, Alex, who told me that someone had taken her checking account number and created and used checks with her information.

She had become the victim of identity theft, the fastest growing crime in the USA.

In the weeks following, Alex encountered nothing but frustration as she couldn't use her credit cards, draw money from the bank, or travel until she was able to prove that she was who she said she was. The matter hindered every aspect of her life until it was finally cleared up weeks later. Her life ceased to function effectively or move forward while she had no "identity."

As a result of this experience, Alex has gone to great lengths to stop the problem from ever happening again. She has new passwords on her accounts; she no longer has her phone number on her checks; she never gives her credit card details on the Internet unless it's a secure site; she is super careful at ATMs; and she is sure to shred or safely file all important documents. This might sound like a case of paranoia, but in fact, she is just taking all necessary precautions to protect her identity.

In the same way, it is crucial we do all we can to protect our identity in Christ. If we're not careful to take the steps designed to protect our blood-bought identity, then we can easily become complacent and run the risk of the enemy stealing our true identity from us.

While it is true that the enemy comes to steal, kill, and destroy, he can only take from us what we allow him to take. If we're confident about who we are in Christ, then nothing and no one can rob us of that.

MOMENT OF REFLECTION

How do you think it would feel to have your identity stolen?

January 19

Let Go of the Past

See, I am doing a new thing! Now it springs up; do you not perceive it? I am making a way in the wilderness and streams in the wasteland.

ISAIAH 43:19

I have an obsession with purging my house, office, car, and any other space of needless junk and clutter. If something has not been used recently or is simply taking up too much space, out it goes. Nick and the girls often leave notes on their possessions begging me to leave their stuff alone and not to give or throw it away. I admit that I may go a little overboard, but I have discovered that when it comes to moving into our future, we have to get good at purging the things from our past that can limit us or hold us back. If we spend our time rehashing and replaying every scenario from our past where someone hurt us, abused us, or disappointed us, or where we failed, then we will never be able to reach forward to grasp the future God has prepared for us.

Sometimes we hang on so tightly to past memories, feelings, or experiences—as if they are happening in the present—that we end up missing out on our "all" for now. It takes courage to simplify our lives and let go of the weights we have been holding on to for years. Whether those are actual, physical things in which we find our identity (such as clothes, cars, jewelry, or houses) or less tangible weights (such as relationships, bad habits, wrong thinking, or emotional baggage), we need to rid ourselves of them if we are going to have hands free to hold what God wants for us.

Even me, the Queen of Purging, occasionally falls into the trap of holding on to things a little too tightly. To continue to pursue the God-adventure for my life, I must constantly follow the prompting of the Holy Spirit to simplify and eradicate the excess weight, those ways of thinking or patterns of behavior that burden me. Remember, so much of what we think is absolutely essential for fulfilling our destiny just isn't that important!

MOMENT OF REFLECTION

How will you begin the process of getting rid of excess weights in your life?

January 20

Authenticity

One generation commends your works to another; they tell of your mighty acts.

PSALM 145:4

As Christians we have an awesome responsibility to impact and influence the young people in our lives, to help the next generation find their way to God. It does not matter who you are; everyone is older than at least one other person. Therefore we each have the opportunity of being a role model for someone. Jesus taught his disciples by example, which is always the most effective way. If we are going to follow in his footsteps, we must be the godly role models he has called us to be.

Our example—how we live—speaks much louder than any

words we say. We must ensure that we are authentic from the inside out because what is within will eventually come out.

If we have unresolved areas of pain, rejection, bitterness, pride, arrogance, or insecurity, they will manifest themselves in our external actions, priorities, and responses. If we do not let the Spirit of God bring healing and wholeness to our own areas of brokenness, then we will pass that brokenness from one generation to the next. Hurting people hurt people, and broken people break people.

Young people want to see that the gospel is working in our own lives before they will believe that it is true.

Today we can build profiles on social media that depict an image of who we would like to be even if it is not who we are. We can say we are one person but in reality be someone else. We must be careful that we don't build an external profile that does not mirror our internal reality. If we are going to truly impact the young people within our sphere of influence, let's make sure that we are who we say we are and that we do what we say we will do.

MOMENT OF REFLECTION

Are you living the kind of life young people would want to follow?

January 21

Trials Will Come

And we know that in all things God works for the good of those who love him, who have been called according to his purpose.

ROMANS 8:28

Life will eventually turn every person upside down, inside out. No one is immune. Not the mom in the suburbs who finds out her teenage daughter is pregnant. Not the husband who is entangled in an affair with a woman who is not his wife. Not the kid whose parents are strung out on drugs. Not the girl entrenched in human trafficking. Not the boy with HIV or his brother without enough to eat.

The day that I unexpectedly found out that I was adopted was one of those times. For thirty-three years I thought I was someone else, and then, just like that, I discovered I was not who I thought I was.

But just as life will upend us, so will love.

God's love, which knows us and claimed us before we were even born, can take us beyond ourselves, as it did Jesus, who left heaven to go to the cross and pass through the grave in order to bring us back home. His love can bring us through emotional earthquakes. Love like Christ's can lift us out of betrayal and hurt. It can deliver us from any mess. Love like that can release us from every prison of fear and confusion. And love like God's can fill us up till it spills out of us, and we have to speak about it, share it, spread it around.

It was the assurance of this love that sustained me, strengthened me, carried me, and kept me. Then and now. Lean into and receive the unconditional, unfailing, indescribable love of our precious Savior. When all else is shaken and fails, Love never fails.

MOMENT OF REFLECTION

What issues in your life seem to daunt you?
How have you been handling those issues so far?

January 22

Appearances Can Be Deceiving

What good is it for someone to gain the whole world, yet forfeit their soul? Or what can anyone give in exchange for their soul?

MARK 8:36–37

A college friend of mine was one of those people who seemed to have a Midas touch—everything he touched turned to gold. Martin had a charisma about him; every person who met him was naturally drawn to him. He was the whole package: good-looking, athletic, very bright, a dynamic speaker. No one was surprised when he made law his career of choice and breezed through college and law school without needing to study much at all.

While Martin appeared to have it all together, we had many long talks throughout college about his desperate desire to be accepted by his father. He felt that nothing he did was ever good enough for his dad, and this was his biggest motivation for always being the best.

Upon graduation, Martin was courted by several prestigious law firms, all of which offered an unbelievable salary. It appeared that every part of his life was coming together perfectly. In only a few years, he was climbing the ranks within the company, becoming very wealthy, and being considered for promotion.

About that time, however, many of Martin's colleagues developed a habit of getting "casually high" (as they called it), and with Martin's desperation to be accepted and popular, it wasn't long before his six-figure salary afforded him a full-blown addiction to cocaine. Soon he was finding it harder and harder to make it to work on Mondays, and almost as hard to wait until Friday to begin his drug binge. His wife wanted to start having children, but she was beginning to doubt Martin's fidelity (and with good reason). On the day he found out that he didn't get the promotion, he came home to find that his wife had left him and taken most of their possessions. Faster than it took to rise to the top, Martin's life came crashing down around him.

The condition of Martin's inner world was starting to be revealed by the collapse of his external world. It is always dangerous when our gifts take us to a place where our character cannot keep us.

MOMENT OF REFLECTION

Which would you say is stronger,
your gifts or your fruit (character)?
Why do you think so?

January 23

The Light Quenches the Darkness

Though I sit in darkness, the LORD will be my light.

MICAH 7:8

Darkness is everywhere. We live in a world full of fear and in need of light. Each time I listen to the stories of the girls rescued from human trafficking—stories of treachery and horror, rape and murder—I am reminded of how dark it really is out there.

But Jesus said that we are the light! And the light quenches the darkness, eliminates it. The darkness should be afraid of the light, because the light of Christ will eat it up. Just as morning follows night, the light of Christ is always coming. As his hands and feet, we are the force that conquers the dark. We hold the truth that wipes out fear.

"Keep your eyes on me," Jesus says. His presence in the darkness, in the face of the most primal, serious danger, vanquishes fear. You see him, not the evil or the danger, but the love and the light. Once fear no longer controls us, and Christ is walking with us, we are undaunted—and eager to go find some darkness. Light does not deny that there is darkness. It simply dispels the darkness.

MOMENT OF REFLECTION

Do you see darkness in your life?
In the life of someone you know?
What will you do about it?

January 24

In Praise of Women

Many of the Samaritans from that town believed in him because of the woman's testimony.

JOHN 4:39

When I first became a Christian, I had no concept of my value as a woman. Because of my past abuse and ensuing feelings of rejection and pain, I had spent many years desperately trying to earn my sense of worth. I thought that if I worked hard enough and achieved enough, I would somehow feel more valued by those around me. I wasted the better part of my life doing a lot of activities that led to nothing but frustration and emptiness.

As I began to study the Scriptures, I found that during Jesus' ministry, he encountered many women like me. He did not reject them but lifted them up regardless of their past, forgave them, healed them, and encouraged them on a journey of becoming whole. He gave women opportunities to prosper and to take an active part in his ministry. He always treated them with honor, dignity, and grace, equal in value to men. This unconditional and indescribable love for all people, both men and women, was the revelation that captured my heart and began my own healing process.

Jesus consistently placed value on women and womanhood, even though he lived and ministered in a culture where women were seen as inferior to men. Unmarried women were not allowed to leave their home without their father, and married women were not allowed to leave without their husband. In addition, their heads were to be doubly veiled anytime they entered a public venue, and they were not allowed to speak to male strangers. For most of us reading this today, such a reality seems almost incomprehensible. Yet, despite the social norms, Jesus boldly included women as a part of his life and ministry. In fact, he included everyone—and he still does today.

MOMENT OF REFLECTION

Have you felt Jesus' unconditional love and acceptance?
How will you be part of Jesus' ministry?

January 25

What to Do with Disappointment

The path of life leads upward for the prudent to keep them from going down to the realm of the dead.

PROVERBS 15:24

Our God-given gifts, talents, and abilities can take us only so far and can open only so many doors. Once we have walked through those doors, our ability to keep going is determined by how resilient we are. Can we bounce back from the inevitable pain, disappointments, challenges, obstacles, and offenses that we will face?

I would love to tell you that the faith journey is an easy and trouble-free one, but I would not be telling you the truth. The road to purpose and destiny has many sharp curves, hills, valleys to navigate, and occasional dead ends to back out of. The enemy will continually try to convince you to give up, give in, or go back to where you started. You must determine that you will never allow what happens to you to stop you from realizing the dream that God has placed within you.

The degree to which we continue to strengthen our "inner man" is the degree to which we will persevere. I encourage you to spend more time working on your inner world than developing your gifts and talents and building your networks. What is *in* you will always take you further than what is *on* you. Don't allow the enemy to thwart God's purpose for your life. Determine to make every setback the foundation for a comeback, not a reason to quit. Keep going; the destination is worth the trip.

MOMENT OF REFLECTION

Has anything made you want to give up or give in lately?
If so, what is it and what are you doing to ensure
that you will bounce back and not step out?

January 26

Confronting Your "Frogs"

Moses said to Pharaoh, "I leave to you the honor of setting the time for me to pray for you and your officials and your people that you and your houses may be rid of the frogs, except for those that remain in the Nile."
"Tomorrow," Pharaoh said.

EXODUS 8:9–10

The frog invasion in the book of Exodus must have been a pretty miserable experience for all concerned, so Pharaoh reacted swiftly to summon Moses and ask him to get rid of them.

But look closely at what happened next. Pharaoh told Moses, "Okay, I give in; I don't want these frogs anymore. Please speak to your God." Moses replied, "Okay, I will go and speak to God about it." Then he asked Pharaoh, "By the way, when would you like the frogs to go?" and Pharaoh replied, "Tomorrow."

Weird! Why, given the choice, would anyone want to spend *one more night with the frogs*? What was Pharaoh thinking? Some theologians argue that the reason he said this was because he hoped the frogs would disappear overnight, so he wouldn't have to give God the credit. Whatever his rationale, I just cannot imagine what would compel anyone to spend one more night with a frog infestation if he or she did not have to.

This story serves as a picture of our lives. What "frogs" are we living with that God has offered to remove yet we are still hanging onto for "one more night"?

Everyone has "frogs." We may not like to acknowledge it or think about it, but we have frogs. What frogs have invaded your life that you have learned to live with? Real frogs are, by nature, noisy creatures. They don't just sit quietly; they hop around randomly and they croak incessantly. Just like them, the "frogs" in our lives are croaking and making a nuisance of themselves, but so often we choose to ignore the noise and put up with them. But God wants to help us get rid of those frogs so that we can clearly hear his voice and not have it drowned out by their racket.

I don't know what your specific frogs are, but I wonder why you would choose to spend one more night with them when you have a God who says to you, "I want to set you free." God wants to release us from the pain of our past, from the hurdles and obstacles that prevent us from being all he created us to be. I realize that it's not easy to confront our frogs, and I'm not pretending it is—that's precisely why so many of us say, "I'll deal with this tomorrow"—but life is for living. That's why I say, don't wait until tomorrow. God can set you free today.

MOMENT OF REFLECTION

What "frogs" are plaguing your life?
Stress? Rejection? Addiction? Insecurity?
Are you ready to ask God to set you free?

❧ *January 27* ❧

Stuck in a Moment

The LORD our God said to us at Horeb, "You have stayed long enough at this mountain. Break camp and advance into the hill country of the Amorites; go to all the neighboring peoples in the Arabah, in the mountains, in the western foothills, in the Negev and along the coast, to the land of the Canaanites and to Lebanon, as far as the great river, the Euphrates."

DEUTERONOMY 1:6–7

I love the U2 song "Stuck in a Moment." In it there is a line that says, "You've got to get yourself together, 'cause you're stuck in a moment and you can't get out of it." This describes the lives of so many people I've met over the years—people who suffered a blow at a particular moment in their life emotionally, physically, or spiritually and have lived in that "moment" ever since.

Maybe many years ago something bad happened to you. Perhaps someone violated you and you experienced abuse that devastated you. Maybe one of your parents said to you in anger, "I wish you'd never been born!" and that phrase was seared onto your memory. Maybe an unthinking teacher said to you in frustration, "You're dumb! You'll never amount to anything!" Maybe someone you loved dearly walked out on you. All these things are tragic and deeply hurtful, but what's worse is letting such events continue to dominate and shape the rest of your life. Much worse than being abused for ten years is spending the next twenty or thirty years living half a life because every day is infused with bitterness, anger, and unforgiveness.

I suspect that a great many people, though they are no longer living "in the moment" that fractured their life, are allowing it to totally define their present. All that can possibly mean is that, if the issue is not dealt with, it will totally define their future as well. So many people don't walk in the liberty and life that is theirs because they have never dealt with the past and moved on.

We need to cultivate a spirit that says, "I'm not waiting until my circumstances change—I'm going to get up and do something now!" If we always say, "Tomorrow . . . tomorrow . . ." then years from now we will still be facing the same struggles we have today. It's time to step out and take a chance on God.

MOMENT OF REFLECTION

Is there a particular moment you seem to be stuck in?
How can you stop allowing the past to define your present and your future?

January 28

A Purpose Beyond Our Past

Heal me, LORD, and I will be healed; save me and I will be saved, for you are the one I praise.

JEREMIAH 17:14

Hanging on to past hurts has consequences way beyond our private lives. Some people can't submit to the authority of leaders in the church because they had a dysfunctional relationship with their dad. Some people can never commit to a stable relationship because they have abandonment issues from their childhood. Some people are obsessed with making money and never feel they have enough because of a lack of provision when they were growing up. Others refuse to open up to others or make themselves vulnerable because they were abused in the past. This is how it is if we refuse to deal with the past. The stone has hit the pond and already sunk to the bottom, but the ripples continue to spread.

The Bible is full of people who allowed their situation to shape their lives. Remember the account of the woman who ran after Jesus who had the issue of blood? We don't even know her name. All we know is that she had "an issue." So many of us fall into the trap of becoming known only for our "issue." The issue, whatever it may be, is so prominent that our true identity all but disappears. Worse still, our friends compensate for our issue: "Never mind him, he often gets angry. You get used to it." Or, "Don't get her onto the subject of guys or she'll freak out. She's still nursing the wounds of a breakup she had five years ago."

How tragic that people's lives should be defined by their issue. For many, their whole identity has grown out of their victimhood to the extent that they wouldn't know who they were without their issue. We can use this victim mentality as an excuse to remain where we are: "You would find it hard to forgive too, if you had suffered the same kind of abuse . . . that's why I don't trust people in authority . . ." and so on. But all this achieves is to hinder us from entering into the future that God has for us. We have a purpose way beyond our past. Let's determine to take our issues to the foot of the cross where they have already been dealt with. We do not need to be bound by our past; we can step into resurrection life as a brand-new creation in Christ.

MOMENT OF REFLECTION

Do you genuinely desire God to heal you from your wounds?
If so, what is standing in the way?

January 29

Nothing to Lose

[The four men with leprosy] said to each other, "Why stay here until we die? If we say, 'We'll go into the city'—the famine is there, and we will die. And if we stay here, we will die. So let's go over to the camp of the Arameans and surrender. If they spare us, we live; if they kill us, then we die."

2 KINGS 7:3–4

I love the attitude of these guys! Here are four lepers, which history tells us were the lowest of the low in society—nobodies with absolutely no rights—who decided to take action. They had nothing to lose, so they looked at each other—and I believe this is a word from God for many people reading this devotional—and said, "Why are we sitting here until we die?" I love that logic! In effect they said, "If we stop sitting around and get up and do something, what is the worst that could happen? After all, the alternative is that we die waiting here instead!"

However dire the circumstances of our lives become during the course of our journey, we need to adopt this same attitude. Some of us are sitting around waiting to die when we should be taking action! The lepers headed into the Syrian camp and to their amazement they discovered that God had gone ahead of them and worked a miracle. Could it be true that if you and I get up from where we are sitting, wallowing in our problems, and take a risk on God, he will do something miraculous on our behalf? I believe he will.

MOMENT OF REFLECTION

What do you think about these lepers who had nothing to lose?
Do you think you could adopt their attitude toward healing?

January 30

Don't Dwell on the Past

Brothers and sisters, I do not consider myself yet to have taken hold of it. But one thing I do: Forgetting what is behind and straining toward what is ahead, I press on toward the goal to win the prize for which God has called me heavenward in Christ Jesus.

PHILIPPIANS 3:13–14

Listen carefully to Paul's words above. Hear what he is *not* saying as well as what he *is* saying. First, he *is* saying that we should forget the things that lie behind us and move on beyond the past. He is *not* saying that we should develop amnesia. Some people have developed an unhealthy theology that claims healing by pretending that the past never happened. Well, sorry . . . it did! To pretend otherwise is to establish your life upon a lie, and eventually that lie will crumble as reality catches up. I would not advocate an approach that says, "Just move on, don't think about the past, and everything will be okay." It doesn't matter how many times you chant that mantra—ultimately, it won't help you. Over time, however, God can heal you from the hurts of the past if you give him access to your soul. The blood of Jesus can cleanse you, restore you, and make you whole. Jesus' blood can give you a life beyond your past and release you into the future that God has for you.

Second, when Paul says "forgetting what is behind," he is referring to the whole of his past, both good and bad. If we had the chance to chat with Paul, he would probably say something like, "The past is the past." Neither Paul's failures nor his successes were important to him—all he was focused on was moving forward with God, taking another step toward his ultimate destiny in Christ. We need to cultivate this same attitude. When bad stuff happens, we let God in, ask him to heal us from the hurt, and take another step forward. When good stuff happens, we rejoice in it, thankful to God for his blessing, and take another step forward. We are grateful for God's every intervention into our life, but we move on, not dwelling on the past.

I don't know about you, but I don't want to find myself reveling in the nostalgia of something God once did while he is someplace else doing something new and exciting. I want to be a part of what he is doing now!

MOMENT OF REFLECTION

What are you holding onto from the past—
both failures and the successes?
How can you let those go to become a part
of what God is doing in this moment?

January 31

What Are You Afraid Of?

For the Spirit God gave us does not make us timid, but gives us power, love and self-discipline.

2 TIMOTHY 1:7

So many people live one life on the outside and have another entirely unused life on the inside. When they get to the end of their days, they discover that they never did truly live. We tend to settle for an existence instead of an abundant life. We crave normalcy, comfort, convenience, predictability, and ease on one level, yet we are desperate for so much more on another. Sometimes we even decide that this will be the year of change, growth, and risk-taking ... and then we are in another year, and then another.

We tend to put things off because we fear that we might fail. The truth is that there are no guarantees. But one thing is certain: as long as we do not start, we can be sure that we will not succeed.

At some point we must step out of the boat and take a risk. That's the only way we can know whether or not something is going to work. Until we take a leap of faith, we will always wonder, "What if?"

I realize that it seems daunting to exchange what we know for the great unknown. But we cannot continue to do things the same way and expect a different result. As hard as it is, we must make the decision that we are going to deal with our past, let God heal our wounds, confront our fears, and jump into the great unknown. The faith life is a great mystery and adventure. I've learned that if we are willing to lose control so that God can have control, we are in for the ride of our lives!

MOMENT OF REFLECTION

Are you willing to allow God to be in the driver's seat of your life?

February

HEALING IS A PROCESS

February 1

The Process of Healing

Every good tree bears good fruit, but a bad tree bears bad fruit. A good tree cannot bear bad fruit, and a bad tree cannot bear good fruit.

MATTHEW 7:17–18

My life before I became a Christian made me a perfect candidate for the *Jerry Springer* show. I was adopted at birth and abused in my past, which, needless to say, left me with feelings of rejection, betrayal, shame, guilt, and fear. Obviously, I had accumulated baggage over the years, but when I became a Christian, I had no idea I needed to deal with it. I embraced my new life with passion and enthusiasm, choosing to forget those things that were behind me, and pressing forward to those things that were ahead. I was not trying to deny my past; rather I sincerely believed that because I was in Christ, I was a *new* creation—the old had gone and the new had come. What I did not realize was that this Scripture spoke of my new *spiritual* condition, not about the condition of my *soul*. The damage and weaknesses that were in my soul realm before I became a Christian lingered after I made the decision to get my life right with God.

Think about it this way: If our physical body has cellulite on it before we become Christians, then even after we've prayed the sinner's prayer, we will still have that cellulite (and we will continue to have it until we stop eating those donuts!). In the same way, if our soul is damaged or wounded before we become a Christian, it isn't miraculously "zapped"—we aren't instantly made whole.

I wondered why I did not seem to be walking in victory in my Christian life even though I was earnestly praying, fasting, attending church, reading the Word of God, and doing everything I knew to do. I seemed to keep defaulting back into patterns of destructive thinking and behavior because I did not realize that I had a deeply wounded soul. I needed to allow God into those dark places of my soul to bring healing and restoration. I had to become vulnerable, transparent, and honest about my struggles so that God could begin the healing process.

MOMENT OF REFLECTION

Have you been confusing heart and soul issues with spiritual issues?

February 2

Seven Times

Naaman's servants went to him and said, "My father, if the prophet had told you to do some great thing, would you not have done it? How much more, then, when he tells you, 'Wash and be cleansed'!"

2 KINGS 5:13

Healing doesn't happen overnight. The Bible tells us that Naaman was told to dip seven times in the Jordan River in order to be healed of leprosy. He couldn't go to one of the prettier rivers with cleaner waters and just dip once. He had to get in the Jordan and bathe there again and again and again. Healing was a messy process, a choice he had to make. It works the same way in our lives. We have to *choose* to heal, and trust that if we do what God, the Great Physician asks —forgive those who have wounded and damaged us—there will be a change, a good result, strength, and wholeness. That means we can:

- **Forgive every time we feel anger or mistrust or bitterness.** Instead of dwelling on the emotions that are eating us alive, we can dwell on all that is good.
- **Stay in the present moment or think on the future.** Instead of rehearsing old injustices and letting our lives revolve around the past, we can find a greater reward by thinking on the future.
- **Love others enough to let them make their own choices.** Instead of loving the need to control and insisting on our own choices, we can love others enough to let them decide for themselves.
- **Let go of the idea of our perceived power and focus.** Instead

we can focus on God's work in every person and on the power of the cross. We can't heal our own hearts. But God promises to be strong when we are weak.

- **Stop trying to punish those who hurt us with anger and hate.** Instead, we can let God deal with them. Unforgiveness harms only you, and the damage is considerable. It keeps you cowardly and stunted, isolated and alone, ugly and bitter. Jesus said to forgive seventy times seven because no matter how much you forgive others, he has forgiven you even more.
- **Stop trusting in ourselves.** Instead we can trust in God and follow his leading. When we do, he promises to direct our paths.
- **Believe our wounds can make us stronger.** The hard work of therapy makes the wounded parts of our hearts even stronger.

Although this list may seem difficult to put into practice, I know from personal experience that following this process *does* lead to freedom. Despite what you feel right now, I know that in the strength of Christ, you can do it.

MOMENT OF REFLECTION

Have you chosen healing for your life?
What circumstances or influences brought you to that choice?

February 3

No Quick Fixes

O LORD my God, I cried out to You, and You healed me.

PSALM 30:2 NKJV

When life hurts us, we want the quick fix, instant newness, wholeness. We want God to take care of the problem. But most often, damage doesn't happen overnight—and neither does healing. Some wounds heal over, but scar tissue remains. Complete healing takes time and goes deep into painful places.

Once, on an embarrassing wipeout down a ski slope, I ruptured major ligaments that connect the bones in the knee. I needed emergency surgery. Afterward, as the doctor unwrapped the dressing for that first post-op look, he warned me that my leg would look abnormal due to the swelling. Still, I was shocked.

"Don't panic," he said. "This is perfectly normal, given the trauma of the surgery. Give it time, and your leg will return to normal. I should warn you though that the pain of the recovery will be much greater than the pain of the injury."

The doctor explained that scar tissue had developed from my initial trauma and then the further trauma of surgery. As my body attempted to heal itself, protective fibers grew around the injured ligaments. My range of motion, circulation, and even sensation in that leg were affected. Unless those protective fibers of scar tissue were broken down, I would never regain full range of motion; I might even have to wear a leg brace the rest of my life. The only way to break down the scar tissue would be an ongoing process of rehabilitation and an unrelenting commitment on my part.

The scar tissue in my knee is no different from the scar tissue that had closed off my heart. Years of haunting memories after abuse or an attack of any kind can last longer than the actual events. The heart, broken in an instant when we learn of an adulterous affair, can keep us from loving for years—if ever again. The harsh names we're called on the schoolyard as a child can echo in our ears for the rest of our lives. So many things can injure us, break our hearts and spirits, wound our souls, and change us forever, leaving our hearts overlaid with fibers of mistrust, bitterness, self-condemnation, guilt, and fear—all the things that keep us from stepping out, risking, moving ahead.

We want God to heal us quickly and without pain. But the healing of our hearts takes time, hard work, and a strong commitment, just as physical healing does.

MOMENT OF REFLECTION

In what ways can you prepare your heart for God's healing touch?

February 4

All in Good Time

Trust in the LORD with all your heart and lean not on your own understanding; in all your ways submit to him, and he will make your paths straight.

PROVERBS 3:5–6

I have been a runner for more than twenty years, and a while ago, I noticed each time I ran I'd get a sharp pain in my right hip. At first, I just ignored it because I couldn't be bothered to get it checked out. However, the pain became so intense that I had no choice but to visit a physiotherapist—which was better than going on record as the youngest recipient of an artificial hip replacement.

At my first visit, I said (in true Christine style), "Can we deal with this quickly? I have a half-marathon coming up, and I need it to be healed by then." After he examined me, he laughed and said, "Christine, your entire hip and all the surrounding muscles have been totally damaged. It's taken years of poor form and lack of stretching for it to get like this—it's going to take a long time for it to heal. There isn't going to be a half, quarter, or any portion of a marathon this year."

It took almost a year of constant therapy for the pain to subside and my hip to be healed. Because I committed the time needed for the healing process and was open to learning new patterns of exercise and stretching, my hip is better than ever. Now I'm confident I'll be able to run for many decades to come.

Having a truly prosperous soul happens the same way. It often takes years for our souls to become damaged and deeply wounded. We'd love to see healing come overnight, but God is into the process of healing. The one thing I can assure you is that it always takes longer than we thought or hoped it would, but the results are always immeasurably better. If we determine to commit to the healing process no matter how difficult it may seem, we will find that our God is truly faithful.

MOMENT OF REFLECTION

How do you know God is faithful to heal even when your healing seems to be slow in coming?

February 5

Beating the Bully

For Christ's sake, I delight in weaknesses, in insults, in hardships, in persecutions, in difficulties. For when I am weak, then I am strong.

2 CORINTHIANS 12:10

Difficulty is the bully that steps into your path and tries to arm-wrestle you to the ground until you cry uncle. No matter what you're trying to do, if it's worthwhile, he will try to outshout both God and your own thoughts, confusing you. He tries to loom so large that you can only see what's right in front of you—the problems, the obstacles, and the walls. Difficulty sings an old song: "Whatever it is you're trying to do will take too much time, money, risk, comfort, health, strength, willpower ..."

In fact, Difficulty's tune is as old as Moses.

When Moses led the children of Israel out of slavery, Difficulty was there every step of the way, singing, "Can't, won't, don't." Pharaoh granted the people freedom, and Difficulty laughed and said that it would cost the Israelites blood, sweat, and tears.

Even after God got the Israelites through those things, Difficulty was singing in the distance, "It's not over!" Difficulty is like that. He hangs around. He lurks. When he saw the Israelites win their freedom, he said, "Don't think you're leaving *me* behind." He was with them at the shore of the Red Sea, and in the desert where there was no water or food and no clear path to the Promised Land.

And why? He wanted the Israelites to stop—to return to Egypt.

If they had, they might be enslaved there to this day. Still building their oppressor's kingdom, and his temples, instead of God's. They would have continued to suffer injustice instead of enjoying the freedom of the Lord. They would have languished under Pharaoh's thumb instead of grabbing all that God was calling them to.

We can't let Difficulty keep us from daring to go where God wants us to go. God will make a way.

MOMENT OF REFLECTION

What is your answer when the bully named Difficulty tells you your God plans are doomed?

February 6

Laying a Foundation

Your servant has killed both the lion and the bear; this uncircumcised Philistine will be like one of them, because he has defied the armies of the living God.

1 SAMUEL 17:36

Most of us prefer instant results to having to go through a preparation process. When things don't happen as quickly as we would like, we tend to give up or drop out. How many diets have we started and never finished? How many New Year's resolutions have we made and never followed through with? How many books have we bought and never read? The list could go on and on.

We are often guilty of "talking a great game" and then not following through with our actions. Lip service and heart commitment are two very different things! For the runner, there must be an absolute commitment to training in order to sacrifice the time needed to discipline, test, and strengthen the mind and body. It is the same for us in our spiritual lives. We have to lay a foundation that will support us in the future. If David had not been keeping his father's sheep in anonymity and obscurity, he would never have had the training to kill a lion or a bear. If he had not killed a lion or a bear, he would have never been prepared to fight and defeat Goliath. He built his strength in the preparation process.

Even though one of my primary gifts is that of preaching and teaching, I rarely ever preached when I was a youth leader in my local youth ministry. During that season of my life, I served by using my car to drive young people to youth meetings, setting up the youth auditorium, vacuuming the floor, cleaning the toilets, and doing whatever else needed to be done. Although I had a dream and a desire in my heart to preach all over the world, I knew that God needed to do a deep work in me so that he could do a great work through me in the future. While I found this preparation phase incredibly frustrating, lonely, and sometimes tedious, I know that if I had not stayed committed to the preparation process during those years, I would not be doing what I'm doing today.

MOMENT OF REFLECTION

How willing are you to stay with the preparation process no matter what?

February 7

The Mind of Christ

Let this mind be in you which was also in Christ Jesus.

PHILIPPIANS 2:5 NKJV

We must never underestimate the importance of the mind, as it is vital in making our internal transformation an external reality. Strong heart and soul muscles reveal our potential, but it is the mind muscle that unleashes it. Our thoughts are like a train; they take us somewhere.

Proverbs 23:7 teaches us that as we think in our hearts, so we are. In other words, who we are today is a result of the thoughts that we have been thinking lately. Similarly, who we will be tomorrow will be the result of the thoughts we think today. And I'm not talking about the thoughts that we *think* we're thinking about ourselves; I'm talking about what we *truly* think about ourselves deep down.

So many of us believe that who we are today is the result of our upbringing, socioeconomic background, education, gender, or ethnicity. Of course, all those factors have played a role in forming who we are, but ultimately our true identities are a result of the patterns of thinking we have developed as a *response* to our background and circumstances. In short, if we want to change our lives, we must change the way we think.

The strength of our mind muscle is not determined by our IQ level, how well we did on our college entrance exams, or how many academic degrees we have obtained. Nor does it depend on how much biblical or theological knowledge we have. The quality of our mind muscle depends on how much of God's truth (as found in his Word) we believe and apply to our everyday lives. Our thoughts—which for many of us have been shaped by the forces of culture, tradition, our religious experience, the media, and our family and friends—have to be supplanted by the truth of the Word of God.

There is only one surefire way for us to strengthen our mind muscle, and that is by committing ourselves to the process of renewing our minds. It helped me move from the prison of my past into the future God had for me.

MOMENT OF REFLECTION

What do you consider to be the greatest factor in shaping your thoughts? In what ways do you think your thoughts need to change?

February 8

Right Place, Right Time

[Elisha] set out to follow Elijah and became his servant.

1 KINGS 19:21

The Bible records the fact that a man called Elisha arose to become one of the most outstanding prophets of God ever to walk the earth. He followed in the footsteps of his mentor, Elijah, and his life was marked by faithfulness. Elisha went on to become twice as powerful as Elijah—a "double anointing"—and the key to his success was preparation.

During the early years of his preparation for ministry, Elisha served only Elijah. That was it! "Go and get that for me," Elijah would say, and Elisha would go. "Do this for me," and he would do it. There was not necessarily a "please" or "thank you." Elisha just did it. While he was busy serving, God was grooming him for greatness, whether he realized it or not. As Elisha cooperated with God's training program, he was sure to be in the right place at the right time when his promotion came due.

Many people are not where they are supposed to be when it comes time for God to promote them, simply because they have not been committed to preparation. As a result, they miss out on or defer the progress of their destinies. We live in a culture that places little value on preparation. Instead of understanding that it is a vital part of our overall journey, people look for a shortcut!

When it came time for Elisha to be released into his destiny, he "took the mantle of Elijah that had fallen from him." It turned out that timing and position were absolutely vital to the fulfillment of Elisha's destiny. Had he not been fully committed to serving Elijah and doggedly pursuing him, he would not have been in the right place at the right time to take up Elijah's mantle. We have to learn that every part of the preparation process is important.

MOMENT OF REFLECTION

What do you think would have happened if Elisha had not been there to take up Elijah's mantle?

February 9

Focus on the Finish

Let your eyes look straight ahead; fix your gaze directly before you. Give careful thought to the paths for your feet and be steadfast in all your ways.

PROVERBS 4:25–26

On those days when we feel depleted, exhausted, and like we are about to give up on the race of life, it may be because we have lost sight of the finish line. I have found that the only times I've ever wanted to give up have been when I've become overwhelmed with my circumstances and lost sight of the bigger picture. Because I lost focus and became consumed with the pressing issues or feelings of the moment, I was tempted to quit. Realizing that I am actually in this race to finish it helped get me back on track.

At my fortieth birthday party I remember looking around at all the wonderful people I have "done life" with. One thing that we all had in common was that we'd each had serious obstacles to overcome and disappointments to process. Some of us had lost loved ones; some had come back from financial ruin; others had dealt with broken dreams, fought cancer or other health issues, coped with betrayal, and parented rebellious children.

As I reflected on this, I realized that the decisive factor that made each one of us "winners" in our individual races was that at every juncture, we chose to see the bigger picture and focus on finishing our race. I often wonder how many destinies have never been realized because people abandoned their dreams and purpose due to failure, pain, discouragement, or disappointment. Somewhere along the journey they lost sight of the destination and gave up. Let's determine to be people who never become so consumed with our present circumstances that we end up losing sight of the finish line. We must keep our eyes fixed and focused on Jesus.

MOMENT OF REFLECTION

At what part of your race are you currently?
Are you struggling to stay focused?

February 10

Learn to Say No

Am I now trying to win the approval of human beings, or of God? Or am I trying to please people? If I were still trying to please people, I would not be a servant of Christ.

GALATIANS 1:10

I have discovered that *no* is often one of the most difficult words to say, but one of the most important if I want to ensure my spiritual fitness. In my own life, this has been a great challenge for many different reasons.

Apart from the fact that by nature I love to be involved in everything, in the early days of my Christian walk, I was still wounded and broken because of the abuse I experienced in my past. I had lived with rejection, abandonment, guilt, shame, and unforgiveness. In an attempt to feel loved, valued, and accepted, I never wanted to disappoint anyone, craving the approval of man at times above the approval of God.

So I accepted every ministry invitation, regardless of the toll this took on my body and my relationships. What's more, I felt I had to personally help every person who had been wounded or broken, so I accepted an unhealthy amount of counseling appointments. Obviously this was not a sustainable way of life or ministry, as you can't please all of the people all of the time. I ended each day feeling depleted, emptied out, exhausted. Everything I was doing was good and helpful to people, but clearly there was a problem.

This pattern of constant activity and striving continued until I accepted personal responsibility for my choices and embarked on the difficult journey of dealing with my own brokenness. I knew that instead of being a wounded healer, I needed to establish healthy boundaries and learn to say no to others (and myself) so I could say yes to God.

MOMENT OF REFLECTION

How good are you at saying no?
How would saying no make a difference in your life?

February 11

Guard Your Heart

Above all else, guard your heart, for everything you do flows from it.

PROVERBS 4:23

Protecting our heart is so important that the Bible tells us to guard it above all that we guard! In the Hebrew, this word *guard* alludes to a very aggressive protest. So, it's not like the kind of guarding you might do when someone is trying to take a bite of your hamburger;

it's the kind of bulldog tenacity by which you guard the last few bites of your piece of dark chocolate cheesecake!

It's no wonder God gives us such strong advice because our destiny flows directly out of our hearts. When our hearts are healthy, whole, and right with God, then it won't be difficult to keep our destiny on course. But if we let down our guard and allow bitterness, unforgiveness, lust, greed, fear, or anxiety to take root, our hearts will become clogged, thus slowing or potentially halting our ability to flow smoothly from one season to the next. It's time to take an inventory of what kinds of things we might be harboring in our hearts. We must allow the Holy Spirit to bring healing to every part.

If we keep our hearts locked up with toxic thoughts and emotions, they will become diseased and damage our every decision and interaction. Sometimes we respond in certain ways to certain situations and are not even sure why. If we take the time to examine our hearts, we will often find that the root cause of a particular reaction stems from an unresolved issue there. We must remember that the goal of our faith is not behavior modification but heart transformation. If we allow the Holy Spirit access to every area of our heart, we will see results in every area of life.

MOMENT OF REFLECTION

What area of your heart needs healing?

February 12

Certain Uncertainty

You know that the testing of your faith produces perseverance.

JAMES 1:3

I'm more aware than ever before of the uncertainty and volatile nature that defines the world we live in today. It only takes a few minutes of flipping through a newspaper or watching a news broadcast to figure this out. In addition to the tumultuous situations facing the planet, each of us has our own private storms we have to navigate through from time to time.

As student, mother, wife, boss, employee, or any of the multiplicity of roles we play, we're inevitably going to face trials and periods of life when we simply don't know how in the world everything is going to work out. I wish I could tell you that if you simply pray the right anointed incantation, then—*poof!*—everything around you would magically fall into place. But the truth you already know is, there's no such prayer.

We must realize that just because we're going through a trial doesn't mean we've failed in some way, missed God's direction for our lives, or that we should shrink back from having and doing all that God has purposed. As long as we're breathing, we're going to encounter challenges at one point or another. That's why it's critical that we learn how to endure rather than just merely survive these difficult times. Perseverance is the key to overcoming.

There is no use wasting time wondering if we will face trials, because we all will. But when we choose to proactively develop and maintain the spiritual muscle of endurance, we will be able to continue to fulfill our God-given destiny and purpose . . . even in the midst of inevitable obstacles and hurdles.

MOMENT OF REFLECTION

What areas of your life seem most difficult?
How can you strengthen your ability to endure?

February 13

Remember the Good

Do not be afraid; you will not be put to shame. Do not fear disgrace; you will not be humiliated. You will forget the shame of your youth and remember no more the reproach.

ISAIAH 54:4

I'm not going to lie to you; sometimes I can have a very selective memory. Like when Nick and I are having a "passionate discussion" about a particular topic, and I realize he's wrong, I can remember exactly what he said, how he said it, what he was wearing, where he was standing, and what we ate for lunch later that day. But when the tables are turned, and I realize I'm the one who is mistaken, my memory can tend to get a bit murky. "Huh? What? Ummm ... yeah ... I can't seem to recall anything about that day. Nick, are you sure you didn't dream up that conversation?"

So often, we can vividly remember those things we ought to forget and completely forget those things we ought to remember! In life, choosing to remember the right things can help us to have great endurance ... especially during the difficult seasons.

Let's make the choice to remember the good and not the bad. We can choose to remember and dwell on the incredible things God has already done in our lives, rather than get so wrapped up in the problems of today, along with the junk that happened yesterday, and the negative stuff that we think might happen tomorrow!

MOMENT OF REFLECTION

Are you remembering the right things and forgetting those things that keep you beaten down and powerless? Why is that important?

February 14

Nothing Can Stop Them

As for us, we cannot help speaking about what we have seen and heard.

ACTS 4:20

On several occasions recorded in the Gospels, Jesus healed individuals and then warned them to say nothing to anyone about what he had done for them. Sometimes, though, those whose lives he had touched did not keep quiet. One man, a leper, first went to a priest who would pronounce him clean, and then he began to tell everyone that Jesus had healed him. The same thing took place when Jesus healed a deaf mute. The more Jesus told him to stay quiet, the more he proclaimed his healing.

Just like the leper and the deaf mute, when people have genuinely encountered Christ, nothing should keep them from talking about him. It is not a manufactured or forced behavior. It is a spontaneous response to an encounter with God.

By God's grace we have received the gifts of salvation, forgiveness, freedom, healing, restoration, and more. If our faith is genuine, we will be unable to resist telling our friends, neighbors, everyone we encounter about what Jesus has done for us.

Sometimes we pull back from doing so because we have encountered resistance, ridicule, or opposition from family, friends, or coworkers; but we must determine that nothing or no one can stop us from declaring the good news. Of course we require wisdom, love, and grace when we share our faith. More often than not, timing is everything, and with this in mind, let's be prepared every single day, in season and out of season, to share the great things that our wonderful Savior has done. People are more ready to hear than you might think. Never forget that for many people we are the only Bible they will ever read and the only disciple of Christ they will ever meet. We are God's love letter to this world.

MOMENT OF REFLECTION

When was the last time you spoke about Jesus to someone for the first time?

February 15

Could It Be Me?

Each of you must take responsibility for doing the creative best you can with your own life.

GALATIANS 6:5 MSG

Nick and I were recently in a meeting where I was encouraged to ask myself a question that I had never actually stopped to think about before. That is, "What is it about me that keeps me from becoming the best me that God wants me to be?" What a great question! Invariably, though, this question led to numerous other questions that concerned everything about *me.*

My thinking . . . my attitudes . . . my perceptions . . . my opinions

. . . my experiences . . . my expectations . . . my friends . . . my associates . . . my knowledge . . . my understanding . . . my tolerance . . . my emotions . . . my reactions . . . my health . . . my fitness . . . my diet . . . my prejudices . . . my biases . . . my preferences . . . my routines . . . just to name a few!

To be honest, I would definitely prefer to just blame outside forces for *me* not being all that I can be. (After all, this would be far easier and a lot less painful.) But ultimately, the only person I can change is *me*, and if I want to step up and into the purposes of God for my life and fulfill my life assignment, then I must take full responsibility for my own growth. This starts and ends with *me*!

MOMENT OF REFLECTION

What is it about you that keeps you from becoming the best you that God wants you to be?

February 16

Build Gradually

For precept must be upon precept, precept upon precept; line upon line, line upon line; here a little, and there a little.

ISAIAH 28:10 KJV

In order to improve the body's ability to sustain high-intensity effort for long periods of time, marathon runners have to increase their exercise volume by training longer, working harder, and increasing their speed. They do this gradually, over time. If they overdo an increase in mileage, intensity, or speed, they will burn out or, worse yet, sustain an injury. Many runners starting out make the mistake of running too fast, too far, too soon. (I am an example of this kind of runner.) In reality, you can't run flat out or for very long every single day. You have to train for endurance first and speed later.

Our Christian life is all about running our race so that we can go the entire distance. This is why God cares so much about endurance. He is not as concerned about how quickly we run as much as he is concerned that we endure and complete our course. The race of the

Christian life is not a competition—we don't need to try to keep up with anyone else. We just have to run *our* race and finish *our* course. We must stay focused on that which God has called us to do and remember that God builds gradually.

Isaiah introduced the principle of building "line by line." We can apply this to every area of our lives. It is the way in which we build strong marriages, great families, good friendships, healthy bodies, prosperous businesses, and fruitful ministries. In other words, it is consistency and commitment that wins races. As an old Indian proverb states, "You walk a mile one step at a time." Today, determine to take the next step, not the next mountain.

MOMENT OF REFLECTION

Are you stressed out trying to hurry up and do what God has called you to do?
How will you slow down and let God set your pace?

February 17

Don't Bypass the Process

Yes, my soul, find rest in God; my hope comes from him.

PSALM 62:5

I have learned that being made whole is a *process*, and if we try to bypass this process, we will remain weak at the core. As a result, eventually all areas of our lives will begin to deteriorate. The walls I once built around my life to protect myself were a clear indication of my unresolved issues. I thought that by burying my past and building walls around the burial site that I had dealt with them. I was not aware that God wanted to redeem all that had happened to me and he would do that very thing if I gave it to him instead of trying to take care of it myself by hiding it.

I developed very destructive coping mechanisms. To ensure I would never be hurt again, I did not allow people to know me too intimately. So fearful was I of not being in control of my circumstances that I demanded control of everything and everyone in my life. Determined to never be rejected again, I became a perfectionist with little tolerance for mistakes or failure. I was often impatient and harsh and thought that if I could just keep succeeding, everyone would need me and want me.

With all of this turmoil in my soul, it is no wonder my life began to unravel. But God wanted me to find freedom. He showed me that although I was born again, my soul muscle was so emaciated, weak, and small that it was nearly impossible for the Holy Spirit and his fruit to flow. I had to allow God to heal my wounds and strengthen the weak places in my soul before I could truly walk in freedom.

MOMENT OF REFLECTION

Have you tried to rush the process of healing from pains of the past?

February 18

In Christ Alone

God made him who had no sin to be sin for us, so that in him we might become the righteousness of God.

2 CORINTHIANS 5:21

Isn't it comforting to know that our righteousness is found in Christ alone and that there is nothing we can do to earn it? It is a gift that has been given to us, not a reward that we receive based on our performance. It has taken me a long time to allow that truth to sink deep into my heart and soul. I had experienced so much abuse and pain as a child that I thought there was something wrong with me. I thought that if I could only *be* good enough and *do* enough good things, then perhaps I could compensate for the things that were obviously wrong with me. I brought that thinking into my relationship with God and almost burned myself out trying to become good enough for a God who, through Jesus, had already made me what I was trying to become.

I will never forget the liberty I felt when I finally stepped off the performance treadmill and reveled in God's acceptance of me just as

I was. When I stopped trying to be made right through my own good works, I found that the grace of God was readily available to help me up when I fell down and to keep me going when I wanted to quit. Nothing saps the life out of us quicker than trying to make ourselves right with God. It is only faith in Jesus Christ and his redemptive work at Calvary that brings us into right standing with God.

Over time I stopped thinking about all of the things that were wrong with me and started thinking more about all of the things that were right with Jesus. I have discovered that you become what you behold, and as I beheld him, I started to become more like him. What I could never do in my own strength began to happen in God's strength.

So put away the performance treadmill and put on the righteousness of God in Christ Jesus. Stop trying to become what you already are!

MOMENT OF REFLECTION

Do you find yourself trying to earn right standing with God through good works?

February 19

Seasons of Submission

But for you who revere my name, the sun of righteousness will rise with healing in its rays. And you will go out and frolic like well-fed calves.

MALACHI 4:2

The world we live in is consumed with instant gratification, and it can be easy to desire a quick fix when it comes to the wounds in our souls. If we allow this desire to rule us, instead of our trust in God, then we will inevitably step out of his plan and purpose for our lives. We need to be willing to submit to his healing process.

It is impossible to "fast-track" this process because it is during this time that God is preparing us for all that he desires to do through us. Only the healing power of Jesus Christ, at work in our hearts, will allow us to walk in wholeness and accomplish all he has called us to do. We'd love for this change to happen overnight, but God's ways cannot be compared to a microwave. (He operates much more like an oven!)

Artificial soul replacement is simply not an option. We have to work with what we've been given. But don't worry; God is faithful and will bring healing if we are willing to commit to his plan and his process.

I have had to work through so many issues in my life that I often wanted to give up or thought that God had given up on me. I wanted to see results so much faster than I did during long seasons when I thought I was making no headway at all. As I look back, I now realize that those times were when God was doing his deepest work in me. I could not yet see the fruit because he was still cultivating the soil of my heart and planting new seeds that would take time to sprout. I am so grateful that I did not destroy his work because of my impatience and frustration ... although I will admit I did often come very close.

MOMENT OF REFLECTION

Have you committed to healing as a long-term proposition, or do you get impatient with yourself — and with God — that healing seems to take so long?

February 20

Are We There Yet?

We do not want you to become lazy, but to imitate those who through faith and patience inherit what has been promised.

HEBREWS 6:12

If you have ever set out on a road trip with children in the car, then you will have heard those familiar words, "Are we there yet?" Seasoned parents will tell you that no point in the journey is too early for this question to be raised — it can come literally any time between five minutes after you've pulled out of your driveway to just before you are halfway there, but certainly no later! We can forgive kids for their impatience, though. After all, they're just kids, and they haven't yet learned the virtue of waiting for things like us adults. They don't understand that certain things in life just take time.

We'd like to think that as adults we have learned these truths ... but have we, really? The truth is, when it comes to our relationship with God, we are just as guilty of shouting, "Are we there yet?"

You've heard it said that life is a journey. This is especially true of the life of faith in Christ. Once we give our lives to him, God takes us on a journey that will mold us, shape us, transform us, and ultimately release us into our destiny in him. We must always remember that destiny is obtained through faith and patience.

MOMENT OF REFLECTION

Remind yourself today, as often as necessary, that life is a journey. But it is a journey that we are not asked to take alone — God is always guiding our steps.

February 21

The Journey, Not the Destination

You need to persevere so that when you have done the will of God, you will receive what he has promised.

HEBREWS 10:36

God is much more interested in the details of our journey than he is in getting us to our destination. The trouble is, we often find ourselves frustrated and bewildered by that process. "Why can't God just propel me into my destiny now?" we want to know. "Why all this waiting?" We live in a world that rushes everywhere and knows very little about journeying. As Christians, we are often infected with the same virus. We want God to act in our lives *now*, and we become impatient and tired if we don't see any evidence of him moving. We need to pause to understand what God is doing in our life now and view events in the context of our whole journey, instead of restlessly trying to push ahead to the next thing.

The question that most of us want answered in life is: "What is happening when nothing seems to be happening?" What is God up to when there is no evidence of him answering our prayers or moving us along in our journey? We must remember that God is always preparing us for what he has already prepared for us. He never forgets us.

MOMENT OF REFLECTION

What slow changes have happened in your life over the past few years? How has God transformed your heart? Taking time to recognize those changes and thank God for them opens your heart still further for God to work even more.

February 22

"And It Will"

Ask and it will be given to you; seek and you will find; knock and the door will be opened to you.

MATTHEW 7:7

Asking for things is second nature to children. No one has to teach them to ask for anything; they are just born knowing how to do it: "Mummy, can I have that?... Daddy, I want this ... can I have it?... I want it!" In the same way that kids plague their parents for everything they want or need, God invites and expects us to do the same. "Ask," he says, "and you will receive."

It sounds simple, doesn't it? But wait. This is a loaded phrase and there is more here than meets the eye.

We tend to think that we can pray and—*zap!*—God will answer our prayers, just like that. But there are three little words separating the "ask" and the "receive" in this prayer equation: *and it will*. Jesus said, "Ask, *and it will* be given." In my Bible those three words take up about half a centimeter of space, but I can tell you from experience that the "and it wills" of life can sometimes take between ten and fifteen years. God forgets to tell us that! Asking is easy and receiving is fun, but in between the asking and the receiving there is always an "and it will" of unspecified length.

All we can do in the "and it will" phase of the process is to trust

God. I think the Lord does that so we do not get so caught up with the receiving that we forget the very One who is giving. The process of waiting helps us to become more dependent upon and intimate with the One who is supplying our request. The purpose is to become closer to Jesus, not only to receive the benefits of God.

MOMENT OF REFLECTION

What have you asked God for that you are still waiting to receive? How long have you been waiting?

February 23

Don't Waver

I waited patiently for the LORD; he turned to me and heard my cry.

PSALM 40:1

Often we throw ourselves into things and make big promises to God. We tell him that we will serve him unreservedly, do anything for him, and then we wait expectantly for him to do his part and open up our life purpose and destiny before us. But when God doesn't respond immediately, we begin to waver. "Hang on, God," we protest, "I've asked but still haven't received. What's going on?"

Some of you will feel like you have done a lot of asking of God and want to know, "When is the receiving?" You may have been praying for a particular person to get saved, for a marriage or other relationship to be restored, for a business or financial breakthrough, for a miraculous healing. You've asked, but you've not yet received. I want to encourage you not to give up. Here is where most Christians abort their destiny. We waver, because we don't want to wait any longer, and drift off course from the purposes of God.

Don't waver. Keep believing and keep waiting patiently. He who promised is faithful.

MOMENT OF REFLECTION

Can you identify an area where you've given up hope because you've been impatient?

February 24

Keep Marching

See, I have delivered Jericho into your hands, along with its king and its fighting men.

JOSHUA 6:2

Maybe you are about to give up because you think your situation is different from those of others. "Chris, you don't understand. My problem is insurmountable and what I've asked God for is just too big to believe for." I sympathize with you, but nothing is too big for God. The children of Israel experienced similar feelings when faced with the insurmountable walls of Jericho. The Promised Land was just on the other side of that wall. It was right there within their grasp, but there was a big obstacle to overcome—a wall that separated them from their promise. Like them, some of us are saying to God, "Lord, how is that wall ever going to come down? It's just impossible, naturally speaking."

The facts of the situation were this: the Bible says that the walls of Jericho were so tightly shut up that no one ever came out of the city and no one ever went in. Those were the facts, yet God had a different perspective. He informed Joshua, "See, I have delivered Jericho into your hands, along with its king and its fighting men." At that point God had spoken and the promise was a done deal, but Joshua and the people still had a process to go through. The receiving of the promise would take another seven days—seven days during which they would have to march around the city, probably feeling pretty silly.

Some of us have taken our eyes off the promise of God and all we see is a wall. All that fills our vision is this great, impenetrable obstacle that is keeping us from possessing what we've waited for so long. We are so close to receiving, yet so far away.

None of us is smart enough, rich enough, talented or well-connected enough to bring down a barrier which God has allowed in our life in order to shape us, stretch us, and mold us according to his purposes. It will come down when he is ready. Our job is to keep marching, marching, marching, until he gives us the order to shout because our promise has arrived!

MOMENT OF REFLECTION

What will it mean for you to "keep marching" today?

February 25

Why Is It Taking So Long?

The Lord is not slow in keeping his promise, as some understand slowness. Instead he is patient with you.

2 PETER 3:9

Often in life, God has to work *in us* before he can release what he has *for us* into our hands. I think of it in terms of a woman becoming pregnant and waiting nine months for her baby to be born. During those nine months a woman becomes a different person—a mother! It doesn't happen overnight; it happens long before the baby is actually born. God uses that period between conception and birth to change a woman's outlook and personality, to prepare her for motherhood, to prepare her to build a family.

Often when we have received the promise of God, we think we have achieved our goal. But in fact, God has not achieved *his* goal—it is only the beginning. God is much more interested in our journey as a whole. When a woman gives birth to her baby, that is not the end of that chapter of her life—it's only the beginning! It is the start of a whole new phase of her journey. The same is true of the promises of God. When God answers our prayers and we think we have reached our destiny, we are still early in our story. There is still so much ahead of us that we haven't bargained for.

The question we most want answered when we have prayed and prayed about something is, "God, why is it taking so long?" God's answer to this question is nearly always, "I need to do something in you so that when I get this answer to you, I can do something through you." God is teaching us to be faithful. He wants us to be faithful with the small things he has placed in our hands, faithful when we haven't yet received the promise, so that we will be good stewards when we do receive it.

MOMENT OF REFLECTION

What are the "small things" that God has placed in your hands? As you journey toward wholeness, how can you be a faithful steward of those "small things"?

February 26

A Journey of Discovery

Simon Peter answered, "You are the Messiah, the Son of the living God."

MATTHEW 16:16

I love that moment when Peter has the revelation that Jesus is truly the Son of the Living God.

I received this revelation for myself after I had been a Christian for a while. I had plenty of opportunity to wallow in self-pity and to label myself a victim, but one day Jesus helped me realize that I wasn't an ex-abused, unnamed, unwanted, poor, marginalized member of an ethnic minority in a foreign country. I was, in fact, a child of Almighty God! I understood who God was to me and who I was to him. Notice that as soon as Simon Peter acknowledged Jesus' identity, Jesus immediately spoke out *Peter's* true identity: "Let me tell you who you are! You're not Simon Bar-Jonah. You're Peter and your purpose is to be the rock on which I will build my church!"

When we get a revelation of who Jesus is, then he will tell us who we are and what we are on this planet to do—and it is so much more than the limitations of our past and present. So much more! But we know that Peter did not immediately become the "rock" that Jesus told him he was. First, he would go on a journey of discovery, fail miserably, and then be healed and raised up by God, humbled and now fully reliant upon him. Although Jesus spoke out Peter's destiny, Peter had to *become* that destiny by cooperating with God's shaping and molding process. He had to let God do what needed to be done.

Once we have a revelation of the purpose of God for our lives, we must commit wholeheartedly to the process of becoming who Jesus says we are and doing what he says we can do. Do not remain limited by who you once were or who you are not, but find out who Jesus says that you are and then undertake the path to becoming who you already are. Yes, I meant what I just wrote.

MOMENT OF REFLECTION

Are you on the path to becoming who Jesus has said you already are?

February 27

God Wants to Invade Your Life

Lift up your heads, you gates; be lifted up, you ancient doors, that the King of glory may come in.

PSALM 24:7

You know how it is when you are expecting visitors at your house. You clean up the lounge, run round with the vacuum cleaner, then the duster, and then spray the air freshener. You round up all the garbage in the kids' rooms and shove it in their cupboards. You run into the bathroom and quickly replace the sandpaper you normally use with the really nice, soft toilet paper reserved for special occasions. You hide all the cheap drinks in your fridge and buy some expensive ones for your guests. Then the visitors come, you all have a nice time together, and eventually they leave—and in no time at all, the kids have wrecked their rooms, the lounge is a mess, the cheap drinks are back in the fridge, and you're staring at the sandpaper again.

This is how we can be with God a lot of the time. We clean the place up really well and invite him in for a visit, but there is no lasting change and soon everything is back to normal.

I don't believe God is into "visitations." My observation is that he is much more into "invasions." He wants to invade our lives and do the things that need to be done so that we will be set free and released into our purpose. When one country is planning to invade another, they don't phone up and say, "Next Wednesday around three o'clock, a few missiles and our army are going to drop in—if that's alright with you." They simply launch an invasion and in they go—and their purpose is generally to overthrow the existing regime and establish a new order. This is what God wants to do with us. He doesn't want to visit with us—he wants to move into our heart, throw out the old, and establish a whole new way of doing things. But we have to allow him to do that now—*today*. Not tomorrow. We have to let him bring his healing and restoration into our lives today.

MOMENT OF REFLECTION

What would it mean for God to be in your life not as an occasional visitor but as someone establishing a whole new order? How can you allow his healing and restoration into your life today?

February 28

Process = Transformation = Freedom

Create in me a clean heart, O God, and renew a right spirit within me. Cast me not away from your presence, and take not your Holy Spirit from me. Restore to me the joy of your salvation, and uphold me with a willing spirit.

PSALM 51:10–12 ESV

Getting past the past is one of the most difficult things we will ever do. It would be so much easier if when we gave our lives to Christ we developed a case of selective amnesia and could simply leave behind all the things that have hurt us or that we have done and wish we hadn't. The fact is, we remember what we have done and what was done to us and often we carry the wounds of our past into our future.

I experienced so much abuse as a child that I developed a number of very unhealthy defense mechanisms in order to protect myself so that I could not be hurt again. If I was going to fulfill my destiny, I was going to have to allow Jesus to tear down the walls that I had built to protect myself because they had now become a prison. My tough exterior and refusal to let anyone close so that they could not hurt me was destroying me and causing my heart to harden.

I tried to avoid dealing with the pain of my past for as long as I could, but if I was ever going to get out of the prison that I helped to put myself in I would have to allow God's Word to penetrate deeply into the darkest places of my soul to bring life, healing, and wholeness. Let me tell you, there is no easy way, no shortcuts. You must do the hard work to be free. Denial does not work. Hiding does not work. Running does not work.

Healing is a process. But if you commit to the work required, then you WILL BE FREE.

MOMENT OF REFLECTION

Are there any wounded areas of your heart and soul that need to be penetrated by Jesus' healing touch?

March

LEARNING TO TRUST

March 1

In the Midst of Loss

For he has not despised or scorned the suffering of the afflicted one; he has not hidden his face from him but has listened to his cry for help.

PSALM 22:24

I will never forget the time Nick and I walked through an unexpected and very challenging experience. We found out we were pregnant with our second baby, and we were ecstatic. Then one day, I went to a routine doctor's appointment, excited to hear my baby's heartbeat for the first time. As the doctor began to listen for the heartbeat, I held my breath and waited for the rapid, miraculous sound of the tiny life inside of me. But the doctor seemed to be taking a long time to find it, and the look on his face told me that something was seriously wrong. After several minutes, he said the words no expectant woman wants to hear: "Christine, I'm so sorry, but I can't find a heartbeat."

To say I was utterly shocked is an understatement; at that instant my mind was bombarded with many destructive thoughts. Could I still believe that God is good, even when my circumstances were not? Would I be able to trust him? Was I willing to apply the truth of the Word to this situation despite the disappointment?

In the days following my loss, I took care to be constantly in the house of God. It was during one of these times of worship that I had what can only be described as a supernatural encounter with God in which he healed my heart. He took my grief and filled me with a renewed hope for my future. I believe this happened because I had made a choice to worship him in the midst of my challenges and adversity.

Holding on to God in the midst of a painful season or trial might not always be the easiest thing to do, but trust me: if I can do it, anyone can do it. The same Holy Spirit who helped me is available to help each one of us.

MOMENT OF REFLECTION

Have you suffered a loss that has left you reeling? As you learn to trust God, what first step can you take to receive God's healing?

March 2

Surviving Disappointment

And at three in the afternoon Jesus cried out in a loud voice, "Eloi, Eloi, lema sabachthani?" (which means "My God, my God, why have you forsaken me?").

MARK 15:34

Disappointment is a sad and terribly lonely place. We all land there at some point in our lives. Our children move away and never call. Colleagues betray us. The company to which we've devoted our years downsizes, and we're on the layoff list right along with the newcomer and the slacker. The man we love doesn't love us back. The perfect child we dream about and tend in pregnancy is born with defects that will make the rest of our lives, and all our family members' lives, nothing less than challenging. We get a disease or suffer an injury for which there is no relief or cure. Our investments dwindle. Friends disappear. The one we've prayed to find Jesus never does. Our dreams shatter and our best-laid plans go astray. Other Christians fail us. People disappoint us. We can disappoint ourselves, and at times we may even feel that God himself has let us down.

The long series of disappointments we accumulate in a lifetime can stop us from moving forward into all the goodness God has planned for us—and that means they'll be stopping not only us but also those God has destined us to reach along our life's journey. After all, how can we convince others of the wonder of God's promises if we doubt them ourselves? How can we share how God has saved us when we don't feel saved at all?

Why is it that we can know in our heads that God has our good in mind and that he can redeem any and every circumstance, and yet we can still feel hugely disappointed and deeply despondent? Our heads tell us God is trustworthy—but in a moment of aching disappointment, our hearts tell us he's not even there.

In these places of deep disappointment, we must remind ourselves of those things about God that we know to be true, though they might not *feel* true at the moment. We must conclude for ourselves that the valley of death through which we are walking truly is a shadow, and that shadow does not define our lives. Christ does.

MOMENT OF REFLECTION

Think back over the disappointments you've had in your life. Did they help you learn to trust God more, or to be wary?

March 3

Losing Everything

Though he slay me, yet will I hope in him.

JOB 13:15

The book of Job tells us the story of a man of great wealth who, in a terrifying series of events, loses everything—his children, his money, even his health. Sitting in the dust, surrounded by friends who have come to help him probe why such things have happened to him, Job laments his losses and asks the great existential questions: "How many wrongs and sins have I committed? What has been my offense? Is there any hope for me?"

Job's friends speak up, offering him the world's wisdom, which is no help at all. Finally God speaks—but even he does not answer Job's questions. Instead, he merely says that he is God, the great I AM, all-powerful and all-knowing, and that Job has no reason or right to question him. Job humbly repents—and God chooses to restore all that Job has lost, and more.

In the entire story, God never finds it necessary to explain himself. We will never understand, this side of heaven, why bad things happen to us and those we love. Nor will we understand so many unexplainable tragedies in this world, from war to famine to human trafficking to earthquakes. But this doesn't mean that we should stop trusting God, who has proven again and again that he loves us. We, his creation, have no right to tell God how to express that love. We can know, for sure, that his choices will not be our choices.

Is God unfair? Unjust? No, in fact, our very definitions of justice derive from God. Is he silent? He may choose *not* to speak to us directly; the psalmist often speaks of God's silence. And yet he *has* given us his Word, full of his messages to us, messages of love and reassurance.

Remember this: While there is breath in your lungs, there is hope —the promise of a new day. The key is that we continue to trust God even when everything screams for us to doubt his goodness. I don't know what you may be going through right now, but God does. He knows. He cares. He tends.

MOMENT OF REFLECTION

What questions do you have for God? Write down the three most pressing and surrender them to God as an act of trust.

March 4

Something Better

But we had hoped that he was the one who was going to redeem Israel. And what is more, it is the third day since all this took place.

LUKE 24:21

Two heartbroken and bitterly disappointed disciples, leaving Jerusalem after Jesus' burial, were on the road to a town called Emmaus. They had hoped and believed that Jesus was the one sent to redeem Israel. But those hopes were shattered just as his body was shattered, and then beaten, bruised, crucified, and buried. Their dreams died on the cross with him.

A man met them on the road and walked along with them as they talked of these things. But they were so downcast, so crushed, they never took a good look at their fellow traveler. Their heads, like their hearts, were bent in despair.

"What are you discussing?" the man asked.

Amazed, they stopped. "Are you the only one visiting Jerusalem who does not know the things that have happened there in these days?"

"What things?" the man asked.

"The chief priests and rulers handed Jesus of Nazareth over to be sentenced to death, and they crucified him," the men replied. "It is the third day since all this took place."

It was then that the apparent stranger began explaining to them how Israel *was* going to be redeemed. He knew the promises of God by heart and explained how those promises would be fulfilled in such a way that they would change the world. A new kingdom was at hand.

When they reached Emmaus, the disciples urged the man to have dinner with them. When they all sat down to eat that night, he took bread, gave thanks, broke it, and began to give it to them.

Suddenly their eyes were opened. The one walking with them through their disappointment, the one who gave them hope that God had a plan—a plan so big that even a crucifixion couldn't stop it, a plan that would in fact use the crucifixion to redeem the world—was Jesus himself. He was not only alive but here, right in front of them, blessing them, feeding them, walking them through their deepest disappointment. He had not left them; he had not forsaken them.

Sometimes, like the disciples, we're so blinded by disappointment that we can't see Jesus walking with us through our heartache, leading us to something better ahead. He wants to show us that God has made a way for us that leads far beyond disappointment.

MOMENT OF REFLECTION

Think back through your life. Are there any occasions when a bitter disappointment has turned out to be a great blessing?

March 5

Divine Appointments

So Pharaoh said to Joseph, "I hereby put you in charge of the whole land of Egypt."

GENESIS 41:41

Isn't it interesting that the word *appointment* comes from within the word *disappointment*? I've often marveled at that because I've seen again and again how disappointments take something from us: a dream, a piece of our hearts—maybe whole chunks of it. But disappointment leaves something too: a gift, an opportunity, the possibility of creating change. This means we can move from the valley of the shadow of death to new horizons and bring others with us on that road.

The enemy would like us to feel such a depth of disappointment that we never find our way back to the plan God has for us. If he can convince us to stay stuck in our disappointment, we'll miss many of our future God appointments. I realize that some disappointments seem so big that we can't imagine ever being able to move beyond them. We ask deep questions and they go unanswered.

Joseph could have become bitter when he ended up in the pit, was sold into slavery, and thrown in prison through no fault of his own. His dream appeared shattered by disappointment. Yet, because he did not lose hope, he finally stepped into his divine appointment and was put in charge of Egypt.

We too will encounter many disappointments along our journey and must decide ahead of time that we will not allow them to derail us. So much of our Christian walk has to do with learning to trust the goodness and faithfulness of God despite what happens to us or is happening around us. This sounds much easier to do than it actually is. When your emotions are screaming and your heart has been betrayed, the door of opportunity has closed, or that relationship has broken down, the last thing you feel like doing is trusting God and continuing the journey. Can I encourage you today with these words? Even if people have disappointed you or circumstances have not turned out as you had hoped or prayed, know that God is with you, cares for you, and loves you. He is working all these things together for your good right at this very moment. There are many future God appointments on the other side of this disappointment.

MOMENT OF REFLECTION

Have you experienced a disappointment that led to a divine appointment in your life?

March 6

Landing Safely

Those who look to him are radiant; their faces are never covered with shame. This poor man called, and the LORD heard him; he saved him out of all his troubles.

PSALM 34:5–6

We live in a dark world. Rain falls. Storms come. Lightning strikes. Our lives can shatter at any moment. The roof can fall in. As long as we live, we will have something to lose—little pieces of ourselves. The people we love, the life choices we cherish—there is always something at risk, something dear, some cause for fear. We can choose to surrender to that fear and let it rule our lives, or we can surrender all those things we love and fear we will lose to Christ and live fearlessly—undaunted.

Once, my paralyzing fear of flying kept me bound to the island of Australia. But because Jesus calmed that fear, the very thing I once dreaded has become my vehicle to minister to others in darkness. I overcame the fear of flying very early in my ministry life, but I have had to make ongoing choices not to fall back into that fear and allow it to rule me. For instance, on a flight from Chicago to North Carolina, the captain informed us that the landing gear was malfunctioning and we would have to return to Chicago, prepared for a difficult landing. As he announced our approach back at O'Hare Airport and gave instructions, I watched the people around me brace for the worst. They held onto the armrests of their seats or the hand or arm of the person sitting next to them. Many audibly prayed.

I closed my eyes.

My hand in Nick's, I prayed silently: "Lord, I am ever so grateful you helped me choose to push through my fear of flying. There were times I never thought I would or could get back on a plane, but I so wanted your will and purpose for my life. How many times have I had to choose to get on a flight afraid—and yet every time, you have been with me, comforting me, enabling me, strengthening me? And because of that I have been able to go to so many cities and nations around the world and reach people I would never have otherwise been able to reach."

Greeted by the sound of rubber hitting the tarmac, the passengers erupted in spontaneous applause. As we gradually decelerated down the long runway, we passed police cars with sirens blasting, fire trucks, ambulances, and ground personnel. Within minutes, the door of the plane was opening, and light was streaming in. Once again I was grateful that I had not allowed fear to have its way in my life. Instead I chose God's power, strength, and a sound mind.

MOMENT OF REFLECTION

What are the three things you fear most in life?
Where will you start to challenge your fears and begin to live undaunted?

March 7

Shame Off You

Adam and his wife were both naked, and they felt no shame.

GENESIS 2:25

Did you know that God's original intent for his children was that we would never feel any shame? The word *shame* in Hebrew denotes something so much stronger than to be embarrassed; it conveys a fear of exploitation or evil. It is amazing to me that from the outset, Scripture records that Adam and Eve were in the Garden of Eden and had no fear of evil. It was important to God that we be free to walk with him and each other in full transparency, vulnerability, and purity.

Although this is how God created us, we know that this is not how things are. When Adam and Eve sinned, their first response was to hide from God because they discovered they were naked, and so they were afraid. Ever since, we have been hiding from God and one another. Shame eats away at the core of who we are. It's our way of telling our Creator that what he fearfully and wonderfully made is not good.

I was abused as a young child and carried shame well into my adult years. I felt that I was a mistake and somehow fundamentally flawed. When you are a victim of childhood abuse, you begin by being ashamed of what is happening to you, but you eventually come to the point where you think it is *because* of you that bad things are happening. A constant recording in your head repeats the phrase, "What's wrong with me?" There is no torment like inner torment.

After many years, I finally discovered that you cannot run from yourself, you cannot medicate yourself enough to numb the pain, you cannot achieve enough to feel better about yourself in the long term, nor can you do enough to rid yourself of the stench of shame. You must bring your shame to Jesus.

Some of us are ashamed of what was done to us; some of us are ashamed of what we have done to ourselves and others. Whatever shame's source, when we surrender it to the healing touch of Jesus, we can finally walk free from the prison it has built around us. Jesus will never dishonor or disgrace us. He took our shame upon the cross, and what God first covered in the garden Jesus once more covered with his blood.

You were not created to live under the unbearable burden of shame and you do not have to. You can bring your shame to the foot of the cross and allow Jesus to take it from you.

You can trust him.

MOMENT OF REFLECTION

Are you still carrying around the burden of shame?
Ask Jesus to lift it off you right now.

March 8

Forget about It

Brothers and sisters, I do not consider myself yet to have taken hold of it. But one thing I do: Forgetting what is behind and straining toward what is ahead ...

PHILIPPIANS 3:13

God has an amazing purpose and destiny for each one of us, but the degree to which we will fulfill our purpose on the planet is largely determined by the decisions we make today about our yesterday. Every one of us had a yesterday, a past. For some, it was wonderful; for others, it was bad; and for others, it was nondescript.

Paul reminds us in this passage that he was determined to let go of everything that was in his yesterday (good, bad, nondescript) so that he could be free to reach forward into his tomorrow. We cannot grab hold of our future if we are still clinging to our past. We must always remember that where we are going is much more important than where we have been.

The key to moving on is letting go. We must courageously and intentionally let go of our past because it does not automatically leave. We cannot erase our past, deny it, outrun it, or escape it. We must *choose* to deal with our past so we don't get stuck there and allow it to define our future.

We can only step into tomorrow by dealing with our yesterday today. We must deal with past rejection, hurt, betrayal, offenses, abandonment, abuse, mistakes, regret, and failures or they will deal with us. At some point, we need to stop playing the blame game and embrace the pain of the process of recovery so that we can move on.

We must stop thinking, talking about, and listening to conversations about "back there" and start thinking and talking about all the good things that God has for us in our future. After all, his plans for us are for good and not for evil; they are plans to prosper and not harm us.

We cannot change the past, but as we deal with it and move on, we can change the future.

MOMENT OF REFLECTION

Do you have any areas of your past that are holding you back from stepping into the future?

March 9

Trust Him

Cast all your anxiety on him because he cares for you.

1 PETER 5:7

It's an easy thing to say we trust God, but it is definitely not an easy thing for some of us to do—especially if we come from a background where our trust has been consistently betrayed. In order to last the distance, we need to strongly develop the habit of not trying to control and orchestrate our lives and futures, but rather give them to God.

It is one thing to plan and prepare for the future, but another to try to manipulate events, people, or circumstances. I have learned that I cannot control people or events. God is sovereign; I am not. When I learned to trust and rest in the sovereignty of God, I found that my life became so much more peaceful. Stress, anxiety, worry, scheming, and fretting will not take you to your destiny any quicker. In fact, they are likely to sabotage your future.

When we believe that God truly cares for us, it is so much easier to cast our cares upon him. No one is going to entrust anything that matters to them to someone who does not care for them. Today, I want you to know that God's plans for you are for good and not evil. God started this work in you, and he will bring it to completion.

If God is for you, then who can be against you? You can trust him with every detail of your life.

MOMENT OF REFLECTION

Can you think of any area or areas in your life that you have not relinquished control to God?

March 10

True Identity

So in Christ Jesus you are all children of God through faith.

GALATIANS 3:26

The truth is that you can't have and do all that God has for you if you don't know who you really are; and who you really are can only be found in Christ. Our identity doesn't lie in our gender, ethnicity, socioeconomic background, education level, or career status. It lies in Christ himself.

For me, the source of my true identity was tested to the core when I was thirty-three years old and found out that I was adopted. The revelation that I was not who I thought I was could have caused me to have a serious breakdown had I not made the choice to focus on who I really was in Christ.

But because I had the Word diligently sown into my heart, I was able to draw on that truth and not be overcome by my circumstances. Day and night, the Word of God became my meditation and helped me keep my head above water during what was a tumultuous period of my life. I honestly believe that years of grief, anger, resentment, confusion—and even therapy—were avoided because of the Word and the fact that I knew my true identity as a child of God.

The enemy will always challenge our sense of identity, but the best and only sure defense is fully grasping who we really are in Christ.

MOMENT OF REFLECTION

Who do you believe yourself to be in God?
What difference would it make in your life if you truly understood that you were a son or daughter of God?

March 11

Peace through Prayer

Do not be anxious about anything, but in every situation, by prayer and petition, with thanksgiving, present your requests to God.

PHILIPPIANS 4:6

We girls love security. We want to know who we're going to marry, how many children we're going to have, whether or not our husbands will get that promotion at work ... then we want to know who our kids are going to marry and how many children they're going to have! From the time we wake up until the moment our heads hit the pillow at night, there are countless issues we could choose to worry about. But do you know what I have found to be true? Almost nothing that I've allowed to consume me or make me anxious has ever come to fruition. And even if it has, God has always showed himself to be much bigger than the situation.

I can't recount the amount of sleep I've lost worrying about things I ultimately couldn't control anyway. I had to discipline myself to intentionally give up all my anxiety, turn my requests over to God, and trust him to take care of things. I have had to learn to substitute my anxiety with God's peace, and this could ultimately be achieved only through prayer.

I believe there's a direct correlation between trusting God and prayer. Prayer is our way to communicate with the Father, our opportunity to bring our gratitude, needs, and concerns before him. Sometimes we think we don't have enough time to pray because we have a zillion other things to do and no extra slot in our schedule. I know that feeling well.

I was not able to find peace in my heart about my prayer life until I discovered this one thing: prayer has no formal location or time-slot requirement! Simply put, prayer is a way of life. When we pray, we are trusting God with our needs and future rather than depending on ourselves. In essence, unceasing prayer means continual dependence upon and constant communion with our Father, and with this comes the supernatural peace that only God can give.

MOMENT OF REFLECTION

How comfortable do you feel when you pray?
Are you comfortable having a conversation with God?

March 12

Anchor Your Soul

We have this hope as an anchor for the soul, firm and secure. It enters the inner sanctuary behind the curtain.

HEBREWS 6:19

I remember being on a boat on the Mediterranean Sea when a sudden and rather brisk storm arose. The boat was rocking like crazy, yet the captain of the ship was as calm as could be. He had dropped the anchor, and as long as that anchor kept a firm hold, he knew his vessel would be fine. Though I've endured much airplane turbulence, I've not had much experience with water turbulence, so the captain's confidence in the anchor brought me great comfort.

This little boat voyage was the perfect visual to the Scripture in Hebrews which describes our hope in God as an anchor for our souls. It holds us safely behind the curtain in God's presence.

As we pursue our purpose, there will most certainly be times when the circumstances around us get rocky. If our hope is in things, our position, or what others think of us, we're likely to find that the "boat" of our life starts taking on water. Before we know it, we'll find ourselves shipwrecked. But if our hope is anchored in Jesus, despite the turbulence we feel, we will never be moved.

MOMENT OF REFLECTION

Who is your anchor during the storms of life?
Is that working?

March 13

It's Good to Remember

[God] has caused his wonders to be remembered; the LORD is gracious and compassionate.

PSALM 111:4

Whenever I'm tempted to give up rather than choose to endure and persevere, I usually pull out old journals and prophetic words that I've received over the years to remind myself of God's faithfulness and specific promises to me. As I do, I recall all the good things God has done, and how he has never left or forsaken me. I realize that as he was faithful before, he is faithful now. I also focus on all the things he has blessed me with—including a wonderful husband, two beautiful daughters, an incredible spiritual family, a fantastic team, great friends, a home, a ministry, and internal healing and restoration.

Every time I look back on the timeline of my own story, I see God's grace, redemption, and protection. It's so important we remember where we have come from, but even more importantly, that we remember the personal defining moments when God has exhibited his faithfulness. These will help to carry us through difficult seasons and give us the strength to endure the future challenges we may face.

Ultimately, we must never forget that trials and struggles will come our way. It doesn't mean that we've blown it, or that our spiritual lives are a wreck. Uncertainty is a constant in life, but it doesn't have to prevent us from pursuing God's purposes. When we choose to endure rather than throw in the towel when times get tough, one thing is certain: we are on our way to fulfilling our God-given destiny.

MOMENT OF REFLECTION

What stories of God's faithfulness do you remember when you face the storms of life?

March 14

Holding On in the Storm

I will say of the LORD, "He is my refuge and my fortress, my God, in whom I trust."

PSALM 91:2

Our life adventure is not about arriving ... it's always about taking off. And like any adventure, there are always new experiences to negotiate, seasons to endure, twists and turns to navigate. On many days (the vast majority of them) the ride of life will be exciting but uneventful, but on other days it will be downright scary. When those times come, we need to know instinctively how to brace ourselves and get into position to weather whatever comes our way.

While the majority of flights I have been on are uneventful, and the most difficult decision I must make is whether I want a whole-grain roll or sourdough bread with my meal, I've also been on flights when the air turbulence has been the worst imaginable. When this has happened, all I can do is tighten my seatbelt and hang on for dear life. My decision then is to pray and simply trust that the pilot knows what he is doing.

Similarly, when it comes to this faith adventure we are on, we must remember that the chief pilot (God) has everything under control. Even in the midst of what may seem like the toughest storm, if we will simply trust him and listen for his instruction, we'll undoubtedly hear him whisper to our heart: "Yes, daughter, right now it all seems impossible. But just stick with me because when you have me in you—surrounding you, ahead of you, and behind you—nothing is impossible!"

MOMENT OF REFLECTION

Who or what do you run to during turbulent times in your life?

March 15

Make God Bigger

Oh, magnify the LORD with me, and let us exalt His name together.

PSALM 34:3 NKJV

It was while sitting in a lecture room at university that I first saw the black dot that came to change my perspective on most things. The professor projected an image of a small black dot in the middle of a very big white screen. He asked us, "What do you see?" Every student immediately responded to his question, "A black dot." He paused for a considerable length of time, and then asked again, "What do you see?"

When we gave the same reply, he told us that he saw a huge white space. While we saw a small black dot, he saw something far bigger. It had been there all along, but each one of us had missed it.

We see what our eyes are trained to see, and it takes effort and time to train our eyes otherwise. How often do we focus on the small things in life instead of the big God that we serve? We notice what we don't have, what isn't working, what didn't happen, what irritates us, what is broken or has disappointed us. We can have twenty great things happening in our lives, but when one thing does not go right, we lose sight of the twenty and focus on the one little black dot.

We must decide to make God bigger than anything else in our lives. The more we focus on him, the smaller the dots will become.

MOMENT OF REFLECTION

What do you see? In what areas of your life have you been focusing too much on what's wrong? What small details have robbed you of the beauty of the big picture? Ask God for his perspective, his vision, and his eyes today!

March 16

Trust That It Makes a Difference

March around the city once with all the armed men. Do this for six days. Have seven priests carry trumpets of rams' horns in front of the ark. On the seventh day, march around the city seven times, with the priests blowing the trumpets.

JOSHUA 6:3–4

The children of Israel had spent forty years in the wilderness. A whole generation had died there in the desert. Even those most committed to the promises of God must have thought, "Lord, I've waited forty years. When am I going to see the Promised Land?" Forty years is a very long time to wait, but even then the walls of Jericho didn't just collapse straightaway. God said, "I want you to do something ..." The final fulfillment of the promise was still another week away.

After waiting for forty years, another seven days doesn't sound like too much to ask, does it, if it guarantees you receiving your promise? But notice what God asks the people to do. They had marched, marched again, and marched some more in order to get where they were going. Now God asks them to (yes, you guessed it!) *march* around the walls, not just once, but once a day for six days, and seven times on the seventh day!

"Lord, not more marching, surely?"

"Yes," God says, "just keep doing the same old thing you've been doing."

You may be saying to yourself, "Gee, here I am in church again. Another service, another offering, another prayer meeting ... what a waste of time! I'm still not seeing the breakthrough I've been trusting God for." Maybe you don't see any way in which that wall can come down just by you showing up—yet, regardless of appearances, what you are doing is making a difference. And that day is soon coming when that seemingly insurmountable wall shall come down.

MOMENT OF REFLECTION

Choose today to trust that all the "same old things" (prayer, reading the Scriptures, going to church, serving others) are making a difference.

March 17

Tear Down Those Walls

Some trust in chariots and some in horses, but we trust in the name of the LORD our God.

PSALM 20:7

We often build walls around our hearts to protect ourselves from pain and suffering. Because I had been a victim of abuse, I did not trust people or God to protect me, so I subconsciously spent many years building defense mechanisms to protect myself. I inadvertently built a prison that was designed to keep danger out but instead kept me locked in.

I deeply mistrusted the need for intimacy and was angry with myself for needing relationships, so I tried to kill this need. I desperately tried to live above my feelings and trained myself to shut down and off in an instant. I lived in constant suspicion of everyone's motives and viewed any legitimate human need as weakness and childish. I never held children or really wanted to be around them. I always wanted to be in charge and in control. I had become emotionally impenetrable because I did not want to ever feel pain again. I had a good heart, but it was a hard heart.

There came a point in my life where I had hit the wall often enough that I realized the problem was not with everyone else but with me. If I was going to step into the destiny that God had planned and prepared for me, I would have to allow the Holy Spirit to do a deep work inside. To work with people, I needed a tender heart. And the only way a hard heart is made tender is by exposing it to life and trusting that God would take care of me.

I had to learn to trust God and to trust people. I had to learn how to become vulnerable and transparent. I had to lose control and learn how to feel again. This was the most painful process of my life. Tearing down walls is never easy and always messy. It had taken me years of careful construction to build them and, unlike Humpty Dumpty, they did not come tumbling down overnight.

As I committed to the process of healing and restoration, I

discovered that our heavenly Father is loving, kind, compassionate, and gracious. In his tender mercy and endless patience, he proved to me time and time again that he is faithful, and just because people had hurt me did not mean that he had. It was other people (who were hurting themselves) who had abandoned, rejected, discarded, and abused me—not God. He had always been protecting me and what had hurt me had hurt him too.

Hurting people do indeed hurt people. The walls I had built to protect myself ended up hurting many others, and I was merely repeating a cycle I was trying to break. The only way to find freedom and victory was to hand over the key to my prison to Jesus and allow him to do what only he could do.

Today, I am ever so grateful I finally trusted God enough to allow him to be God in my life.

MOMENT OF REFLECTION

Can you identify any defense mechanisms you have developed in your life?

March 18

Trust in God's Timing

What do people gain from all their labors at which they toil under the sun?

ECCLESIASTES 1:3

How amazing it is that God is never late for an appointment that he schedules! Yet so often we feel as if we have turned up for our appointment, but God has not.

The reason is the due dates we impose on the promises of God are often very different from God's appointed times. That's because we tend to impose a due *date* on a promise that God has given us rather than a due *season* for the delivery of that promise.

When I was pregnant with my girls, people would always ask, "When is your due date?" I answered based on the date that the doctor had given me, always knowing that it might not be the exact date because how could anyone but God really know that? When Catherine still had not arrived on her expected date, people's question changed to: "How far past your due date are you?" I eventually realized that Catherine was not overdue; she was coming right on time. All that had happened was that there had been an incorrect assessment of the due date. The actual arrival date was not wrong; the estimation of the due date was.

I have found that God rarely turns up on our time, but he *always* honors his. And when he does, we discover that his time is invariably the perfect time.

MOMENT OF REFLECTION

Do you find it difficult to trust in God's timing? Why or why not?

March 19

The Certainty of Jesus

Praise be to the God and Father of our Lord Jesus Christ! In his great mercy he has given us new birth into a living hope through the resurrection of Jesus Christ from the dead.

1 PETER 1:3

As I travel the world and see the plight of humanity, I note above all else the absence of hope. People are despondent, without a sense of purpose, future, or destiny. Hopelessness permeates the media, politics, the arts, finances, and society at large.

I am so grateful that the Scripture teaches that no matter what is happening *around* us, it is what is happening *in* us that actually matters. We must never forget that Jesus is our hope and an anchor for our soul that is both firm and secure. We live according to a different set of principles than people who do not know Christ; therefore, no matter how bleak things seem, we always have an eternal hope. In the midst of uncertainty we can hold on to the certainty of Jesus.

We must become prisoners of hope because we know the One who is the source of hope. If our ultimate hope were in people, things, or what this world can offer, we too would be hopeless. But our hope is in Christ alone, and all we need is in him. Instead of looking around at the hopeless state of the world, why not choose to look up today into the hopeful eyes of our eternal, ever-loving, gracious Savior?

MOMENT OF REFLECTION

Is your hope in Christ alone? Make a list of the things in which you place your hope.

March 20

You Will Find the God You're Looking For

Commit your way to the LORD; trust in him and he will do this: He will make your righteous reward shine like the dawn, your vindication like the noonday sun.

PSALM 37:5–6

I was once biking down a steep hill at a frightening pace. About halfway down I remembered there was construction work at the bottom of the hill and a large pothole that had not been filled. I became very focused on that pothole and was determined to avoid falling into it. I kept my eyes locked on the very place I did not want to go and inevitably ended up hitting the pothole at full speed. Painfully, I discovered that what you look for ... you will find.

In the same way that I looked for and invariably found that pothole, we tend to find what we look for when it comes to God. In my travels, I have met many people who have shared powerful stories of how God has transformed their lives, marriages, and families; how he has healed them emotionally, spiritually, and physically; how he has saved them from a hopeless past and given them a hope-filled future. The God that they see is One who is big in grace, mercy, love, forgiveness, compassion, hope, and purpose—and so their relationship with him is developed from this perspective.

I also have met many other people who feel that God has disappointed them, not answered their prayers, or has even forsaken them. Often, their lives are filled with sorrow, regret, pain, struggle, anger, offense, despondency, resentment, or fear. The God that they see cannot heal, restore, reconcile, forgive, or love. Consequently, they remain trapped and defeated, all because of their perspective.

I am convinced that if we are to fulfill our purpose, it has less to do with gift, talent, anointing, or ability, and more to do with how we see God. If you see God as One who is willing and able to help you overcome the obstacles of your past in order to lay hold of your future, then you will find what you are looking for. If you choose to look for a big God, then you will find a big God. You will see him working in creative and unique ways that others in the same circumstances cannot see.

MOMENT OF REFLECTION

How do you truly see God?
(Remember, what you look for you will find.)

March 21

Your Life Isn't Small

Dear, dear Corinthians, I can't tell you how much I long for you to enter this wide-open, spacious life. We didn't fence you in. The smallness you feel comes from within you. Your lives aren't small, but you're living them in a small way. I'm speaking as plainly as I can and with great affection. Open up your lives. Live openly and expansively!

2 CORINTHIANS 6:11–13 MSG

I will never forget walking into the home Nick was convinced we were going to buy. The location was perfect; it was advertised as having unlimited potential and being a renovator's dream (that should have been a sign); and most importantly, it was listed at a price we could afford. (That should have been another sign.)

As soon as we walked through the front door, I had to stop because there was nowhere to walk. The house was cluttered with books, furniture, ornaments, food items, magazines, newspapers, and a collection of everything conceivable to collect. I could not see the flooring because of the mess and trinkets scattered everywhere, nor could I tell the color of the walls because of everything hanging on them.

Being the compulsive minimalist and tidy person that I am, it was surprising that I did not pass out when confronted by such disorder and chaos. Nick kept whispering, "Christine, you have to look beyond the clutter to see the potential of what we could do with this place." I still think one of the greatest miracles ever is that I agreed to buy that house, though I have to admit Nick was right—the house did end up having the potential he said it did.

The project was a major undertaking, but the difference that it made was remarkable. The shell of the home was the same, but on the inside everything had changed. Once all the junk had been emptied out, I saw how spacious the house actually was. We also knocked down non-load-bearing walls to make the house appear more open and repainted every room. The house always had the potential to look magnificent and to contain beautiful things, but in order for it to realize its potential, we had to clean, purge, and renovate it in its entirety.

In the same way that our future house looked small when I first toured it, I think we often live our lives far smaller than necessary because of excess clutter and trash. This clutter hinders God from having adequate space to be big in our lives. God is a big God, and the only thing that limits him is the clutter within us.

MOMENT OF REFLECTION

In what ways might you be limiting God's work in you?

March 22

The Truth Will Set You Free

Then you will know the truth, and the truth will set you free.

JOHN 8:32

It was a shocking moment when I found out that I was not who I thought I was. In an instant, most of the facts that I thought to be true about my life changed. My parents were not actually my biological parents; my birth certificate was not my real birth certificate; and, most shockingly, all my neighbors and relatives knew the truth about my life but never let me in on the secret.

In that moment I began to wonder what else in my life was not real. What other facts had I believed that were not true? Could I trust anyone or anything else? If I kept on that train of thought, no doubt I would have ended up derailing, but I am ever so grateful that I had spent many years hiding God's Word in my heart. God's Word is living and active and is supposed to interact with us in these critical moments of life. The Word was immediately a comfort, a lamp, a light, and an instructor for me. Because I knew the Word, I could fall back on God's truth, his promises, and what I knew about his character.

There were so many facts screaming for my attention in that surreal moment when I discovered that I was not my parents' biological child, but I had to make the big God that I served bigger than my emotions, questions, pain, and shock. After a few seconds to collect my thoughts, I almost surprised myself with what came out of my mouth: "Oh well, before I was formed in my mother's womb, whoever's womb that was, he knew me and knitted together my innermost parts. I am fearfully and wonderfully made." It was the Word of God and not the word of hurt or shock that spoke.

By making the truth of God's Word bigger than the facts that had been revealed, I could readily ground myself in the great overriding truth that God is who he says he is and could be trusted even when everything else had just shifted in my life. Newly disclosed facts were bombarding me, but the truth never changed.

MOMENT OF REFLECTION

Has the Bible ever provided you with truths about God that helped you to trust him even in challenging circumstances?

March 23

God Is Trustworthy

Sovereign LORD, you are God! Your covenant is trustworthy, and you have promised these good things to your servant.

2 SAMUEL 7:28

We live in times of instability, uncertainty, and fear. We are daily bombarded with negative news reports and projections that everything is getting worse. This includes the economy, the environment, terrorism, crime, and so the list continues. If we do not guard our hearts and minds, it is easy to be overwhelmed by anxiety, stress, and worry. In fact, an increasing percentage of our society is requiring prescription medication in order to combat these very emotions.

If we can remember that God is in ultimate control of the world, then I believe that the anxiety in our lives can decrease. When we can accept what we cannot change, and take responsibility for the things we can, then we begin to make progress. Worry, stress, and anxiety paralyze us with fear. Fear is a strategy of the enemy to stop us from moving forward. It does not add one single ounce of value to our lives and is a great robber of love, joy, and peace.

The only way we can become free from the bondage of worry is to trust God. In order to trust him, you must believe he is worthy of your trust. If you believe that God is good and that he does good, then you will continue to trust him even when your circumstances are not good. Don't worry about anything, but pray about everything. The fact that we can pray about everything shows me that everything can be affected by prayer. There is not one single thing in your life that is not important to God. He cares about you and everything that matters to you. Make a decision today to stop talking to your friends or yourself about things that you cannot change, and start talking to God instead. Worry has never increased productivity nor has it added joy to the adventure of life!

MOMENT OF REFLECTION

What have you been worrying about that you need to pray about instead?

March 24

Pass through the Gates

I will go before you and will level the mountains; I will break down gates of bronze and cut through bars of iron.

ISAIAH 45:2

During a trip to Berlin, Nick and I visited the beautiful Brandenburg Gate. Built in 1778, it is one of Berlin's main landmarks and the only remaining gate of a series through which the city was once entered. Vehicles and pedestrians could travel freely through the gate until the Berlin Wall was built, blocking access from 1961 to 1989. When the Berlin Wall fell, this gate again became a symbol of freedom and the desire to unify the city. In fact, the Festival of Freedom was held there to celebrate the twentieth anniversary of the fall of the Berlin Wall. This gate that had for three decades contained and restricted people once more became the gateway to freedom.

Gates can be swung, drawn, or lowered to block an entrance. They can also provide a means of access. The same gate that blocks a person's path can become the very gate that opens the door to his or her future. We all have various "gates" in our lives. Some of these gates in our lives are glaringly obvious; they are big and appear impenetrable. Other gates, we are not even aware of. It is as if we keep hitting an invisible wall blocking our path, but we don't know what it is.

Some gates are placed in our lives by God because we are not supposed to go down certain paths. These are gates of protection and wisdom. Conversely, there are other gates that we should refuse to sit in front of any longer because they are blocking our dreams, purposes, and destinies, causing them to die. When we remain at these gates, sitting in the same place, looking at the same thing, we end up losing sight of the promise of God that is on the other side. There are so many gates that will try to separate us from the purpose of God, but God is bigger than any of them.

MOMENT OF REFLECTION

Trusting in God does not usually mean simply waiting around for something to happen. Are you sitting at the gate, waiting for entrance to something better than you have now? If so, why are you waiting?

March 25

Walking in Truth, Love, and Forgiveness

So do not fear, for I am with you; do not be dismayed, for I am your God. I will strengthen you and help you; I will uphold you with my righteous right hand.

ISAIAH 41:10

I wish I could tell you that I prayed one single prayer and that I was instantly healed of all the pain of my past, but that would not be true. There was no drive-thru breakthrough for me. I had to travel many valleys and through much pain and struggle to get free from my past and step into the promise of my future.

You and I have spent the first part of this devotional looking inward so that we can identify those things *in* us that stop God working *through* us. Today I am sharing three things that helped bring breakthrough in my life, and I pray that they serve to help you find freedom in yours as well.

Learning to face the truth was a big thing for me. I had to admit that I had a problem and then stop blaming others for the way I was acting. I could not change what had happened to me, but I could take responsibility for my responses now. You cannot move forward if you live in denial or self-deception. I had to bring God into the midst of all my mess so that he could deal with it. I thought if I could just keep up the appearance of having it all together, he would not know that I did not. I was deluded and had to make a decision to invite him into my calamity so that he could get me out.

Learning to receive the unconditional love of God was also profoundly difficult for this performance-driven, rejected, shame-filled, guilt-laden woman. I eventually got to the place where I truly believed God loved me as much in the midst of my mess as he would when I finally got my act together. Grace is difficult to digest, but for a victim of abuse it is harder still.

Learning to truly forgive the perpetrators of the abuse against me was the single most difficult thing I have ever done—and the one thing above everything else that resulted in my gaining true freedom. For a long time I felt that if I forgave those men, it would make what they did to me okay, or that they would get off very lightly. I wanted them to feel the pain that they had inflicted on me. I am ever so grateful that God gave me the grace to release them to him at last. Nothing is more liberating than not having to carry these abusers with me into my future because of my own bitterness and unforgiveness.

Still, I have to make a decision every single day to believe these things if I want to continue to walk in freedom. I must replace my thoughts with God's thoughts. I must daily renew my mind with the truth of God's Word. I must obey God in the small things (and trust him with everything) so that I do not slip back into patterns of destructive behavior. I am not so healed on this side of eternity that I no longer need Jesus.

I need him for my very next breath.

And. So. Do. You.

MOMENT OF REFLECTION

Do you need to work on any of these three things in your life?

March 26

It's Never Too Late

"Even now," declares the LORD, "return to me with all your heart, with fasting and weeping and mourning." Rend your heart and not your garments. Return to the LORD your God, for he is gracious and compassionate, slow to anger and abounding in love.

JOEL 2:12 – 13

No doubt, at one time or another all of us have dropped one or several of the batons with which we have been entrusted in this divine relay of which we are a part. But the good news is that it is never too late to pick up the baton right where you are and once again begin to run your race so that you can finish your course.

It is important to remember that God is bigger than any of our past mistakes and that Jesus has redeemed our lives, so that we can all have forgiveness for our past, a fresh start today, and a hope for the future. His mercies are new every morning, so do not let yesterday's regrets or mistakes stop you from partaking of today's readily available fresh mercy.

I believe that while our lungs still have breath in them, our heart is still beating, and blood is still streaming through our arteries and veins, there is always a hope and there is always a future. God always gives us another chance.

It is never too late to allow Jesus to complete the work of salvation that he started in you. Remember, we cannot change the past, but we can all make decisions today that can change our future. Don't believe the lie that you have been disqualified from this divine relay. Instead, pick up your baton, look unto Jesus, and start to run your race again.

MOMENT OF REFLECTION

Have you dropped any of the spiritual batons God entrusted to you? Are you willing to try again?

March 27

In the Desert

Now Moses was tending the flock of Jethro his father-in-law, the priest of Midian, and he led the flock to the far side of the wilderness and came to Horeb, the mountain of God. There the angel of the LORD appeared to him in flames of fire from within a bush.

EXODUS 3:1–2

We all feel like we're in a desert spiritually sometimes. Long before he ever worked through me, God took me through very dry seasons where he molded, shaped, and refined me on the inside.

During these desert times, it seems that God has abandoned us, that no one knows where we are, nor does anyone care. We feel weary, dry, and forsaken. We can find ourselves in that place in any of our relationships—at home, at work, with career or ministry. We can be tempted to leave that place to find a cool, restful, peaceful spot out of the heat and fire, somewhere nice and comfortable. But if we do not allow God to work in us on the backside of the desert, then we will never be promoted or grafted into the ultimate place of our destiny. We must learn not to despise where we are on the way to where we are going, but to allow God to have his way in us.

It was on the backside of the desert that God showed up in a powerful way in Moses's life, appearing "in flames of fire from within a bush." Can you even begin to imagine this scenario? God came to find Moses in a place that was not prominent or apparently significant. When God wants to find you, he knows your location. You do not have to leave your place to try to find a more noticeable place, in the hope that someone will discover your gifts and talents. You simply need to be in your place. God has the best cosmic GPS system, and when he wants you, he will find you.

MOMENT OF REFLECTION

Do you trust that God sees you and knows your situation?
Do you have faith that God has a future planned for you?

March 28

Everything in Its Place

But in fact God has placed the parts in the body, every one of them, just as he wanted them to be.

1 CORINTHIANS 12:18

I have to admit I am a person of many quirks; don't laugh because I am sure you have your own. One of the things I am obsessive about is tidiness. We have a saying in our home: "There is a place for everything, and everything must be in its place." I have been known to throw things away because they were not put in their place, and have also been seen pulling beloved toys out of the trash because my girls were so distraught about me throwing their toys away. (I already told you I am quirky, but I am working on it.)

I like to remind anyone who will listen that God himself sets things in their place, and the reason he does this is so that everything functions more effectively and efficiently. There is much to be said about everything being in its place.

It is not unusual for me to receive emails and letters from believers all over the world who, for one reason or another, feel displaced or misplaced within the body of Christ. They often outline myriad reasons for why they feel that way, many of which are indeed valid. However, I have found more often than not that it comes back to the fact that they have never *embraced their place.*

There is a place for every believer in the body of Christ—without exception. If we leave our place because of frustration, disappointment, or offense, it will lead to disconnection. If you try to transplant yourself to the place you want to be, you may find that your "organ" is rejected by the body because you are no longer in your place. Ultimately you need to go back, submit to the process, and reconnect with your place. It often takes a degree of pain to fix a broken place, but with the love and grace of God, healing can and does occur. We need to deal with the broken and fragmented parts of the body in order to have a healthy functioning whole.

MOMENT OF REFLECTION

Do you trust that there is a place for you in the body of Christ, no matter what you have been through?

March 29

An Issue of Trust

Father, if you are willing, take this cup from me; yet not my will, but yours be done.

LUKE 22:42

Over the years, I have learned that we cannot always be doing what we want to do, when we want to do it, and how we want to do it, and still be following Jesus at the same time. We must commit to being about our Father's business at all times, regardless of the inconvenience, risk, or hardship that it causes. His business must always be our first priority.

I spent many years in full-time youth ministry and watched countless times as young people walked away from God's plan and timing for their lives because they wanted other things first. They wanted to follow Jesus, but on their time schedule. We need to learn to go when Jesus calls, and to trust him with all the other details that may arise. God is a good God and has a great plan for our lives, but we must learn to trust him. The issue of "first" is really an issue of trust. The question we must ask ourselves is, "Do we trust God enough with the outworking of our future that we put his priorities before our own?"

In order to fulfill our destiny, there will be many moments where we must subordinate our will to that of the Father. We can rest confidently in the truth that anything God has for us is better than anything we may think we want. God's will, purpose, and plan is so much greater than ours, and will always work together for our ultimate good. Always.

MOMENT OF REFLECTION

Do you trust God enough to put his priorities before your own?

March 30

Moving into the Future

There is surely a future hope for you, and your hope will not be cut off.

PROVERBS 23:18

I once spoke at a women's conference in Bedworth, England, a short drive away from Stratford-upon-Avon, the birthplace of William Shakespeare. Having a major in English literature, I could not pass up the opportunity to visit this beautiful village, the home of one of my favorite playwrights.

As I traversed the quaint cobblestones, imagining William himself walking along the very same streets, I noticed a shop that specialized in family trees and heritage. Nick's family origins trace back to England, so I thought I would check to see if we were perhaps related to royalty. I sat at the computer and typed in Nick's name and the names of relatives that I knew, and then waited for the printout, all the while thinking to myself, "Who knows who we could be related to—perhaps even the queen herself!"

A few minutes later, the assistant handed me the results of Nick's bloodline, which were very different from what I had anticipated. Instead of being related to knights or lords, my husband was a descendant of convicts, criminals, thieves, and pirates!

The truth is, there is nothing we can do to change our ancestors—or even more recent personal history. But though we cannot change the past, we can make choices today that will determine our future.

I am so grateful that I chose to trust God and make him bigger than my past. This decision not only impacts me but also everyone around me, including the generations that will come after me. My daughters will one day walk into a similar shop and receive the computer printout of their family tree. The first part will be the same as the one I received, but when they get to March 30, 1996, everything will change. That is the day that Nick and I were married and made the decision to draw a line in the sand when it came to our bloodlines.

While the past was still the past, we chose to move into the future that God prepared for us.

MOMENT OF REFLECTION

Do you trust that God has a future hope for you?

March 31

Reject the Labels

But because of his great love for us, God, who is rich in mercy, made us alive with Christ even when we were dead in transgressions—it is by grace you have been saved.

EPHESIANS 2:4–5

It is so easy to allow ourselves to be defined by the limitations or labels that others place on us. So, in order to walk into the purpose that God has ordained for us, we need to shake off those labels and be defined by the truth of God's Word. I grew up with so many different labels and limitations that nothing short of Jesus Christ himself could have rescued, redeemed, restored, and reactivated me.

Although we now live in an inclusive multicultural world that embraces diversity, that was not the case in Australia when I was growing up, especially when it came to accepting immigrants with a Greek background. My family was demeaned and ridiculed because of our ethnicity. Because of this, I grew up feeling that we were all somehow second-class citizens—that I did not belong anywhere or would ever be accepted by anyone. I was riddled with anger, insecurity, and low self-esteem.

What's more, I grew up in a housing commission area that was at the bottom of the socioeconomic ladder. My neighbors were frequently arrested and imprisoned for drug possession and dealing. No one seemed to have aspirations or high hopes for their future. Instead, it appeared as though everyone was just trying to find a way to exist, to make it through another day.

I also grew up in a culture that did not teach a woman to dream or aspire to anything beyond getting married and having children. We were not encouraged to pursue further education or a career. Male and female roles were clearly defined, stereotyped, and pretty much inescapable. In fact, I was actually ridiculed and chastised by my family when I told them that I had enrolled in university because it "was not something that Greek girls did."

The reality is that we all have negative things in our past, but it is our decision whether or not to allow our past to determine the outcome of our future. We cannot do anything to change the past, but we can decide to stand up today, change our perspective, and walk boldly into the future that awaits us. If we choose to make God bigger than our past, then we can be redefined by who we are in him.

MOMENT OF REFLECTION

Do you trust that God can empower you to overcome your past?

LOVED

April

CHOSEN AND ACCEPTED BY GOD

April 1

God's Workmanship

Before I formed you in the womb I knew you, before you were born I set you apart; I appointed you as a prophet to the nations.

JEREMIAH 1:5

We each arrive on the planet differently. Some babies are planned over, prayed over, and loved by conscientious parents. Others are surprises. Some are unwanted by their parents. While some are conceived in love, others are conceived by force. Some babies are born prematurely. Some are born breech. Some arrive by C-section, and others are pushed out in a few minutes. Some are brought home to lovely nurseries, handpicked strollers, and handmade cribs. Others get hand-me-downs—or nothing at all. Some of us may not like or know the circumstances of our births, but not one of us needs to be defined by or limited by those circumstances. Each of us has the chance to be born again in Christ, a second birth, to connect with our eternal purpose.

Before even the making of the world, God says we were designed and made to do good works in Christ. No matter how we got here, no matter the particulars of our births, we each were chosen in eternity long before we ever arrived in time, on earth.

Regardless of what our parents may have planned or intended, from God's perspective, there was nothing accidental or unintentional about our births. We were not an accident, unknown, unnamed, or unwanted. God has always known who we are.

MOMENT OF REFLECTION

What difference does it make knowing that you were intentionally created by God for a purpose?

April 2

You Are Mine

Yet you, LORD, are our Father. We are the clay, you are the potter; we are all the work of your hand.

ISAIAH 64:8

When we understand that every single human being is created in the image of God and is full of God-given purpose and destiny, we can no longer overlook the grocery clerk at the checkout stand or the downcast person we pass on the street. Instead, we should choose to recognize their value and call out their worth. It means caring enough to help the mom at preschool whose child won't come when called; loving enough to offer a word of cheer or humor to the receptionist at the doctor's office struggling to answer phones and still respond to every question at the counter. It means thanking the garbage man lifting bins at the curb, recognizing the God-made-and-paid-for soul in every person we encounter throughout the day. But we won't—we can't—help others know they matter unless we first recognize how much God loves and chooses each of us. And that's a challenge we must face inside.

As I've mentioned, I was shocked when I learned that I had been adopted. My mum wasn't really my mum. But then I asked her about the day she got the call from the hospital telling her that I had been born. How had she felt? What expectations had she had? Her eyes lit up. With enthusiasm, she explained that she and my dad had been desperately hoping for a girl, since they already had a son. But there were no sonograms back then to reveal whether you were having a boy or a girl. Mum was very close to her sister, who had four boys of her own and also hoped for a girl, so they would chat often about names and dreams for me.

One day my aunt suggested, "Why not Christine?"

"I like that," my mum said. And so the decision was made over a cup of tea. There was nothing deep or spiritual in that decision—they just liked the name Christine. Yet I know that my name, Christine, is derived from the Greek and Latin and means *Christ follower.*

The Christ I follow has given me another name too—a name by which he calls me. And he calls you and others by that same name—a simple name; one word; just four letters, like *love*—that rings loudly through time and space because we have all been chosen before time. He calls us: *Mine.*

MOMENT OF REFLECTION

How does it make you feel to know that God himself has claimed you as his own? Do you see everyone as a child of God?

April 3

Lost and Found

Jesus told them this parable: "Suppose one of you has a hundred sheep and loses one of them. Doesn't he leave the ninety-nine in the open country and go after the lost sheep until he finds it?"

LUKE 15:3–4

If you have one hundred sheep and one wanders off, Jesus tells us, that's the one you hurry to rescue. Isn't that one as valuable as each of the ninety-nine who have been accounted for? In natural disasters and times of war, medical personnel often perform something they call *triage.* It means that they examine the injured and determine which have the best chance of living. They concentrate their efforts on those they think they can save—and, with regret, allow the others to die, or perhaps to rally and recover on their own.

But Jesus doesn't do triage. He leaves the healthy ninety-nine safe in their pens while he goes out into the night looking for the one who is lost, sick, depressed, disappointed, wounded, or enslaved. When he has found it, he lays it across his shoulders and calls together his neighbors to celebrate. How could an almighty God do any less?

That, I believe, is why Jesus told story after story about how easy it is to be lost—and how remarkable it is to be saved. Stories of people hopeless and hurting. People who need living water, people whose souls are tattered, people who are watching the dark close in around them, people whose time is running out.

In Luke's gospel, chapter 15, he told of a lost sheep. This story, he told his followers, is intended to remind them of something he wants them (and you!) to always remember: "No matter how deep the pit or dark the night, I will always look for you and rescue you because I love you with an everlasting love. You are precious to me. Even when you mess up, even when you're careless or mistaken or afraid or broken or weak, I still love you. Even when you are incapable of doing anything for anyone, including yourself, I still love you. And just as I come to you, I come for all those who have made mistakes, who are overlooked, who have been devalued and despised."

Jesus comes for all the wrong people—the careless and uncared for, the merry and the miserable. He comes for the lost.

MOMENT OF REFLECTION

Have you ever felt lost and alone?
How did God reach out to rescue you?

April 4

Little Princess

You are a chosen people, a royal priesthood, a holy nation, God's special possession, that you may declare the praises of him who called you out of darkness into his wonderful light.

1 PETER 2:9

Catherine Bobbie is our firstborn. She's a beautiful, wonderfully charismatic little princess. And when I say "princess," I mean princess! I'm not referring to one of those little girls who like to play dress-up and act like a princess. I'm talking about an honest to goodness, tiara-wearing, legitimate princess—or so Catherine was convinced when she was a toddler. Of course, Nick and I encouraged this behavior. We have given her authentic Disney princess costumes, including gloves, crowns, shoes—everything short of the prince (by order of Nick). What we didn't take into account was the fervor and zeal with which she would embrace her faux royalty (the "faux" part is just between you and me, of course, as Catherine will hear none of that).

She would wear one of her favorite princess outfits *everywhere* we went. Dressed from head to toe, she would visit her subjects at the grocery store, the shopping mall, restaurants, and anywhere else we visited. On a dinner outing, Catherine noticed one of the seating areas in the restaurant was closed off—and made a beeline for it. When the waitress graciously pointed out that there was no seating in that particular section, Catherine looked up and said very sweetly and sincerely, "I'm a princess. Can't I sit anywhere I want to?"

I have to admit that I love this quality about my daughter. She truly believes that she is special. This is a stark contrast to what I believed about myself when I was a child. It took me years (okay, maybe decades) to walk with the confidence and love for myself that Catherine so naturally exhibits. Nick and I are determined never to quash this quality in her.

I can't imagine a better start in life for Catherine than knowing who she is in Christ. After all, God calls us his sons and daughters—and that makes us royalty! We truly are sons and daughters of a king, the apple of our heavenly Father's eye. As we come to understand this, it becomes easy for us to declare his praises to others.

MOMENT OF REFLECTION

How does knowing that God calls you "chosen" and "royal" change the way you think about yourself?

April 5

God Delights in Me

[God] brought me out into a spacious place; he rescued me because he delighted in me.

PSALM 18:19

When I was in my late twenties, I was the head of a community-based youth center and on the way to leading a major Christian youth movement in Sydney, Australia. I was passionately serving God and so busy that my weeks literally felt like one long day with a series of naps (and these were rare). It was a very exciting time for me.

God had given me gifts of leadership and speaking, and many doors of opportunity were opening. I felt like I was living the dream, yet when I placed my head on my pillow at night—well, actually, in the early hours of the morning—I felt like I was dying inside.

When everything was quiet and it was just God and me, the successes from the day would fade away and all that would be left was what felt like a gaping chasm in my heart. No matter how much I accomplished or achieved, I just couldn't seem to find contentment and joy. In order to fill this void, I kept working harder and keeping longer hours, hoping sooner or later my heart would feel fulfilled.

Eventually, the stress and intensity of my schedule took its toll on my body, and I collapsed. Quite literally, in fact. I threw my back out, and my life came to a screeching halt. For the next three weeks (which felt like an eternity!), my days were spent lying on the couch, keeping very still to avoid the pain of movement. I was forced to stop doing and simply be still.

As I lay there feeling like a completely useless Christian, I picked up my Bible. As I flipped through the pages, I came across the verse in Psalms that begins this devotion. It was like God had a megaphone and was screaming to get my attention: "Christine, I delight in *you*. Not just the thousands of young people you minister to, not just in all that you accomplish in my name, but in *you*, my own precious daughter." God delighted in *me*—in me with all my faults, me with all my failings, me with my broken past . . . me immobile on a couch!

And guess what? He delights in you too. Just stop and ponder that thought.

MOMENT OF REFLECTION

Do you feel contentment and joy in your service to God?
How do you feel knowing that God delights in you—just because?

April 6

Learning to Relate

See, I have engraved you on the palms of my hands; your walls are ever before me.

ISAIAH 49:16

When I watch Nick interact with our daughters, I am often moved to tears by his tenderness, love, delight, generosity, protection, and provision. Nick is not detached, aloof, distant, or rigid with the girls; rather, he is involved with them and their *whole* lives.

If our second daughter, Sophia Joyce, comes to her daddy to share with him the newest outfit she just got for her doll or to show him her most recent work of art, he always responds with genuine interest and excitement. Even if he thinks the doll's dress looks identical to the rest of her wardrobe or he cannot make out which of her drawings is him and which one is the dog, he knows these things are important to Sophia. That makes them important to him.

The most wonderful aspect of Nick's love for the girls is the fact that it's *unconditional*. He does not expect the girls to do anything for him to merit his affection—he is simply besotted with them for who they are. His devotion is not forced or manufactured; it just bursts forth from his heart of love. This is *exactly* how God the Father loves us! It's such a blessing for me to see this, because it took many years for me to know I could have a personal relationship with God like the one Nick shares with our daughters.

I'm sure it must grieve God to have paid such a great price for our salvation and freedom only to find so many still shackled by the bondage of religion. He does not want us to try to relate to him through tedious ritual or religious protocol, but rather to enter boldly into his throne room of grace, full of joy and expectation. Dare to open up your heart and life to the freedom of a relationship with your heavenly Father!

MOMENT OF REFLECTION

How would you describe your relationship with your heavenly Father? What aspect is most important to you?

April 7

Letting Ourselves Be Loved

The LORD appeared to us in the past, saying: "I have loved you with an everlasting love; I have drawn you with unfailing kindness."

JEREMIAH 31:3

From the time Catherine started formulating sentences, she has asked, "Mummy, can you come and play with me?" or "Mummy, can you read me a book?" I always reply, "Yes!" That is one of my greatest pleasures in life! As a result, I now have a little girl who is convinced at the very core of who she is that her mummy loves spending time with her, listening to her stories, watching her twirl at dance classes, and talking through any questions she might have. (And I get to do it all over again with Sophia!)

I truly delight in Catherine, in everything about her, not just in what she does—because there are definitely things she does that I do not delight in. I am captivated and thrilled simply by who she is and who she is becoming.

I am so happy that Catherine is entirely confident in the devotion that Nick and I have for her, because this is an area of life that I struggled with for many years. I found it very difficult to believe that *anyone* would actually delight in me simply for who I am. I saw myself as not good enough, not smart enough, not cool enough, not *anything* enough.

It took me a very long time to renew my mind and to truly believe that in the same way I love my precious daughters—totally head over heels for no other reason than the fact they breathe air—God loves me. Just as I love their personalities, little quirks, laughter, dimples, cute questions, so too God loves *me* purely, totally, and unconditionally, simply because he made me and is my Father.

MOMENT OF REFLECTION

Do you believe that God loves you?
Why or why not?

April 8

Only You Can Be You

But who are you, a human being, to talk back to God? "Shall what is formed say to the one who formed it, 'Why did you make me like this?'" Does not the potter have the right to make out of the same lump of clay some pottery for special purposes and some for common use?

ROMANS 9:20–21

All of us can struggle with feelings of inferiority, insecurity, and self-doubt, especially when we compare ourselves with others. It is easy to forget that God made us unique, special, and perfectly fitted for his purposes when we spend all our time looking at how others have been shaped and molded. How many times have we asked God, even subconsciously, "Why did you make me like this?" We seem to be dissatisfied with who we are and think that our lives would be so much better if we were anything or anyone else.

We feel that we are not as good looking as someone else—or as happy, smart, talented, eloquent, artistic, creative, holy, fit, or thin. Instead of rejoicing in who God has made us to be and pursuing his purpose for our lives, we focus on our limitations and everyone else's strengths. This comparison trap is paralyzing. No one wins except the enemy.

When you discover who you are in Christ and what he has uniquely fashioned you to do, you will be better being you than anyone else ever could be! Why waste all your time trying to be someone else when everyone else is already taken? Determine to be the best you that God has made you to be.

MOMENT OF REFLECTION

Have you found yourself wondering why God made you as he did? Right now, begin to list all the strengths that God has given you.

April 9

God's Masterpiece

For you created my inmost being; you knit me together in my mother's womb.

PSALM 139:13

In the early 1990s, there was a huge stir in art communities all over the world when a famous Caravaggio painting, considered to be lost for two hundred years, was discovered hanging on the wall of a Jesuit's home in Dublin, Ireland. The painting, *The Taking of Christ*, a masterpiece by one of Italy's most famous and influential Baroque painters, had disappeared in the late eighteenth century. Through a series of exciting events, starting with a random discovery by two graduate students in Rome and ending with an art scholar's visit to a priest's residence on the other end of Europe, the painting was recovered.

For many years, it had been wrongly identified as a painted replica by another artist, and as a result, had been devalued and passed casually through several hands before landing on the Jesuit's wall. When it was found, there still was a question of its authenticity, but as layers of dirt and discolored varnish were painstakingly removed, the high technical quality of the painting was revealed. From that point on, it was viewed as the extremely precious and priceless treasure it truly was.

To God, *you* are his masterpiece, and *you* are extremely precious to him. Yes, today you might feel like you are used goods—damaged by your own poor choices or abused and discarded by people who did not realize your true value. But none of these circumstances have ever changed God's perception of your priceless value.

No matter how covered you think you are with layers of the world's dirt, grime, and pain, God has always had a plan to restore you to your original and priceless value. His eye has been focused on you since the day you were conceived in your mother's womb, and his desire has always been to bring you back to the image in which he originally created you ... which is his own. It is only when you understand your true value that you can begin to have and do all that God has for you . . . because sometimes all it takes is realizing that you're worth it.

MOMENT OF REFLECTION

What is the value you place upon yourself?

April 10

Who Are You?

We do not dare to classify or compare ourselves with some who commend themselves. When they measure themselves by themselves and compare themselves with themselves, they are not wise.

2 CORINTHIANS 10:12

It seemed simple enough. Hoping for some relief from all the traveling and activity, I had determined that I would become a cookie baker extraordinaire. Sure, it was a stretch, but I wanted to feel normal, like my life was predictable for a change. I was going to be like the other moms at Catherine's school and bake treats for the fund drive instead of buying something on the way to school in the morning. After following every single one of the cookbook's instructions, all I can say is that the cookie baking resulted in a smoky kitchen and burned cookies.

Later that night after putting the girls to bed, I distinctly heard the Lord ask me, "Who exactly are you trying to be?" I sat down to spend some time with God so he could help me make some sense out of the last few days. He simply reminded me that he had made Christine Caine unique from every other person on this planet and that being unique is okay; in fact, it's his intention.

I felt God say to me, "The reason you are not like someone else is because I don't need another someone else—I need a unique you." Instantly, I felt like a weight had been lifted off my shoulders, and I realized that just because I'm not super-cookie-baker-extraordinaire, it doesn't mean I'm not exactly the kind of woman God created me to be. The reason I had become discontent was because I had allowed my focus to shift from pursuing my own unique life-print to the life-prints of some of the women around me.

This experience taught me that nothing good comes from comparing our unique call from God with someone else's. We definitely want to be wise women (and men), so let's decide we are going to discover God's life-print for our lives and fulfill it. We are each graced for our particular race and not anyone else's.

MOMENT OF REFLECTION

What are two things about your life that set you apart from your family and friends?

April 11

A Designated Lane

Do you not know that in a race all the runners run, but only one gets the prize? Run in such a way as to get the prize.

1 CORINTHIANS 9:24

God had a plan for our lives even before we were born. He had a lane marked out on the track of life with our name on it and a specific race for us to run. God has plucked each one of us out of eternity, positioned us in a certain place in time, and given us special gifts and talents for the purpose of serving our generation. There are certain things he wants us to achieve while we are on this side of eternity.

When we stand before God one day, we will have to give an account of what we did with our lives. God will want to know what we did with the time he gave us, what we did with the talents he gave us, and what we did with the treasure he placed in our hands.

Therefore, it's imperative that we all ask ourselves these questions:

- Where am I in my race of life?
- Am I running my race in *my* lane, pressing on for the prize that God has for *me*?
- Am I crawling along somewhere, stumbling and tripping, not really knowing where I'm going?

- Am I running in my lane but distracted because I'm looking around to see how others are doing?
- Am I envying how others are running their races and what lane God has placed them in?
- Am I collapsed somewhere along the way, because discouragement, disillusionment, and disappointment have caused me to stop running?
- Have I become a spectator who sits in the grandstands watching the race I should be running?
- Have I been sidelined by a sin that has left me feeling guilt and shame?
- How can I get back in the race, ready to run and win?

MOMENT OF REFLECTION

Are you confidently running in the lane God has purposed for your life?

April 12

You Count

The number of the men who had eaten was five thousand.

MARK 6:44

It never ceases to amaze me that God chooses to use people that other people do not count. In the story of the fish and the loaves, Scripture tells us that there were five thousand men counted on the mountain that day and yet God used the lunch of a little boy who had not been counted to perform a miracle. If you feel discounted, then perhaps you have the ingredients for a miracle right where you are.

Miracles are often produced not from the things that we count as useful to God—such as our accomplishments, qualifications, gifts, connections, heritage, and talents—but from things that we think do not count. God will use anyone who is willing to be used, regardless of whether or not others think they are qualified. He is not looking for our *ability* as much as he desires our *availability*. I have found that, more often than not, God has used me in particular situations simply because I have been the only available option he has. Never underestimate the power of willingness.

I wonder whether the little boy's mother thought that she was doing anything significant the morning she packed five loaves and two fish into her son's lunchbox. Undoubtedly, she had done the same thing countless times before, but because she was faithful with the task she had been assigned, she too was part of a miracle. Never underestimate the significance of where you are and what you do. As this story illustrates, you do not need to be a famous celebrity or gifted athlete or highly educated person to do a small thing with much love that will yield a mighty harvest.

You matter to God. Your contribution to his kingdom *does* count, so do not let anyone devalue you or your contribution. I think that there were many lunches in that crowd on the hill that day, but there was only one boy who offered his and therefore became a part of a miracle.

We are so often overwhelmed by the magnitude of a need that we don't do anything because we can't do everything. God is not asking any one of us to do everything, but simply to do something —and then he will do the rest. The ingredients for a miracle are always in our midst, but we must release them to God—however small they may seem—so that he has something to work with. Let's decide today that we will put our little into the hands of a big God and watch him do the impossible with it.

MOMENT OF REFLECTION

What do you have in your midst that you could offer to God to multiply, even though you may think it does not really count?

April 13

Life-Prints

Your eyes saw my unformed body; all the days ordained for me were written in your book before one of them came to be.

PSALM 139:16

It is no coincidence that God gave each of us a distinct set of markings unique to every person alive or who has ever lived: the fingerprint. Even identical twins aren't 100 percent identical because each has a different pattern on their fingertips. I believe this is one of the ways God reminds us that each of us is an original, a unique person with a unique purpose. He prepared for each of us a "life-print" that is completely our own.

Sadly, many people never truly discover their divinely given life-print because they're too busy trying to "fit" into someone else's. This is as silly as Cinderella's stepsisters' attempts to stuff their big feet into the tiny glass slipper. Remember that story? The stepsisters so desperately wanted to fulfill a purpose never meant for them in the first place that they went to extreme measures to squeeze their feet into that slipper. In fact, in the original version of the story, they even cut off a few toes to try to make the slipper fit! And before you get too grossed out, haven't we all gone to some pretty harsh measures to make fit that pair of designer shoes that were 75 percent off—and three sizes too small?

Most of us tend to devalue our own uniqueness and instead attempt to become a carbon copy of those we admire. We look at others whom we deem to be "successful" or godly Christian women or men and, rather than taking principles from their lives and applying them to our own, we try to become exactly like them. Ultimately, this leads to frustration because those shoes just weren't made for us!

Make a decision that from this day forth you are going to walk in your own shoes. You'll find they are the perfect fit and will take you much further than anyone else's.

MOMENT OF REFLECTION

What are some of the aspects of the life-print God prepared uniquely for you?

April 14

God Loves You

But you, O Lord, are a God merciful and gracious, slow to anger and abounding in steadfast love and faithfulness.

PSALM 86:15 ESV

It seems to me that every single day of our lives we need to remind ourselves that God loves us. The enemy of our souls will daily and relentlessly bombard us with thoughts and feelings of inadequacy, guilt, shame, condemnation, insufficiency, insecurity, fear, doubt, and rejection. He is an accuser constantly trying to make us feel that we have blown it so badly this time that God could not possibly want us back.

Satan wants to undermine our trust in God's unfailing, indescribable, and unending love. If he can do that, he will paralyze us, make us quit, and keep us from stepping into the fullness of our purpose and potential. The only thing that can ultimately keep us running our race is the knowledge that God loves us. Once we begin to doubt that, our very foundations are shaken and everything else begins to crumble.

I want to remind you today that no matter what you have said or did not say, what you have thought or have not thought, what you have done or have not done, what you have accomplished or have not accomplished, God loves you and always will.

Love is not only what God does, it is who God is. He cannot stop himself from loving us because God is love. His love far surpasses any earthly love we may have experienced. It is based entirely on his character, not our performance. There is nothing you can do to make God love you less or make him love you more.

Decide today that you will not listen to the lies of the enemy but to the truth of God's Word. God has always loved you and he always will.

MOMENT OF REFLECTION

What Scriptures speak strongly to your heart?
Write them down and hold on to them as reminders of God's love.

⁂ *April 15* ⁂

Be Yourself

Each one should test their own actions. Then they can take pride in themselves alone, without comparing themselves to someone else.

GALATIANS 6:4

Have you ever been shopping and found an outfit that looks identical to the one your favorite celebrity wore on the red carpet—and for a fraction of the price? So you buy it only to realize it doesn't quite look like it did on the waif-thin actress. And, besides, you don't quite feel like yourself in it. That's probably because, while the outfit looks great on the celebrity, it's not your style! I can't tell you how many times I've wanted to buy something, but after trying on the "look" in the dressing room, I quickly discover this 5'2" Greek woman simply can't pull it off!

Way too often, we women (men too sometimes!) get so caught up with trying to be like someone else we forget how special we are. Comparing your life, your calling, your schedule, or even your way of doing things with someone else's will only bring frustration.

For instance, my neighbor is a brilliant stay-at-home mom raising several children, an effective member of the PTA, a freelance graphic artist who volunteers this gift once a week at her church—and still she is able to cook a gourmet meal each night for her family. What if she looked over her fence into my life and decided that having and doing it all meant she needed to do all the things she's wired to do *and* everything she saw me doing ... even though she absolutely hates traveling and public speaking? Now, that would be a problem! Her husband and kids would be frustrated that she was gone so often pursuing something she doesn't even enjoy; plus she'd eventually get kicked off the PTA for too many absentee votes, and her church would be forced to revert to using clip art. And I don't even want to think about the chaos my family would experience if I tried to accomplish her "all," while simultaneously traveling and preaching around the world and helping victims of human trafficking.

Clearly, we should each pursue having and doing our own unique "all." So relax . . . love yourself and be who God made you to be.

MOMENT OF REFLECTION

Are you comfortable being yourself?
Who are you trying to emulate?

April 16

Do You Love You?

As I have loved you, so you must love one another.

JOHN 13:34

Strengthening our spiritual core is not just for our benefit—it's also for the benefit of others. Remember, God has called us to love him *and* to love others. But to obey Jesus' command to love our neighbor as we love ourselves, it is imperative that we actually love, value, and esteem ourselves.

So often, we find it difficult to love one another because we do not understand how to receive the love that God has shown us. We think we must somehow earn that love or make ourselves more perfect in order to receive it. Yet it was while we were still sinners that Christ loved us and that unconditional love is what he desires us to give to others.

Since it is impossible to offer what you do not have, we must first receive his love in order to give that love away. The truth is that God loves you so that you can love yourself in a healthy, godly way. And the natural outflow of loving yourself as God does is that you will love others likewise, with a love that only God can give you.

Try loving yourself today so that you can love others in the same way God loves you. Remember, there is a huge difference between loving ourselves as Jesus does and walking in arrogance and pride. One will enable us to love one another as Christ loved us; the other will destroy us.

MOMENT OF REFLECTION

Do you truly believe that Christ loves you unconditionally? If not, does that hamper your ability to show his love to others?

April 17

Blessed and Broken

Taking the five loaves and the two fish and looking up to heaven, he gave thanks and broke the loaves. Then he gave them to his disciples to distribute to the people. He also divided the two fish among them all.

MARK 6:41

When the disciples brought five loaves and two fish to Jesus, it was never going to be enough to feed the multitudes. But instead of complaining about how little food there was, Jesus blessed the little. He did this because the miracle was never about the loaves and fishes; it was about what the boy's offering had the potential to become in the hands of a miracle-working God.

I have learned that until we can be thankful for what is not enough, then the little that we have cannot be multiplied into what can become more than enough. Imagine how different our lives would be if we stopped cursing what we don't like, what we don't have, and who we are not and began to give thanks instead. We could start by saying; "God, this is not the job I wanted, but I thank you that I have a job. This is not the house I wanted, but I thank you that I have a roof over my head. This is not the marriage I expected, but I thank you that we are working on it. These are not the ministry results I was praying for, but I thank you I'm in the ministry. This child is not living up to my expectations, but I thank you for this child. Lord, I know this is not enough, but I lift it up and give you thanks for what I have."

The key is to begin to thank God right where we are for what we do have and believe him able and faithful to perform the miracles necessary to take us where he wants us to go and to give us what he wants us to have.

Once Jesus blessed what was never going to be enough, he then broke it . . . and that is where the miracle of multiplication began. The blessing is in the breaking; it is those very things that we thought would take us out because they broke us that become the things we feed to others. If we put our broken lives, relationships, bodies, finances, emotions, dreams, and hopes into the hands of our gracious and redeeming God, he will use them to feed the multitudes. Our brokenness does not disqualify us from being used by God; it is the very thing that qualifies us.

When you believe that God works all things together for your good, then you know that he can take the broken pieces of your past and make it work for his glory. The very thing that the devil meant for evil is what God will use for good. The power is in the broken pieces.

MOMENT OF REFLECTION

Do you have any broken places that you have been trying to hide instead of giving them to God to be used for his glory?

April 18

Learning about the Love of God

The LORD your God is with you, the Mighty Warrior who saves. He will take great delight in you; in his love he will no longer rebuke you, but will rejoice over you with singing.

ZEPHANIAH 3:17

My initial view of God was shaped as a young girl forced to attend church with my family almost every Sunday morning. In all those years of going to church I cannot remember a single time where I was told that God loved me (or for that matter anyone else) or that he had a plan and purpose for my life. I am sure that many of the church leaders believed this to be true; it is just that no one told me or I simply did not hear or understand it. For me, church was a very somber occasion and so boring that my weekly goal was simply to try to stay awake during the service. This might sound disrespectful, but I was subjected to a weekly two-hour liturgy, all in ancient Greek, full of symbolism and tradition that made no sense to me. I cannot recollect hearing one sermon that was applicable to my everyday life.

I would often ask my parents what was going on during the church service, and why we needed to attend something we did not understand, but was only chastised for my rudeness and ignorance. My perspective of God was formed by the conversations of relatives and friends who had no revelation of the God of the Bible because they had never been encouraged to read the Bible for themselves. These were sincere and good people, but they were sincerely wrong about God. My understanding of God consisted of old wives' tales, superstition, and mysticism.

It is hard to believe that the same girl today travels the world teaching the Bible and telling people about the love of God and how to find their purpose in him. All I know is that somewhere along the journey I encountered a life-transforming relationship with Jesus Christ, and the Jesus unveiled in the Word of God was so much bigger than the one I had been exposed to growing up. The God of the Bible is big in grace, big in mercy, big in love, big in forgiveness, and big in justness, and he has a big plan and purpose for each of our lives. Let's spend our lives taking down any barriers that would obscure people's view of the true God of the Bible. The sooner people are exposed to his love, grace, mercy, righteousness, and holiness, the sooner they will flock to him. Jesus is irresistible.

MOMENT OF REFLECTION

What were you taught in childhood about the love of God?

April 19

God's Love Is a Gift

For I am convinced that neither death nor life, neither angels nor demons, neither the present nor the future, nor any powers, neither height nor depth, nor anything else in all creation, will be able to separate us from the love of God that is in Christ Jesus our Lord.

ROMANS 8:38–39

So often we base our relationship with our Father God on the one we had with our earthly father. This can be limiting on every level because even the best, strongest, most loving earthly relationship pales in comparison to the one we can have with our heavenly Father.

Perhaps your experience with your earthly father was negative or nonexistent, but you must not allow yourself to believe that who he was or how he felt about you is in any way a reflection of God. I do not know who my biological father was, and although I had a wonderful relationship with my adopted father, he died when I was nineteen years old. I felt rejected by one and abandoned by the other. But I discovered that I had a heavenly Father who truly loved me and would never leave me nor forsake me. I find great comfort in that thought.

Our heavenly Father loves us unconditionally because we are his children, with full access to him and all that is his. This is almost incomprehensible to us, and so we feel that we must do something to earn his love. We can easily get caught up in thinking God will love us more if we do more good deeds, but unconditional love is not given based on qualification. Our actions cannot guarantee his love, because his love is not earned; it is a gift. There is absolutely NOTHING we can do to make God love us more than he already does. Perhaps the one thing we *can* do is to learn to receive more of the unconditional love that he wants to pour out.

MOMENT OF REFLECTION

Do you find that you keep trying to earn God's love?
Do you believe the promise that his love is unconditional?

April 20

Male and Female

God created mankind in his own image, in the image of God he created them; male and female he created them.

GENESIS 1:27

The original spirit-man that God created possessed all of the qualities of the masculine and the feminine. In Genesis 2, the Bible says that God took this spirit-man and placed it into two physical forms—the male and the female—for the purpose of fulfilling his eternal plan on the earth.

In fact, God created Eve out of the same substance from which he created Adam; that's why the Bible says that she was taken out of man. Eve was not a separate creation but a separate expression of the same creation. From the outset, it is clear that God didn't make either the male or the female superior: they were both created from the same spirit-man and are of the same essence. Essentially, man and woman are equal but definitely different.

We know this because God said that the man should not be alone and that he would make a helper for him. Note that God didn't say, "I'll make a slave for him" or a "mistress" or a "baby incubator." He called Eve a "helper." In the Hebrew, this word is *e'zer* which refers to someone who is strong, with no connotations of weakness. In fact, *e'zer* is often a word used to describe a characteristic of God. When he created the woman, it was not as a subordinate for man, but as a completer to man—someone who, united with Adam, would be equally responsible for fulfilling God's purpose.

It is so important that as women of God we understand that we are created equal but different. When we get a revelation of our equal value, we can begin to understand that God has a great purpose for us. I realize that for some of you this is a given, but you can pray for the multitudes of women who still do not recognize their value or worth as daughters of the King. Entire cultures still devalue women and do not understand their worth. Every day our safe houses at The A21 Campaign are full of young women rescued from sex slavery.

Why does this happen? Because people still do not understand that women are equally created in the image of God and have a divine purpose and destiny.

The more we live and model this truth, the more captives we will help to set free.

MOMENT OF REFLECTION

Why do you believe that you are God's unique creation?

April 21

Nothing Is Impossible

For no word from God will ever fail.

LUKE 1:37

The God we serve is big, strong, and mighty. He made this world; he keeps it all together; and he has created each one of us to play a unique part in his redemption story. This big God is not aloof or distant, but ever present, loving, and compassionate. He has the ability to solve any problem, to heal any memory, to reconcile any relationship, to forgive any sin, to stretch any budget, to feed every mouth, to clothe every body, to free any captive, to break any habit, to cure any disease. Nothing is irredeemable with God. He is able to work all things together for good. The truth is there is simply nothing our God cannot do. If you truly believe that God has the power to create and sustain the universe, then surely there is nothing in your life that is beyond his power to mend, heal, or restore.

I believe God wants us to live wide-open, expansive lives that bear witness to the truth that he is mighty and magnificent, and that through him all things are possible. But to do that we must see him as he is—a God who is big around us, in us, through us, and beyond us.

MOMENT OF REFLECTION

The God who created the universe also created you as his unique and special child. When do you most feel God's love for you?

April 22

God Loves You in Your "Broken State"

Then they cried to the LORD in their trouble, and he saved them from their distress. He sent out his word and healed them; he rescued them from the grave.

PSALM 107:19–20

When I was in the process of dealing with my childhood abuse, one thing that I had to learn was how to receive the unconditional love of God. This was such a challenge for me at first, because the hurt and abuse I had experienced had deeply woven into my mind and soul the belief that I had no worth or value to God or other people. Deep down, I believed that the only way I could be loved or have any worth was to earn it through performance. As a result, I found my identity in everything I did rather than who I was in Christ. I had to replace that false belief with the truth that the magnitude of God's love for me did not hinge on the degree of my abilities or accomplishments. It was rooted in the simple fact that I existed and that I was his child. I had to come to the place where I understood that God loved me just as much in my "broken state" as he ever would in my "perfected state." It didn't matter what I had gone through, what I had or didn't have, what other people had said about me; the truth was that God delighted in me and my core identity was in him.

MOMENT OF REFLECTION

Do you believe at your core that God loves you in your broken, imperfect state? That his love is not based on what you are doing but in the fact that you are his child?

April 23

God Uses Other People to Help Us

A friend loves at all times.

PROVERBS 17:17

Sometimes we can't stand up on our own, so God uses other people to help us rise as well as to stabilize us until we can walk with him into our future. One of the people he used to help me overcome my past was my friend Holly. I like to describe the way that she came into my life as being one of those people who stick their arm in the elevator just as the doors are already closing, and there is nothing you can do about it. Once in the elevator, she is not one of those who follow proper elevator etiquette by keeping a safe distance, looking forward, and making no eye contact. Rather, Holly will get right into your personal space and begin chatting with you like she has been your best friend since birth; and by the time you are ready to get off the elevator, both you and your entire extended family have an invitation to her upcoming Christmas party.

Holly was precisely the carefree, fun-loving, no-concept-of-personal-space kind of friend I needed to help pull me out of my reserved, distant, resistant shell. I remember when she took me shopping to help diversify my wardrobe of black, black, and more black. I was so stiff, awkward, timid, and scared of anything that would heighten any awareness of my body. But Holly simply loved me where I was, and by using her gifts of friendship, laughter, and acceptance, she helped me to gradually introduce navy blue to my wardrobe.

I always felt so uncomfortable around her open and vivacious demeanor because it was the total opposite of my inhibited one. Yet it was exactly what I needed to help me stand up and start walking away from my past into my future. I am so grateful she did not give up on me, because God used her to help me find the real me hidden beneath all the layers of defense mechanisms I had formulated.

If we are willing to embrace the discomfort and awkwardness of change, then we will start to see both God and ourselves differently.

Often God uses other people in our lives to show us his love and to initiate the growth he desires.

MOMENT OF REFLECTION

How has God used other people to communicate to you how much he loves you?

April 24

Listen to the Voice of the Lord

The tongue has the power of life and death, and those who love it will eat its fruit.

PROVERBS 18:21

When I was in second grade, I received a school report card with the following comment from my teacher: "Christine is a great motivator, but she must realize that she cannot always be the leader." Can you believe that a teacher would write such a thing? Well, that single sentence totally devastated me, and I remember as an eight-year-old child making a deliberate decision to take a step back and never volunteer for any leadership role again. I thought that my teacher wrote that comment because something must be wrong with me, and so I allowed her perspective to limit my potential for many years.

How many times have we succumbed to the limitations that others have placed on us? I have discovered that if the enemy cannot convince us directly that we are not enough, he will endeavor to use others to hold us back. So often we finally develop the courage to rise up and trust that God can use us; and before we are standing upright, someone will cross our path to tell us we are not capable of doing the thing we believe the Lord is asking of us.

Sometimes we share our dreams and aspirations with friends and family only to be met with responses such as, "Who do you think you are? You could never do that. You are so bad at that. Why don't you try something else?" If our own doubts are not enough to stop us from getting up, then there will always be a multitude of other voices trying to keep us down. Unfortunately, it is often the voices of those who are closest to us that echo the loudest and to which we tend to listen most. We must determine to listen to the voice of the Lord more than any other voice in our lives.

MOMENT OF REFLECTION

What is the Lord trying to tell you about yourself—specifically about your strength, passion, and calling?

April 25

Your Days Are Precious

Why, you do not even know what will happen tomorrow. What is your life? You are a mist that appears for a little while and then vanishes.

JAMES 4:14

I have a deep love for perfume. I love the whole process of spraying perfume and allowing the fragrance to touch everyone I come into contact with. I wish I could spray it on once and have that scent remain on me all day, but I find myself having to reapply it to keep the smell alive. Once the vapor is sprayed, the bottle empties a little more, and before I know it the perfume has been used up.

In his epistle, James reminds us that this precious gift called life we have been given lasts only about as long as a vapor. Our days on the earth are limited and very precious; we must not waste a moment.

So the next time you spray yourself with a fragrance, take a moment to observe how quickly the vapor fades. It is there, and then it is not. In light of eternity, this is how long our lives last. We are here one minute and then gone the next.

We must ensure that while we are here on the earth, we do not waste a second. We have a mandate to fulfill, an objective to accomplish, and we only have as long as the clock is still ticking. Stop wasting time and start investing this time you have been given for the sake of eternity.

MOMENT OF REFLECTION

Does it frighten or comfort you to think of the brevity of life?

April 26

The Place God Has for Us

But seek first his kingdom and his righteousness, and all these things will be given to you as well.

MATTHEW 6:33

Sometimes we do not find our place because we confuse the concept of a place with having a position. We expend a lot of time, energy, and resources preparing for a position that we think we want rather than embracing the place that God has already prepared for us or is preparing us for.

Because God made us, he knows how and where we will be most fulfilled, functioning at our maximum capacity. So much of the frustration we experience is because we try to fill a position for which we were never designed. We may do this by trying to live up to someone else's expectations or maybe even our own dreams or ambitions, but we will never find true fulfillment until we assume the place God has for us.

If we truly believe that God *is* good and that he *does* good, then surely we can believe that he has prepared a good place in his body for us. Nothing will satisfy us like the place he has prepared for us. God made us and knows where we will flourish; all we need to do is to step into that place and trust him with our future.

Instead of chasing what we want or what others say we should desire, let's determine to seek God and find our place in him. When we do that, we will find peace, love, joy, patience, kindness, goodness, perseverance, self-control, blessing, prosperity, strength, faith, hope, courage, grace, and mercy are all in that place too.

MOMENT OF REFLECTION

Have you found God's place for you,
or are you chasing a position you desire?

April 27

What Is the Theme of Your Heart?

My heart is stirred by a noble theme as I recite my verses for the king; my tongue is the pen of a skillful writer.

PSALM 45:1

The theme of our hearts determines the story of our lives. If our hearts are full of God, his Word, and his promises, then they will overflow into every area of our lives. Indeed, the story of our lives is written out of the overflow of our hearts. The question we need to ask ourselves is, "What are we allowing into our hearts that then sets the course of our lives?" If we want a great life story, then we need to have a healthy heart.

If our hearts are full of fear, doubt, unbelief, negativity, bitterness, unforgiveness, envy, pride, lust, or greed, then those traits will characterize our lives as well. Conversely, if we choose to fill our hearts with love, joy, peace, hope, kindness, faith, courage, grace, compassion, and purpose, then those traits will determine our story.

The good news is that we get to choose. We may not have had the opportunity to determine the story line thus far, but we can make a decision today to deal with the toxic things in our hearts that are sabotaging the story line that God has purposed for us.

Why don't you determine that your heart is going to be set on course with Jesus and his Word, and that the ensuing story of your life is going to be a great one. Don't just settle for a quick, nondescript short story when you can have an epic novel, a daring adventure, and a Holy Mystery.

It all starts and ends in our hearts.

MOMENT OF REFLECTION

What is the theme of your heart?
What do you hope that the story of your life will be?

April 28

The Lord Looks at the Heart

So Saul said to his attendants, "Find someone who plays well and bring him to me."

1 SAMUEL 16:17

So often we place limitations on others (or allow others to place them on us) based on external factors. We think they should have a certain level of education, look a certain way, speak a certain way, or need to be connected to the right people. But God does not limit himself by these factors; he looks at the condition of someone's heart. Only the Lord knows what is hidden there—and he can use anyone with a pure and willing heart. We regularly overlook the very people that God wants to use in our midst because we are too busy focusing on the obvious choices based on looks and abilities.

Samuel the prophet thought that Jesse's oldest son, Eliab, was surely going to be the next king—he had all the obvious requirements. But God had not chosen Eliab. Can you imagine how David would have felt knowing that the prophet himself had not considered him as his first choice?

Not only did the prophet get it wrong, but the father of the house also missed it. Jesse made seven of his sons pass before Samuel, thinking one of them must be God's choice. He never even considered that his youngest son, David, who was tending the sheep, would be a candidate. Can you imagine how demoralizing it would be to have your own father think that you are not good enough to be all that God has purposed for you to be? But ultimately, it does not matter what anyone else thinks; the key to fulfilling our destiny is being preoccupied with what God thinks and says about us.

Wherever you are, God is there and he knows you are there. Ultimately, it does not matter what anyone else thinks; God will have his way. God does not choose in the same way that man chooses. God always has and always will look at the heart before anything else.

Keep your heart right and trust the Lord.

MOMENT OF REFLECTION

Have you ever felt that someone had passed you over and not recognized your worth? How did you respond?

April 29

God Made You to Be You

A heart at peace gives life to the body, but envy rots the bones.

PROVERBS 14:30

Comparison is extremely destructive. It makes you feel less than you really are and leads to self-deprecation, self-rejection, depression, and fear. All these factors will hinder you from rising up and being all you can be and doing all you can do within the body of Christ.

Spending your time looking at what you are not, what someone else is doing, or what you wish you could be doing only serves to shrink God in you. God did not make you to be someone else or to do someone else's ministry. He made you to be you, and when you become the best you that you can be, there is more of you to be filled with God.

Competition is healthy on a sporting field, but not within the body of Christ. We should be inspired by one another, stir one another to good works, and pray for each other. But we should never envy or compete with another part of the body.

We are all a part of the same body; comparison and competition only serve to destroy it. We are called to *complete* each other, not *compete* with one another.

Let's remember that we are on the same team, fighting for the same cause, serving the same master: Jesus Christ.

MOMENT OF REFLECTION

Do you ever envy other Christians? Remind yourself often that God designed you to be you, and no one else.

April 30

The Church That Jesus Is Building

And I tell you that you are Peter, and on this rock I will build my church, and the gates of Hades will not overcome it.

MATTHEW 16:18

I love the opportunity that Nick and I have to build the local church throughout the world. I love the diversity of the church—the differences in worship expressions, culture, tradition, music styles, people, programs, and services. It would look boring and bland if everyone were the same everywhere, if there were only a single expression of God's greatness.

No one denomination, tradition, church, ministry, or tribe displays all of God's greatness any more than one star reflects all the glory of God; but together we certainly reflect more than any of us do alone. The diversity of his church is breathtaking. She is stunning throughout all the earth, truly the hope of the world.

We must be very careful that we only speak words of life and hope about the bride of Christ. In the same way that no groom would like anyone to make a negative comment about his bride, her wedding dress, makeup, perfume, character, or personality, let's ensure that we do not make negative comments about the way somebody different from us chooses to worship Jesus. Unity is not uniformity, and it is our differences that make Christ's bride sparkle and dazzle. Let's not ever divide what should always be united.

Let's determine to love, serve, and build what Jesus is building: his church.

MOMENT OF REFLECTION

Do you love God's church,
even the parts that are different from you?

May

FOLLOWING IN LOVE

❦ *May 1* ❦

True Followers

I have been crucified with Christ and I no longer live, but Christ lives in me. The life I now live in the body, I live by faith in the Son of God, who loved me and gave himself for me.

GALATIANS 2:20

All too often we compartmentalize our lives, each segment demanding a different "us." We become actors, taking on the role we think we're supposed to play—depending on our audience or circumstances. For example, at church or with our Christian friends, we're supposed to be a Christian, so we act like one (some of us could win an Oscar for our performances). At work, we try to act like a Christian because we're supposed to be one, but there we don't have to play the role too well because our coworkers are not quite as familiar with the Christian "script." When we go home, we act like our real selves, because we believe that our secret is safe with our family. Then the doorbell rings. It's amazing how quickly we can shift and play the part of the perfect family, even if moments before, our house was more like the perfect storm.

Living in this cycle is exhausting and, more importantly, it is not the abundant life that Jesus came to give us. He wants us to have an integrated life in which we are the same person everywhere, to everyone. If we find ourselves playing different roles in different places, then we need to stop and ask ourselves why. Jesus came to set us free; when we have to pretend, we are not free.

Allow Jesus access to every part of you everywhere you go, and you will find that you will increasingly be conformed and transformed into his image. The more you meditate on his Word, the more like him you will become and the less like the old "you" you'll need to act. Transformation is possible. Consistency is possible. Authenticity is possible.

MOMENT OF REFLECTION

Are you the same person everywhere you go?
If not, then why?

May 2

A Spiritual Workout

"Love the Lord your God with all your heart and with all your soul and with all your mind." This is the first and greatest commandment.

MATTHEW 22:37–38

In the first great commandment, Jesus describes our spiritual core muscles as the heart, the soul, and the mind. These three muscles enable us to love God wholly and completely. So how do we effectively exercise these spiritual core muscles?

Just as our physical muscles are connected, giving us the ability to stand, walk, sit, and run, our heart, soul, and mind are also interrelated and must be exercised if we are to be spiritually healthy. Our core muscles are often the ones that require the most work and are the least enjoyable to exercise, but they are also the ones that provide strength to the whole body.

Let me explain it this way: A body builder wouldn't go to the gym week in and week out and only focus on building his biceps. He knows that without an exercise routine that develops his body as a whole—not just his biceps—his other muscles would atrophy and eventually become useless. Similarly, we have to focus on strengthening and growing all three muscles that make up our spiritual core—or we risk growing stagnant, complacent, and lukewarm, which would hinder all God wants to do in and through us.

Being spiritually strong is no different from being physically strong. It means working our spiritual core muscles every day. Think about how much easier it will be to conquer the challenges in our lives if we are indeed spiritually fit.

MOMENT OF REFLECTION

Of your body, soul, and mind, which do you feel will be the most difficult to strengthen as you learn to follow God? Which will be the easiest? Why?

May 3

A Healthy Relationship

I am jealous for you with a godly jealousy. I promised you to one husband, to Christ, so that I might present you as a pure virgin to him.

2 CORINTHIANS 11:2

The Bible teaches us that we, the church, are the bride of Christ. In the same way that a husband desires complete devotion from his bride, God requires our complete commitment, passion, faithfulness, and fidelity. He wants a relationship with us that is heartfelt, spontaneous, vibrant, alive, and reciprocal. In a healthy marriage, neither person wants the other to begrudgingly fulfill his or her marriage obligations out of guilt, condemnation, or force but rather from a genuine heart commitment, conviction, and desire. If the husband or wife is merely going through the motions of being married, the marriage becomes nothing more than an empty, boring, passionless living arrangement. The two people involved in this union are simply acting like a married couple rather than enjoying the benefits of truly being married.

It is little wonder that Jesus said the greatest commandment is to love the Lord our God first and foremost with all our hearts. He longs for authentic relationship with his bride, not a mere religious obligation or empty ritual. God is not at all impressed by empty words or heartless platitudes. In fact, it makes him angry when our words and actions are not sincere. We must be careful that our Christianity does not become mere lip service or hollow actions. God wants genuine relationships that stem from our hearts.

Make sure that you cultivate a love affair with your Prince. He is so worthy.

MOMENT OF REFLECTION

God has promised to give us a new heart and spirit.
Have you seen this change manifested in your own life? If so, how?

May 4

Burn Some Bridges

So in everything, do to others what you would have them do to you, for this sums up the Law and the Prophets.

MATTHEW 7:12

I have always heard people say, "Don't burn bridges because you may need them someday." Although I understand what is implied by this statement—and am aware we must be sure to never burn *people*—if we are going to fulfill God's plan and purpose for our lives, there are some bridges that we *must* burn. In fact, when we are indecisive about leaving certain things behind, we may end up thwarting the plans and purposes of God for our lives.

Some bridges keep pulling us back to the past. Perhaps there are some relationships that are hindering us, places that we should no longer be visiting, habits that are destroying us, activities that are time wasters. If we stay too attached to such bridges, we will never have the strength to cross them and enter into our future.

We cannot get to where we are going without leaving where we have been. If we are going to pursue God's plan A, we cannot have a plan B. There must be no bridge that can take us back when it feels like following Jesus is becoming too costly, risky, or difficult. Once we have decided to follow Jesus, we must also determine that there is no turning back. Ever.

Ultimately, it is only by burning some bridges that you will discover you do not need them to get to where you are going. God himself is the One who can take you there.

MOMENT OF REFLECTION

Are there any bridges that you need to burn?
Have you given yourself options in
case the Christian life does not turn out?

May 5

Guarding Our Hearts

I hold this against you: You have forsaken the love you had at first.

REVELATION 2:4

When we are in love, we will do anything to be with the one who has captured our heart. In fact, we not only long to be with that person but would literally do anything for him or her. Many of us begin our relationship with God overwhelmed with a revelation of his love, grace, and mercy, and there is nothing that we wouldn't do to try to please him. Our earnest desire is to be with him and become like him.

We love to spend hours in his presence, his Word, and his house. It seems as though every sermon was written just for us and that God is speaking directly to us. We see his providential hand guiding us and acknowledge his presence and provision constantly.

It is only by continually strengthening our heart that we will be able to sustain this kind of passionate commitment to God for the duration of our Christian walk. In the same way that a natural relationship left alone will just fizzle out and eventually die, so too will our relationship with God. We all have a honeymoon phase in our relationship with Jesus; and then comes the work of building a relationship that will endure. And, as in every relationship, it takes work to make the relationship work.

I have found that, after all these years, my love for the Lord has deepened so much that I would not even want to return to the honeymoon phase. There is something that happens when you walk together through mountaintop experiences and the deepest valleys —when you discover in your darkest hour that he is still God, he still loves you, he still cares for you, he will never leave you, and that all things ultimately work together for good.

This love affair need never diminish, grow stagnant, or cold.

It can continue to remain red-hot and passionate as long as God's Word, not Hollywood, is your standard for love.

MOMENT OF REFLECTION

How has your love for God changed over time? Is it deeper now than at first? If not, what do you need to do to get closer to Jesus? He has not moved.

May 6

Following Wholeheartedly

But because my servant Caleb has a different spirit and follows me wholeheartedly, I will bring him into the land he went to, and his descendants will inherit it.

NUMBERS 14:24

When Nick and I exchanged our wedding vows, we committed 100 percent of our hearts to one another. If we had entered our marriage only halfheartedly, we would have set ourselves up for inevitable failure. We knew that the only way to make our marriage work was to invest our *whole hearts* in it.

When we embrace God and his purpose wholeheartedly, it is easier to stay passionate about our faith, our spiritual disciplines, and every other aspect of our spiritual walk. All our actions and activities flow from our love relationship with God rather than from an obligation to fulfill a Christian requirement. We possess a love for others, for church, for reading our Bibles, for praying, and for giving and serving. We love what God loves and desire to do what he does; it is the natural outflow of our hearts.

Because love is so important, we must ensure that we continually strengthen our heart, this core spiritual muscle. We can do this by spending quality time with God, staying in close communication with him, and remaining obedient to his Word. It is through an intimate and daily relationship with God that we are able to give ourselves up to him—wholeheartedly!

MOMENT OF REFLECTION

Does God have 100 percent of your heart? Really?

May 7

Embracing God's Plan

Each person should live as a believer in whatever situation the Lord has assigned to them, just as God has called them.

1 CORINTHIANS 7:17

Children are so much fun to watch because they shamelessly demonstrate many aspects of human nature, while we adults have learned to cleverly mask the socially unacceptable ones.

Human nature is such that we spend much of our time focusing on what we do *not* have and what someone else *does* have. Catherine and Sophia each have many different toys, but I can guarantee the only one each wants is the one the other is holding. Catherine can be sitting surrounded by twenty-seven toys, and Sophia only one—and *that* is the one Catherine desperately needs to complete her collection. I work with them, teaching them to be satisfied with what they have and trying to help them to stop comparing and coveting what the other one has.

As Christians, we must learn this same lesson. God has a great plan and purpose for each one of us and has given each of us many gifts and talents, but so often we are like Catherine, sitting surrounded by all our gifts but focusing on and desiring the talent someone else has. If we allow ourselves to continue down this path, we will miss out on the only destiny that will bring us deep satisfaction.

God desires for us to live with a deep contentment in our hearts, but we can only experience this when we embrace *his* plan. There is no use desiring to be a worship leader and coveting that position or title if that is not what God has ordained. We must keep our eyes focused on Jesus and learn to love and be content with his plan and purpose for our lives.

MOMENT OF REFLECTION

Are you content with God's plan and purpose for your life? How do you know?

May 8

True Love Always

And now these three remain: faith, hope and love. But the greatest of these is love.

1 CORINTHIANS 13:13

Remember in junior high school when the girls used to doodle all over their notebooks, drawing huge hearts with their initials and some boy's initials inside the heart? Invariably there would always be a "TLA" nearby, meaning "True Love Always!" Or if the girl was not interested in boys yet, she would have her name plus her best friend's name with a big "BFF" next to it, meaning "Best Friends Forever!" In our youth, we were just beginning to understand the joy of close friendships, and we wanted to make sure we let everyone know about it.

When Nick and I started dating and falling in love, I was past the stage of doodling "Mrs. Christine Caine" on every available scrap of paper, but I must admit that I did have to make an effort not to make Nick the center of every conversation. The trust, love, laughter, and closeness I was experiencing were new to me, and I was so happy about our relationship that I sometimes just couldn't help myself. And once we got married and had children, all restraint was thrown out the window! I cannot help talking about my loving husband and my beautiful princesses, and God bless any person I am sitting next to on a plane as I have an entire photo slideshow of my family ready to go on my iPhone.

When our relationship with Jesus is fresh and passionate, it is the same way. We cannot help but proclaim how much we love him and how he has changed our lives. Now, I'm not suggesting we plant huge signs in our front yards that say "I Heart Jesus, TLA!" Or "J.C. + Me = BFF!" We simply need to ensure that our conversations with our neighbors leave room for expressing the joy and sense of security that flow from our relationship with him.

When we are in a love affair with Jesus, we can't keep quiet.

MOMENT OF REFLECTION

Think of one person in your world whom you would characterize as "loving." Then explain why you attribute that quality to this person.

May 9

Continually Stretching

Not that I have already obtained all this, or have already arrived at my goal, but I press on to take hold of that for which Christ Jesus took hold of me.

PHILIPPIANS 3:12

If we are going to continue to press on in our Christian walk, we must make sure that we have the strength and energy to do so. To "press on" implies that we exert a steady force against something; and I think one of those somethings is a hardened heart. Often unknowingly, we allow little things to build up inside of us. Slowly, these small subtle obstructions form very large blockages, which over a period of time clog our spiritual arteries and harden our hearts by depriving them of access to their life source. We must do whatever it takes to ensure that these blockages have no place in our lives as followers of Jesus, because they hinder our ability to run freely.

We must never think that we have arrived, for the moment that we do, we become stagnant and complacent. Instead, we must always fervently seek after the heart of God. We will never "arrive" on this side of eternity because there is always more of God to press into and so much more to accomplish for his purpose and kingdom.

We must commit to continually pressing against those things that would pull us back and toward those things that make us run unhindered. If Jesus has left us on planet Earth, then there is obviously still more ahead for us to do; he did not leave us here so that we could retire. Determine to never stop but to keep pressing on. Don't allow complacency, apathy, weariness, indifference, hurt, offense, insecurity, fear, doubt, bitterness, or unforgiveness to clog up your arteries. Keep your heart strong and free so that you can keep pressing forward.

MOMENT OF REFLECTION

Do you feel that you have arrived, or are you still pressing on? Identify some of the things that Jesus has "laid up for you" that you have not yet obtained.

May 10

Holding On to the Passion

Because of the increase of wickedness, the love of most will grow cold.

MATTHEW 24:12

I remember a time before Nick and I started dating when he found out from a friend of mine that I swam at the local swimming pool at six o'clock each morning. I had been doing these early morning swims for almost a year, and up to that point, I had never seen Nick at the pool. All of a sudden, I began seeing him there each morning, already in the pool and doing laps by the time I got there.

There is nothing pleasant about doing laps at daybreak—the water is cold and getting out is even colder! But alas, Nick was in love and on a mission. After about a week, we "accidentally" (actually a well-planned accident on Nick's part) bumped into each other, and I asked him what he was doing at the pool so early in the morning. He looked at me indignantly and exclaimed, "What do you mean? I'm always here at this time." Of course, only later were my suspicions confirmed. No one had to convince Nick to do it, because he had a passion for a petite Greek woman and he was going to do whatever it took to take home his prize! And his passionate affection won the day—we eventually were married.

Many of us begin our relationship with God like this. But just as marriage partners must work proactively to sustain their passion for one another, we too must work to keep our passionate commitment to God fresh and strong for the duration of our Christian walk. This means spending time with him in vital communication through his Word, prayer, and making ourselves at home in his presence.

MOMENT OF REFLECTION

How are you working to keep your relationship with the Lord fresh and strong?

May 11

Higher and Bigger

Then Caleb silenced the people before Moses and said, "We should go up and take possession of the land, for we can certainly do it."

NUMBERS 13:30

When that old bully named "Difficulty" pops up, God wants us to see and hear something more—something beyond the difficulty. Camped on the edge of the Promised Land, Moses sent twelve scouts to scope out the land. Ten of the scouts brought back a negative report, but Joshua and Caleb kept their eyes on God, who was higher and bigger. (God is *always* higher and bigger.) Rather than being distracted by all that looked impossible, they saw all that was possible. The song in their heads was not the old, sad song of Difficulty, but rather the song of all that God had promised. And instead of fixating on the problems, they remembered God's promise—a land of plenty for their people. They could see it, feel it, taste it.

They knew that the same miracles that God had performed to get the children of Israel out of Egypt would suffice to take them into the Promised Land. This task was no harder, and the miracles required were no bigger. The same God who did that was the same God who could do this. It never was about what they could not do; it was always about what God could and would do if his people would only believe in him to do it.

MOMENT OF REFLECTION

Concerning the giants in your life, can you say with God, "We can certainly do it"? As you strive to follow God more closely, how will you confront the giants in your path?

May 12

What Faith Is

Faith is confidence in what we hope for and assurance about what we do not see.

HEBREWS 11:1

What is it that God does? He shows up. He speaks out. He shines. When you're convinced something is hard and difficult, when everyone tells you that it's impossible, God is able to make a way where there is no way.

When difficulties get in the way of us daring to do what God has called us to do, we must ask ourselves, "Who am I going to believe: the rational or the supernatural, the factual or the true?"

The Bible tells us that Moses and the Israelites, and Abraham before them, all got to the destination God had ordained for them by faith. Their journey made no sense. Leaving everything they had, the safe and familiar, for the unknown wasn't rational or explainable, definable or predictable. But the exercising of faith requires the unknown, along with the unexpected and unpredictable and outrageous.

Faith is required when you're in doubt, when you're in want, when things are difficult and unclear. We can't touch faith, but it can move mountains. The Bible puts it this way: We may not be able to hold faith or wrap it up in a box, but it is real and powerful and can conquer kingdoms, administer justice, gain what was promised. It can shut the mouths of lions, quench the fury of flames, escape the edge of the sword, raise the dead, end torture, and release the imprisoned. Faith can take you right where God wants you.

MOMENT OF REFLECTION

Are you walking by faith or sight?

May 13

The Little Things

Let perseverance finish its work so that you may be mature and complete, not lacking anything.

JAMES 1:4

Unwavering commitment to preparation and training is a major determinant of how successful we will be in the marathon of life. Training is essential because it not only strengthens our physical capacity but also prepares us for possible obstacles and hindrances that we may encounter along the way.

Just as marathon runners are constantly in training, Christians must be constantly in training as well. Every day, we need to make the effort to do the things that will determine our level of success in the future. These daily disciplines include: reading the Bible, praising and worshiping God, and asking him to fill us afresh with the Holy Spirit. Strangely, it is the small, seemingly insignificant things we do every day that determine whether we will win or lose in life.

Athletes cannot live any way they want and expect to be in peak condition on race day. They have to follow a tightly disciplined regimen. It's exactly the same in our spiritual lives. God has given us moral guidelines for living and certain spiritual disciplines that we need to maintain in order to win in life. We must keep up those disciplines in order to keep our spiritual lives on track.

It seems as though the longer we walk with God, the more we let the small things slip. Endurance is built by paying attention to the small things. The simple disciplines of the faith are ones that no Christian ever outgrows. They may appear boring and mundane to some, but they are actually the invisible force that is continually moving us forward in the purposes of God.

MOMENT OF REFLECTION

How are you doing with your spiritual daily disciplines?
How can you improve in that area?

May 14

My Prayer

I have fought the good fight, I have finished the race, I have kept the faith.

2 TIMOTHY 4:7

My prayer is that we will never give up before we reach the finish line in our lives. I want us all to finish as winners—doing all that God has called us to do, becoming all that he has called us to be. But I also know that there is an area, maybe two, maybe more, in each of our lives where we feel we have "hit a wall." Whenever this happens, we're tempted to back off, slow down—or quit! But God wants us to press through and carry on.

My friend Kylie is a marathon runner and, without exception, in every single race she hits "the invisible wall." It does not matter how much she prepares for it or even knows it is coming, it never makes hitting that wall any easier or any less painful. After more than a dozen marathons, the only difference is that she knows that if she just keeps running she will get through it. It still hurts just as much physically and mentally, but she knows she will get to the other side if she does not stop.

Today, I simply want to encourage you to keep going.

We do not always have to charge forward at a hundred miles an hour and take the next hill. We need only take the next step.

Sometimes all you can do is place one foot in front of the other and let God carry you.

MOMENT OF REFLECTION

Have you ever hit a "spiritual wall"?
How did you keep going?

May 15

Small Beginnings

Who dares despise the day of small things?

ZECHARIAH 4:10

If King David had not spent untold hours looking after sheep, he would never have been able to kill a lion and a bear. If he had not had to contend with lions and bears, he would not have had the courage to tackle Goliath. And if he had never faced Goliath, he would have probably remained in obscurity. There was a clear development from one stage of his life to the next. Too many people want to shortcut their foundational training program, but they are only shortening their ability to go the distance.

Focusing on strengthening our spiritual foundations now will increase our capacity to run to win in the future, as God presents us with bigger challenges. We should not despise the seemingly insignificant things we are doing, for they may turn out to be the very things God is using to prepare, train, and shape us for what we will be doing for him in the future.

If we are faithful in the small things God has given us to do, he will be able to trust us with bigger things down the road. Everything that is now big was once small; if we cannot be good stewards of a small thing, how will we ever be trustworthy with the big things? We need to grow to go where we need to go . . . and our faithfulness in the small things grows us.

Let's ensure that we never try to shortcut God's training program for our lives. If we want to take out a giant, we must first master the bear.

MOMENT OF REFLECTION

What little things is God using in your life to help you establish a foundation for your destiny?

May 16

Swept Away

The king said, "Stand aside and wait here." So he stepped aside and stood there.

2 SAMUEL 18:30

No matter what we do, we cannot run ahead of God's timing. If we do, we are in danger of being swept aside and overwhelmed by the discovery that we are not up to the task at hand. We always want to reach our destination sooner rather than later, but God will have his way—and the person who is meant to be fulfilling a certain task at a certain time will be there! We have to learn to run our races in the time that God has ordained.

One of the major lessons that I have learned in life is that everything always takes longer than I thought it would. Every big promotion in my life has come "suddenly," but each "suddenly" was usually preceded by ten years. There have always been more challenges than I anticipated, but in the end, God's will and promises prevail. My personality type is such that I want everything to happen "yesterday"; nothing ever moves quickly enough for me. But no matter how hard I have pushed, I have discovered that God has set a pace for my race. If we can all just learn to accept that, our lives will be full of much more joy and peace!

There is no doubt that God is more concerned about building endurance in us than he is about getting us to our destination quickly. Therefore, we must stay focused on what it is that we are meant to be doing right now and resist the urge to rush ahead of God.

MOMENT OF REFLECTION

How will you resist the urge to rush ahead of God?
How will you follow instead of lead?

May 17

Obedience Produces Success

Keep this Book of the Law always on your lips; meditate on it day and night, so that you may be careful to do everything written in it. Then you will be prosperous and successful.

JOSHUA 1:8

The Bible is living, vital, and relevant. God knows how to maximize our potential and his Word shows us how to live our lives passionately and with purpose. Society has created hundreds of thousands of laws and bylaws, rules and regulations, but no one has ever been able to improve on the Ten Commandments.

Winning in life is a natural by-product of obedience to God's law. Conversely, failure or disqualification can be a by-product of disobedience. If we break God's rules, there are consequences. Disobeying God's rules is like deciding to drive on the wrong side of the road late at night. We have the power and choice to do it, but we are likely to end up killing ourselves and someone else as a consequence.

Like any good parent, the boundaries that God establishes for us are there for our protection. Since God is good and does good, then surely the law that he gave to the children of Israel was good and for their good. The problem was not the law; it was what man did to the law that turned it into religious bondage. When God says that we shouldn't be sleeping around, committing adultery or fornicating, it is because he knows that such activities lead to sexual diseases, broken hearts, damaged emotions, and wounded souls. When God tells us not to covet things that belong to other people, it is because he knows we will never be truly happy until we are content with what he has already blessed us with.

Many pay lip service to living God's way but aren't really prepared to obey his Word when the crunch comes. We live in a world that is self-absorbed and self-indulgent, where people do what is right in their own eyes. Against this backdrop, God's Word is still powerful, true, relevant, and prophetic. It is not some archaic, legalistic, irrelevant book, but rather the way to true life, abundance, health, success, and prosperity. Do it God's way—it always has been and always will be the best way.

MOMENT OF REFLECTION

How do you believe the Ten Commandments are relevant to your life? How do they help you in your quest to follow God?

May 18

The Utopian All

Keep me free from the trap that is set for me.

PSALM 31:4

For years, we have been told we can have it all, be it all, and do it all. So inevitably, we have aggressively set out on a pursuit to achieve this utopian "all." We roll up our sleeves in true "Rosie the Riveter" style (to reveal our femininely chiseled arms, of course) and belt out the lyrics to "I Am Woman, Hear Me Roar" in our best Helen Reddy voice. We get up an hour early to exercise, another hour earlier to pray, and still race to get the kids ready and packed for school. We are consummate organizers, jugglers, and problem solvers as we manage husbands, children, church commitments, friendships, finances, groceries, mealtimes, child taxi service, quiet time with God, and whatever else is on the agenda.

Then, at the end of the day, we stay up an hour longer to ensure the house is tidy, an additional hour to read a chapter of the latest bestseller, and one more hour to ensure we spend "quality time" with our husbands. We've set out on this mission to do it "all," only to quickly discover that in order to achieve it, we conservatively need an extra twenty-four hours every day!

The fact is that the pursuit of having and doing it all has left many women disappointed and discouraged, exhausted and defeated, anxious and stressed. Despite our sometimes superhuman exploits, we begin to question the pace and fullness of this "having and doing it all" life. In our disillusionment, we can even begin to think there is no possible way we can manage a strong Christian walk, an amazing marriage, great kids, a fulfilling sex life, fantastic friends, and pursuing our God-given purpose.

The truth is, you *can* have it all and do it all ... but often it's an incorrect perception of "all" that leaves us feeling like we fall short. If we want to do this adventure called life well, and fulfill the purpose God has for us, we need to discover his definition of "all" and go after it.

MOMENT OF REFLECTION

Do you feel trapped by society's image of what the perfect woman should be? How does that image compare with the godly woman depicted in Proverbs 31?

May 19

Draw Near to God

Come near to God and he will come near to you.

JAMES 4:8

I remember back when I was in Bible college, single, and able to spend three hours in prayer and study with God almost every day of the week. And then I got into full-time ministry ... and then I got married ... and then I had kids ... and then ... and then ... and then ... Believe me, I completely understand the dilemma of trying to get a thousand things accomplished each day and still carve out time to spend with God. What Christian woman does not deal with this?

But the fact of the matter is, if we are running so much that we have no time left to talk to God, we are way out of balance. Drawing near to our Source of everything needs to be the highest priority if we want to have and do it all in life, and out of the thousand things that need to be done, spending time with God must be at the top of our list.

Now, before any of you start feeling all that guilt and condemnation, let me say this: Throw out your legalism, find what works for you in this season of life, and stop feeling guilty about it! There is no correct formula for drawing near to God; you must simply do whatever you need to do to be close to him. He will meet you there.

When we take the time to nestle into our Father in heaven, we will find the strength, power, wisdom, and contentment to navigate every season of life.

MOMENT OF REFLECTION

How do you draw close to God?
Do you have a specific plan?

May 20

Two Perspectives

Do not conform to the pattern of this world, but be transformed by the renewing of your mind. Then you will be able to test and approve what God's will is—his good, pleasing and perfect will.

ROMANS 12:2

Essentially, there are two perspectives through which we can view every situation in life. One is the "heavenly" perspective that Paul exhorts us to set our minds on; the other is the "worldly" perspective that he warns us about. We have the power to transition our thinking out of the worldly perspective and into a heavenly one.

This isn't always easy at first. It takes practice and commitment to change your default mind-set. That's why it is so critical to spend time in God's Word daily, meditating on the truth it contains, rather than the facts of our current circumstances. We need to immerse our minds in his Word so we can quickly recall these principles during difficult moments or challenging seasons.

We all want to prove what is good and acceptable and the perfect will of God. After all, isn't that what having and doing it all is really all about—fulfilling our destinies? But in order to do God's perfect will, we have to know what God's will is. This comes from a deep understanding of the Bible and personal revelation from the Holy Spirit.

When we are fueled by God's Word, our thoughts inevitably become governed by his truth, and this truth causes us to be internally transformed.

This transformation is what Paul is referring to when he exhorts us to renew our minds: it has an incredible effect on our actions and responses to people and circumstances. We begin to analyze situations from a heavenly perspective and react accordingly. It's amazing what the appropriate response can do for a seemingly hopeless situation. This is why the truth of God's Word has the power to change the facts of our circumstances.

MOMENT OF REFLECTION

How has your mind been transformed by the power of God's Word?

May 21

Who Are You Listening To?

Every word of God is flawless; he is a shield to those who take refuge in him.

PROVERBS 30:5

I was sitting in an airport (surprising, I know), surrounded by a large crowd of other waiting people. I had taken a moment to put my book down, and in just a matter of minutes I heard people giving dozens of opinions on different topics. One lady was talking about Oprah's newest fad diet; another was giving Suze Orman's latest philosophy on the stock market; another was giving Tim Gunn's fashion advice to her mother; yet another was talking about what Brangelina thought about the environment. I wondered how many of these people had any opinions of their own!

In our fast-paced world driven by media and technology, we have the opportunity to access literally hundreds, thousands, and perhaps tens of thousands of views on every imaginable issue. The real question is: Are we taking time to listen to what God thinks about these issues? It's fine to hear what the media or social commentators have to say about world events, but are we also seeking out God's views? On a more personal level, it's okay to listen to what our friends or our parents have to say about the situations happening in our lives, but more importantly, what's God saying to us about them?

I think sometimes we get lost in the storms of adversity because we haven't stopped to listen to what God is speaking to our hearts, or to follow his directions about how to navigate them. Storm or no storm, it is critical that biblical truth is the overwhelming sound in our lives. This is why every day, I do something to connect myself with God—read a verse, listen to a teaching CD, listen to a podcast, or simply meditate on one of his promises. I want God's truth to echo so loudly in my life that it drowns out any other contrary voice that could possibly distract or deter me.

MOMENT OF REFLECTION

What voices are you listening to?
As you follow God, is God's voice the loudest and most important?

May 22

Knowing Our God Purpose

> *Josiah was eight years old when he became king, and he reigned in Jerusalem thirty-one years.*
>
> 2 KINGS 22:1

It's important to understand that our purpose is always part of God's bigger plan. However, unless we discover our inner sense of purpose (why we are on the planet), any part we might be called to play in a bigger plan will never get off the ground.

So many of us stumble through life crippled and immobilized because we do not know our ultimate purpose. We are designed by God for accomplishment, engineered for success, and endowed with seeds of greatness.

Josiah was born in the midst of Israel's darkest hour and was just eight years old when he ascended to the throne. However, 322 years before Josiah's birth, a prophet mentioned his name and that he would be born to the house of David. God knew Josiah was coming to earth and had a predetermined plan for his life.

The Bible says that Josiah did what was right in the sight of the Lord and walked in the ways of David. He fulfilled his purpose and was pivotal in restoring the house of God, his Word, and worship in the hearts of the Israelites.

God requires that we do for our generation what Josiah did for his. The plan that God has for our lives usually complements the gifts and personality that he has placed in us. His desire is that we use our gifts for his glory, to build his kingdom. In order to do that, we must discover God's purpose for our lives by seeking him, reading his Word, and searching our hearts for the gifts and passions he has placed there.

MOMENT OF REFLECTION

What is your "God purpose"?

May 23

Reaching Out

This is why it is said: "Wake up, sleeper, rise from the dead, and Christ will shine on you."

EPHESIANS 5:14

When we are not fully awakened to God in our lives, we miss the thrill of seeing him at work. It's like the time Nick and I took our girls to Disneyland, and Catherine fell asleep just before the evening fireworks display. All day long, she had been anticipating the show in the sky that night. But we had seen so many sights and wonders that, by evening, she was tired. We let her drift into sleep.

Later, the show in the sky over, she awoke as we were headed back to the parking lot to go home. "Mummy," she cried, "why didn't you wake me up?" She had slept through the only part she had really wanted to see. How many of us do exactly the same thing? We end up sleepwalking through this thing called life, oblivious to the needs of people around us, the pain of our world, and ignorant of the very purpose for which God created us and placed us upon this earth.

What a great tragedy it would be to come to the end of life only to discover that we never really lived, that we were never fully awake. Perhaps today would be a great day to walk around with our eyes wide open, our spiritual ears alert, our hearts tender, and our expectations high. God wants you to colabor with him in his harvest, but a laborer must be awake to work.

A daring adventure awaits the awake.

MOMENT OF REFLECTION

Do you feel like you are awake to the needs of those around you? If not, what have you missed?

May 24

Shed Those Sins

For sin shall no longer be your master, because you are not under the law, but under grace.

ROMANS 6:14

We can live in victory and freedom in every area of our lives if we choose to admit, confess, and deal with those areas that have been holding us back from fulfilling the purpose of God. Because of grace we don't need to be mastered by sin any longer. What a great hope and promise lies in this truth.

Perhaps you are compromising in areas of your life and are destroying your intimacy with God and your relationships with others. Because of the redemptive work of Jesus Christ on the cross, you and I no longer need to be slaves to sin; we have been set free. Praise God!

Sin must be dealt with ruthlessly and cast aside. God won't do that for us; we need to repent of every sin and evil desire. That's the only way to strip sin of its power in our lives. Once we shed our sins, we will no longer stumble along but run freely.

I realize that many people do not like us to use the term "sin" today, but I think it is important that we correctly diagnose a sickness so that we know exactly what to administer to bring health and wholeness. If I had a bottle of poison and ripped off the label, replacing it with a label that said chocolate syrup, you would think I was crazy. And you would be correct—because the milder you make the label, the more potent you make the poison. Let's not put a wrong label on the disease, because if we call it what it is, then we can be washed clean by the precious blood of the Lamb. You can be set free right here and right now.

What can wash my sin away? Nothing but the blood of Jesus.

MOMENT OF REFLECTION

This is your chance to be very honest. What sin has the Holy Spirit been convicting you of that you have been ignoring? Remember sins are not just external actions, but can also be attitudes that we store up in our hearts.

May 25

What Are You Hearing?

Consequently, faith comes from hearing the message, and the message is heard through the word about Christ.

ROMANS 10:17

Who and what we listen to defines what we will do in life, the risks we will take, and who we become. If we constantly hear that we are failures, not good enough, not talented enough, not pretty enough or smart enough, then we eventually begin to believe those lies and settle for a mediocre existence instead of the abundant faith-filled adventure that Jesus called us to live. Listening to the wrong voices will cripple and immobilize us.

Conversely, if we are hearing affirming, life-giving, hope-filled messages from the Word of God, we will take greater risks, because we will have the faith to believe that Jesus is who he says he is and will do what he has promised. God's Word is living and active and breathes life back into dead bones, weary souls, and broken hearts.

In today's Scripture, the apostle Paul clearly tells us that there is only one place where our faith is developed—and that is by listening to the truth of the Word of God. We are bombarded daily with thousands of messages that try to undermine the truth of who we are in Christ; if we are to build our faith, then we need to turn down the volume on all those other voices and turn up the volume to the Word of God.

There are so many ways to access God's Word today that none of us have any excuse for not making the hearing of it a daily priority. Access to the Word in all shapes and forms is no longer the issue; it is a matter of getting that Word *into* us. Bottom line, it doesn't matter *how* we do it; the key is to actually prioritize the time *to* do it.

Faith only comes by hearing the Word of God. Make sure this is what you are listening to more than anything else.

MOMENT OF REFLECTION

Can you identify the voices that are speaking into your life the loudest right now?

May 26

Hearing Loss

[Jesus] called out, "Whoever has ears to hear, let them hear."

LUKE 8:8

It's uncanny to me how I can be at a playground with my girls, send them off to play, and if one of my daughters calls for me, I'm able to decipher her call instantly among the throngs of screaming, excited children. When Catie or Sophia yell for me, I can hone in on their voices and respond immediately.

We all have this ability with certain voices and people in our lives, don't we? As our bodies age, however, our ability to hear and interpret sounds can diminish, and everything can start to sound muddy and indecipherable.

We are exhorted throughout Scripture to constantly have an ear inclined to the voice of the Spirit. In order to fulfill God's purpose in our lives, we need to be able to decipher his voice above all the other voices vying for our attention Let's be real: never in history have we been overwhelmed by so many voices. There are 7.3 million new pages being added to the World Wide Web today, and even more will be added tomorrow. One thousand books will be published today, and the total of all printed knowledge will double in the next five years. If we were to start reading right now, and continue reading for 24 hours a day, 365 days a year, we would never catch up with everything being written. There are five billion instant messages that will be sent today. Our world will make available more information in the next decade than has been discovered in all of human history. I could go on, but I think you get the picture.

So pardon the graphic illustration, but we must ensure that we regularly remove the "wax" from our spiritual ears that can build up over time, so that our ability to hear God's voice is not dulled. If we fail to monitor the other voices screaming for our attention, we can inadvertently miss the voice of God. Ultimately, this is the only voice that will lead us into our destiny.

MOMENT OF REFLECTION

Are your ears open to God's voice?
Who do you listen to each day?

May 27

The Power of Planning

Do not despise these small beginnings, for the LORD rejoices to see the work begin, to see the plumb line in Zerubbabel's hand.

ZECHARIAH 4:10 NLT

If we want to live a life of significance, we need to understand that it won't happen by accident. We must be intentional about the choices we make in relation to our dreams, and set goals to ensure we are moving toward them daily. A question I am regularly asked is how I balance marriage, motherhood, and ministry (a whole other book), and keep my sanity. The truth is, my God-given dream fuels me;

therefore, my life is very focused and uncomplicated. I plan my time according to my priorities rather than letting my life just happen. Most of the year, I work hard traveling and speaking. But as important as it is to book my tickets or organize my speaking schedule, it's no less important to plan dinner dates with my husband, go to the beach or park with my daughters, see a movie with friends, and keep fit and healthy.

Many people "go with the flow," taking life as it comes. They have no strategy or infrastructure in place to facilitate the realization of their dream. The fact is, when it comes to fulfilling our destinies, we can't hit a target we cannot see. Studies show that those people who have written measurable goals and plans are more likely to succeed than those who don't. In fact, one of the primary factors associated with underachievement is confusion and fuzziness when it comes to goals. Goals, accompanied by a burning desire to see them accomplished, dramatically increase the probability we'll achieve our dreams (within reason that is—marrying the future king of England is not impossible, but very unlikely).

As I pursued my dreams, I set very specific goals along the way. I understood that only a succession of small, daily, measured steps would take me into the future I envisioned. Of course, this was coupled with God's favor, anointing, and opportunity. It is not enough to see the future we want; we have to be deliberate about the actions we take to make this future a reality. We need to ask ourselves, "What future do I see for myself, my family, my relationships, my work, my finances, and my ministry?" We need to start envisioning ourselves in the future we want to have, and begin to take small, incremental steps (even if they don't look like much) toward that dream. In the words of the prophet Zechariah, "Do not despise . . . small beginnings."

MOMENT OF REFLECTION

What future do you see for yourself, family, relationships, work, finances, and ministry?

May 28

Small Steps of Obedience

But Samuel replied: "Does the LORD delight in burnt offerings and sacrifices as much as in obeying the LORD? To obey is better than sacrifice, and to heed is better than the fat of rams."

1 SAMUEL 15:22

If God instructs us to do something—whether through his Word, a prompting of the heart, or the words of a godly adviser—we must quickly obey. If we have not been obedient to the most recent thing God asked us to do, we cannot expect to be entrusted with more.

Obedience may be as simple as sending someone a note of encouragement, apologizing to a friend for being short-tempered, volunteering in church, talking to someone about Jesus, giving something away, getting marriage counseling, dealing with an addiction, watching less television, or adopting a child. Whatever it is, we must remember that every small step of obedience has eternal ramifications. If we choose not to obey, our hearts can begin to harden, which will inevitably silence the voice of God in our lives.

So often we want to do everything else but obey God. We will read the Bible more, pray more, worship more, give more, or serve more, when God does not want us to do anything other than obey. If we respond in obedience, however difficult it may seem, it is always for our benefit, because God is for us and not against us. Obedience to God is the key to a life full of love, joy, peace, hope, progress, success, blessing, abundance, and prosperity. Obedience is actually very simple; it's just not easy.

MOMENT OF REFLECTION

As you strive to follow God more closely,
how can you more fully and joyfully obey his promptings?
What is God telling you to do?

May 29

Enter His Gates with Thanksgiving

Enter his gates with thanksgiving and his courts with praise; give thanks to him and praise his name.

PSALM 100:4

Thanksgiving is a *choice* that we make, not a reaction that occurs when good things happen to us. Notice today's verse doesn't say, "Enter his gates with thanksgiving if you've had a good week." We read nothing about giving thanks when we have enough money to pay our bills. It doesn't say we are obliged to give thanks on condition that the kids have behaved like angels and have cleaned up the house whilst asking us, "Mom, how are you today? Can I make you a cup of tea?" Neither does it mention anything about entering God's gates with thanksgiving if our husband has managed to put his own socks and undies in the laundry basket!

I could go on, but you get the point! Regardless of what is going on in our lives, we have to make a decision to enter in God's presence daily with *one* attitude—thankfulness—not based on what is happening to us, but based on who he is—a good God.

The truth is, it's easy to give thanks when everything is going great in our lives. It is how we react when everything is not great that truly defines our character and determines our destiny.

MOMENT OF REFLECTION

As you "enter his gates" today, what is the state of your heart? Are you following God with thanksgiving or a heavy heart?

May 30

Look Up!

My heart is not proud, LORD, my eyes are not haughty; I do not concern myself with great matters or things too wonderful for me.

PSALM 131:1

One year for my birthday I got the most wonderful, bright pink Vespa, which I absolutely adore, and Nick booked me on a riding course to ensure that I learned to drive the thing safely! The course was spread over two days and the whole time the instructor kept on telling me, "Keep your head up. You've got to look in the direction you want to go." He explained to me that (a) I should not look at anything I wanted to avoid running into, and (b) I should always keep looking further ahead than where I was. He must have told me this a hundred times over those two days, but what great lessons for our spiritual life! We need to keep looking up and keep looking ahead.

When it comes to the purposes of God, it's all about perspective. Many of us are locked in the prison of our current circumstances because we have lost perspective regarding his promises for our lives. Instead we have focused on where we are, where we have been, and, worse still, the very things we want to avoid. We will go nowhere until we gain a true perspective and begin to speak words of faith, life, and thanksgiving into our present situation. We need to lift our heads and look forward in the direction in which we want to go. God has a promise for our future that is much greater than where we are right now. God has promises for our marriage, our children, our health and prosperity—every aspect of our lives—all of which are much bigger than we can currently see or understand. We need to look up and begin to see what God has for us, because he has so much more!

MOMENT OF REFLECTION

In your quest to follow God more closely,
how can you keep looking ahead in the direction you want to go?

May 31

Passing the Baton

After that whole generation had been gathered to their ancestors, another generation grew up who knew neither the LORD nor what he had done for Israel.

JUDGES 2:10

If we don't keep our eyes fixed on Jesus, then we run the risk of repeating one of the greatest tragedies in the Bible. Joshua is often spoken about as the model leader. He was, of course, a *great* leader—he did awesome things in his generation; he ran his hundred-meter leg of the divine relay fantastically. But, somehow he did not manage to pass on that baton to the next generation. Joshua did not leave a legacy of faith. It is almost incomprehensible to me that after all the great miracles, signs, and wonders that occurred through his ministry that a generation arose who "knew neither the LORD nor what he had done for Israel." Joshua ran a fantastic personal leg, but ultimately he failed. The next four generations of his people were godless.

Let's ensure that we do everything in our power to pass the baton of faith to the next generation. Take every opportunity that is available to you to share God's Word, truth, and precepts with any young person you come into contact with. And never forget that the most effective way to carry the baton of faith to the next generation is by running your leg of the race with strength, character, focus, and integrity—whether you are a stay-at-home mom, schoolteacher, pastor, or corporate CEO.

MOMENT OF REFLECTION

As you seek to follow God more closely in your own life, how will you "pass the baton" of faith to others, especially the next generation?

June

MORE LIKE CHRIST

June 1

What's at the Core?

Follow my example, as I follow the example of Christ.

1 CORINTHIANS 11:1

Quite simply, the goal of every Christian is to become more Christlike—after all, the very word *Christian* denotes "a Christ follower." Elsewhere in the New Testament Paul writes, "Therefore be imitators of God as dear children" (Ephesians 5:1 NJKV). When I think about this, I wonder exactly what Paul meant by "imitate." Does this mean that we should wear the same style toga and sandals that Jesus wore? Does this mean we should only eat kosher foods?

Probably not.

In fact, I think it is obvious that Paul is speaking about following Jesus' example in terms of his mission, values, motivation, priorities, thinking, teaching, and attitude. In other words, being imitators of Christ happens as the inner core of our being is transformed to become more like him, having his heart and mind. The internal change in turn is reflected in the way we speak, think, and act.

If we simply try to imitate Christ's external behavior—being kind, compassionate, and merciful without strengthening our spiritual core—then we risk missing out on the very process that makes us Christlike. We end up acting like a Christian sometimes, but not truly being a Christian at all times.

Think about Jesus: His actions stemmed from who he was. The *doing* part flowed naturally from the *being* part. This *being* stemmed from his spiritual core. In other words, Jesus did not try to act like anything he was not. Therefore, if we are to be imitators of Christ, we need to stop trying to *act* like Christians (external actions) and instead focus on *being* a Christian at our core (internal transformation). When this becomes our focus, we will discover that it's not difficult to act like a Christian, because we simply will be one. Period.

MOMENT OF REFLECTION

What are the characteristics you most admire about Jesus? Do you see those characteristics in your own life?

June 2

Looking the Part

Blind Pharisee! First clean the inside of the cup and dish, and then the outside also will be clean.

MATTHEW 23:26

It was on the ski slopes in Australia that I experienced firsthand the consequences of trying to act like something I'm not. Although I'd never skied before, I accepted the invitation to be the chaplain on a youth ski trip. My friend, a professional skier, loaned me her very chic, top-of-the-line ski gear. She said, "Well, at least you'll look the part!"

It was apparent that first day on the slopes that looking great on the outside had no bearing on my performance as an actual skier. I didn't have any of the knowledge, skill, experience, or strength on the inside that a real skier needs to have. In the end, looking the part counted for nothing.

The same holds true for us as Christians. We can look the part by having the best gear (our Bibles, our WWJD bracelets, our fish bumper stickers); by refraining from certain behaviors such as smoking, drinking, or cussing; or by going to church and singing in the choir. We certainly can be perceived as successful Christians by looking the right way, having the right "accessories," and acting the right way. But if all of this does not stem from who we really are at our core, our faith is just a sham.

We are supposed to be transformed into the image of Jesus. If we reject the transforming grace of Christ, then we are hypocrites, just like the Pharisees. The fact is that Jesus despises hypocrisy. He wants authentic followers. Unfortunately for our flesh, which craves instant results, this transformation is not something that happens overnight. We have to be willing to work at it. We cannot allow ourselves to be sidetracked by the external quick-fix plan. Instead, we must be committed to strengthening our spiritual core, which is all about an internal work that brings about our transformation into the image of Christ.

MOMENT OF REFLECTION

What are some of the things you do as a Christian that you feel are not authentically you?

June 3

C Is for Compassion

When Jesus landed and saw a large crowd, he had compassion on them and healed their sick.

MATTHEW 14:14

When I first became a Christian, I found it so amazing to read about all the miraculous signs and wonders Jesus performed during his short time in ministry. Many people were healed, delivered and, on more than one occasion, more than five thousand were fed! If Jesus lived today, Hollywood would be begging him to star in their next superhero movie. I can just see it now: famous designers creating a Lycra tunic with a big *M* for Messiah across the chest.

But as I matured in my faith, I began to understand what made these accounts truly remarkable: It was *compassion*—nothing more and nothing less—that undergirded every single thing Jesus did. He never performed a miracle for the purpose of showing off his amazing superpowers, thereby building his ministry faster; he simply loved people and was compelled by compassion each day he walked on earth. He brought deliverance to the demonic; he raised the widow's son from the dead; he broke Jewish laws by reaching out to touch the "unclean" lepers simply because he was motivated by pure love.

Every work Jesus performed externally naturally flowed from who he was internally. He never had to struggle to try to be the Son of God—he simply *was*. His deeds were an extension of who he was at his core.

For you and me, being Christlike is not only about our external actions, including things such as feeding the poor and helping the marginalized and oppressed. It is also about the motives of our hearts. We can do all of the right things, but if we are not becoming more like Christ *from the inside out* and allowing these actions to spring from true compassion, then we are not being truly Christlike.

MOMENT OF REFLECTION

When was the last time you remember feeling Christlike compassion for another person? How did you respond?

June 4

Train of Thought

Set your minds on things above, not on earthly things.

COLOSSIANS 3:2

The phrase "train of thought" certainly is an accurate metaphor. Our thoughts are just like a train; they always take us somewhere. If we want to change our destination, regardless of what area of life we're talking about, we have to change the thought trains we board.

Often, we don't realize we have the ability to choose what we think. Yet Scripture exhorts us to set our minds on things above and not on earthly things. This doesn't mean that negative thoughts won't enter our minds—if that were the case, there would be no need to consciously choose to set our minds on the thoughts of God.

While I was learning to renew my mind, I discovered that many of the trains of thought I had at that time about God, the people around me, myself, and my destiny were completely contrary to what God thinks. They were built on my experience rather than the truth of God's Word. I knew I had to consciously choose what thoughts I would allow to pull into the platform of my mind.

Armed with this knowledge and a firm commitment to exercise my mind muscle, I was ready to go to work. Each time a train of thought contrary to the Word of God pulled into the platform of my mind, I would choose not to get on board. Instead, I would purposefully board trains of thought that would take me to the right destination.

This is why it's so important to read and meditate on the Word of God. If we don't know what thoughts are contrary to God's, how will we ever know what trains to avoid?

MOMENT OF REFLECTION

What are some of the "thought trains" you often board?
How might reading the Scriptures help you not get derailed?

June 5

Peeling Back the Layers

The LORD is near to all who call on him, to all who call on him in truth.

PSALM 145:18

I had a friend who wanted to make those fine laugh lines appear less embedded in her cheeks, so she bought a tube of anti-wrinkle cream. Wanting to stay within her frugal budget, she grabbed one of the more inexpensive brands whose fancy packaging claimed to reduce wrinkles by some insane percentage. A few days later (or I should say a few pimples and dry patches later), she realized that this cream contained no real anti-aging ingredients. The packaging had all been a gimmick!

Seeing my friend's blotchy face after a few applications of that phony lotion reminded me of the importance of having a strong spiritual core. If our core doesn't have the proven "God ingredients," then we're never going to have anything except a flawed Christianity wrapped up in fancy packaging.

So many times, we build layers around our inner core to protect ourselves. We cover ourselves with all sorts of fancy packaging —all the Christian behaviors we know we are "supposed" to have. Eventually we get so good at hiding, we actually believe our own marketing campaign—we have completely forgotten that we even *have* a spiritual core!

We must embark on the process of carefully peeling back the layers to expose our core, because if there is to be any real change in our lives, it must start on the inside. The whole direction of our lives and the outworking of our destinies flow from there! We cannot *act* our way to our future. In fact, unless we are transformed into the image of Christ, we *have* no future. The only way to lay hold of the purposes of God for our lives is to become who we need to be on the inside. It's only then that we will be able to do what we have been called to do.

MOMENT OF REFLECTION

If the layers were peeled back to expose your core, what would people see?

June 6

Being a Pilgrim

When you pray, do not be like the hypocrites, for they love to pray standing in the synagogues and on the street corners to be seen by others.

MATTHEW 6:5

Some of us live our lives as if it were a dress rehearsal for another life in another time. Jacques in Shakespeare's *As You Like It* says, "All the world's a stage, and all the men and women merely players; they have their exits and their entrances, and one man in his time plays many parts." As romantic as this sounds, we must remember that you and I are not actors pretending to be Christians in the drama of life. We are on a very real journey to Christlikeness, and we cannot "perform" our way into becoming like him.

Every interaction that we have *every day* is part of this pilgrimage. This includes the ways in which we respond to our circumstances, the kindnesses we choose to extend or withhold, the irritations we choose to hang on to or let go, and the generosity we choose to offer freely or not. All the challenges and joys of life are part of the process of helping us to be conformed and transformed to the image of Christ.

I grew up in a strict Greek Orthodox home and remember being told each Sunday, "Christine, you'd better behave in church because

God is watching you!" I soon learned that if I ever wanted to have "fun," I had to do it when I was not at church or any other Christian activity. As a result, my life became compartmentalized. I put on an Emmy Award-winning performance as "Christian Christine" for a few hours every Sunday and during the rest of the week, I was the real me and lived the way I wanted.

It was only when I truly surrendered my heart to Jesus that I realized that he was with me in every circumstance, each day, and not just for a few hours on Sunday. It changed the way I live my life. Now I understand that everything matters and that God is with me everywhere. My Christian journey is not about some faraway destination, but is worked out in the details of my everyday life.

MOMENT OF REFLECTION

Are you a different person at church than you are at home or with your friends? If so, why?

June 7

New Thoughts, New Ways

We take captive every thought to make it obedient to Christ.

2 CORINTHIANS 10:5

After I gave birth to our second daughter, Sophia, I was determined to lose the extra pounds I had gained while pregnant. Being somewhat extreme, I emptied my house of all traces of unhealthy food and stocked my refrigerator and cupboards with every variation of lettuce that exists, as well as soups and vegetables. I was determined to lose weight—I thought that being healthy meant being able to fit back into my favorite jeans.

One day I agreed to catch up with two friends at a local restaurant. When the waiter came to take our order, I was determined to stick to my new eating regimen, so I ordered a salad (with no cheese, no croutons, and fat-free dressing on the side) and a glass of hot water with lemon. About ten minutes into our conversation, an appetizer of potato skins arrived. They looked divine! Then came the chocolate shakes, and the main courses of ribs for one friend, bacon alfredo for another—followed by my dry, cheeseless, croutonless salad.

Halfway through the meal, my friends excused themselves to use the restroom. As soon as they were gone, I stuffed a few ribs in my mouth, washed them down with chocolate shake, and spun a forkful of alfredo noodles so thick that I almost got lockjaw trying to fit it in. I emptied the leftover potato skins into my purse and wiped my mouth just in time to welcome my friends back to the table. If they noticed the missing food, they never mentioned it, and I finished off my weeds feeling a bit defeated.

This little episode taught me a lesson: My thoughts about being healthy were not about the type of food that I ate, but rather about losing weight. Because I did not have a healthy mind-set, I was kidding myself if I thought I was going to be able to keep up a healthy diet. My brain needed to be "washed" and renewed before my habits could be modified.

MOMENT OF REFLECTION

Can you identify any areas in your life in which you changed your behavior but not the way you thought about your behavior?

June 8

Good Habits

Do not merely listen to the word, and so deceive yourselves. Do what it says.

JAMES 1:22

If we want to be open to God's divine interruptions in our lives, we must live in a state of awareness. Too often, when we are the answer to someone's prayer, we miss it. We stay busy going places and doing things, intent on our own agendas.

What if we paid a little more attention to the older woman struggling to step down from the curb? Or the fellow trying to balance a bunch of boxes in his arms, one or more of which we could carry for him? What if we *looked* for people who need help, instead of just seeing what we want to get done? We should greet each interruption with a question: "Lord, what is it you really want from me here?"

We also tend to overthink God's interruptions. As we hesitate, our own insecurities, feelings of awkwardness, schedule, and agenda start to stand in the way of the moment of interruption that God has prepared for us. So let's resist that urge and make it a habit to:

- Give an encouraging word to someone standing next to us in line.
- Acknowledge a cashier or waitress or service clerk by the name on his or her nametag, rather than treating that person as our servant.
- Make focused eye contact with those we address in any situation.
- Respond with patience to rude treatment, even though we would really much rather respond in kind.
- Drop a dollar in the homeless man's tin or save small change for donations to the neighbor child's fundraiser.

Allow God to continually soften your heart so that it beats for what his heart beats for—people. It's so easy to stay locked in a selfish cycle of *my* time, *my* objectives, *my* plans. But ask God to transform you into his image—to see what he sees, feel what he feels, love as he loves.

MOMENT OF REFLECTION

What do you think about these five habits?
What are some others you can think of?

June 9

Running to Win

Everyone who competes in the games goes into strict training. They do it to get a crown that will not last, but we do it to get a crown that will last forever.

1 CORINTHIANS 9:25

The word *marathon* takes its name from the legend of Pheidippides, a Greek soldier who ran twenty-six miles to deliver the news that the Greeks had beaten the Persians at the Battle of Marathon. Sadly, after this hero had reached the city and delivered his message, he promptly fell dead. The thing is, he might have lived had he done a few things differently.

Instead of pacing himself for marathon distance, he ran the entire course as if he were running a short sprint. If he had slowed down a little, stopped occasionally, and taken a drink and some food, in addition to tempering his speed on the grueling uphill stretches, it is possible he could have lived.

Similarly, the Christian life is much more a marathon than a sprint. God wants us to be endurance runners—the kind of people who will run the whole stretch of our race and finish victorious at the end. That being so, it is important that we learn to pace ourselves.

Paul emphasizes the importance of training and discipline. His vivid description of running to win in life inspired me to do some research on what makes marathon runners tick. I studied their preparation, their training techniques, mental attitudes, and other aspects of running. I discovered that the very principles foundational for running a marathon in the natural world are equally applicable to running our spiritual race.

I am aware that many people who started this faith adventure with me have dropped out of their races. The absence of disciplined training and good technique in their lives meant they didn't have the spiritual stamina to keep going when the going got tough. Instead of running to win, they have been defeated by disappointment, discouragement, distraction, disillusionment, or disease. Training and discipline in the race of life mean making the right choices today to ensure that we run to win. We can't allow ourselves to be forced out of our races by poor preparation and training.

MOMENT OF REFLECTION

How are you preparing
for your race through life?

June 10

One Day at a Time

His master replied, "Well done, good and faithful servant! You have been faithful with a few things; I will put you in charge of many things."

MATTHEW 25:21

It is the basic spiritual disciplines such as reading the Bible, prayer, waiting on God, praise and worship, and asking God to fill me afresh with the Holy Spirit that have kept me on course and running my race for the last twenty years. We don't need a dozen prophetic words from a dozen different people to remind us what we're supposed to be doing. Being intentional about walking with God day in and day out will do it. If we keep doing the simple things, we won't wander off the track and miss our destinies.

Author Graham Cooke has suggested that we should live in "day-tight compartments." In other words, take one day at a time and seek to keep the simple disciplines going. That way, one day will lead to the next day, the next week, the next year, and eventually a lifetime. When it comes to discipline, it is just easier to think of one day at a time!

I know that if I did not live a disciplined life, it wouldn't matter how much I prayed, fasted, confessed, or believed, I would not be running to win. It is making the right choice with every moment that we have in our hands that determines our destinies. Daily disciplines may not seem glamorous, but they provide us with the foundation to do what we need to do in the future.

MOMENT OF REFLECTION

How would you do living one day at a time?
What advantages do you see in living in "day-tight compartments"?

June 11

Only Jesus

He who began a good work in you will carry it on to completion until the day of Christ Jesus.

PHILIPPIANS 1:6

Many people begin their race with their eyes fixed on Jesus but get distracted and end up focusing on numerous other things: people, possessions, position, status, gifts, their spouses, their careers. They think that these things will complete them as a person and help them achieve their destiny. But the apostle Paul warns us that only Jesus can and will do this for us.

The source of our completion is found nowhere else but in Christ. Nothing else in life can totally fulfill us—not our marriage partner, children, any amount of material possessions, accolades, or achievements—as important to life as they may be. God loves to bless our lives and he gives us many precious gifts in the form of people and material blessings, but these are not the goal of our lives.

Our goal is to complete the course set out for us by God and become more and more like Jesus along the way. Jesus is both the beginning and the end of our race. We must be watchful. When we find ourselves feeling emptied out, distracted, and exhausted, it might be because we have lost sight of the source of our completion. If so, it's time to refocus, fixing our eyes on Jesus once again.

MOMENT OF REFLECTION

What action do you need to take in order to refocus your attention on Jesus?

June 12

Fix Your Eyes on Jesus

Fixing our eyes on Jesus, the pioneer and perfecter of faith. For the joy set before him he endured the cross, scorning its shame, and sat down at the right hand of the throne of God.

HEBREWS 12:2

One of the most important ways to keep ourselves focused on today —on the now—and not get caught in the trap of wishing we were everywhere except for in our present season is to keep our eyes fixed on Jesus.

I made the decision long ago to fix my eyes on Jesus, his Word, and his will for my life daily. I have learned that if my goal each day is to be more like Jesus as a wife, a mom, a leader, a speaker, a friend, a daughter, and a sister, then everything else seems to fall into place.

Even through the most difficult seasons, keeping my eyes fixed on Jesus helped me to see how God was using those tough times to make me more Christlike. This enabled me to embrace the season (sometimes a little unwillingly!) rather than resist it or try to skip over it. Admittedly, I haven't been perfect at this. There have definitely been times when I temporarily chose to focus on the pain, the frustration, or the challenge of the season instead of on Jesus. As a result, instead of moving ahead toward my destiny, I moved toward the pain and frustration! Trust me, it's so much better (and quicker) to keep your eyes on Jesus regardless of the season.

MOMENT OF REFLECTION

How will you fix your eyes on Jesus today?

June 13

Diminishing Vision

Where there is no revelation, people cast off restraint; but blessed is the one who heeds wisdom's instruction.

PROVERBS 29:18

I'm not going to deny it; I love to tease all my friends who have come to the point where they need glasses to read everything. I ever-so-modestly rub in the fact my vision is still 20/20, and even today, I can read any book, no matter how small the typeface, without having to hold it at arm's length. Someday all of this gloating may come back to haunt me, but for now, I'm enjoying the lighthearted banter.

The fact is, as our physical bodies age, one of the first signs is a diminished ability to see! Similarly, a key indicator for growing old spiritually (as opposed to maturing) is that we start to lose sight of God's long-term vision for our lives. That's why we can't afford to cast off restraint; in fact, we must learn to "wear" the constraints of our vision, so that we don't get distracted or settle for short-term gratification.

Some of us desire to be married, have a family, live in a dream home, or work in a dream job. Even if these goals become realities, they can never replace the ultimate goal—fulfilling God's purpose for our lives. We must consciously choose to continue to look up and forward and pursue that purpose.

Many other factors directly related to the condition of our hearts can diminish or impair our vision. For example, if we don't deal with the inevitable disappointment and discouragement that come on life's journey, we'll begin to lose heart and lose sight of the greater vision.

Unforgiveness, offenses, bitterness, jealousy, envy, greed, and the like can cause calluses to form within us—if we could see into the spirit realm, these attitudes are like scales or cataracts forming over our spiritual eyes. So let's choose to keep our spiritual sight clear by daily fixing our eyes upon Jesus, the author and finisher of our faith.

MOMENT OF REFLECTION

What are you doing to keep 20/20 spiritual eyesight?

June 14

Tastelessness

You are the salt of the earth. But if the salt loses its saltiness, how can it be made salty again?

MATTHEW 5:13

A television documentary on aging I once watched talked about the fact that as we get older, our ability to taste things changes or diminishes. Growing up in a Greek household, and eating some of the best food this world has to offer, I can't imagine anything worse! If there ever comes a day when I can't tell the differences between souvlaki and moussaka, or pastitsio and baklava ... I will become very good at fasting! How boring would it be if all food tasted exactly the same?

In a spiritual sense, we need to ask ourselves if our "taste" for God and our destiny is as sweet, intense, and full of flavor as it once was? Or does our daily life have the equivalent taste of a bland bowl of high-fiber bran cereal?

If we feel like parts (or all) of our lives have faded into tastelessness, we *can* do something about it. We all have the ability to get our spiritual taste buds back and to be refilled with joy and excitement for life. Joy is a fruit of the Spirit and something we can allow the Holy Spirit to develop, or continue to develop, in us.

You see, there's a direct correlation between us relishing the God-journey we're on and touching the people we encounter each day. My mother used to say that salt was important when cooking because she could make a dish go from bland to vibrantly tasty with just a pinch.

As Christians, we're supposed to be the "seasoning" in every situation, circumstance, or relationship of our lives. What taste is left in people's "mouths" after an encounter with us? Did they taste the goodness of God through our words and actions, or were they left with a bitter aftertaste?

Our lives are not just about us and our destinies but about the people we encounter along the way—being a beacon that shows them the way to Jesus. In the end, it all comes back to our relationship with Jesus. When we have tasted God's goodness, we can't help but add flavor to our world as well.

MOMENT OF REFLECTION

How are you adding an appealing taste to the lives of those around you?

June 15

The Truth

Jesus answered, "... The reason I was born and came into the world is to testify to the truth."

JOHN 18:37

The most effective way to prove the gospel to this or any other generation is to live it. People want to see that something works before they'll believe it to be true. Jesus did not say that he came into the world to tell the truth; rather he came to bear witness to the truth. He lived an authentic life where his words, actions, thoughts, and deeds all bore the same message.

We live in a world where there is little authenticity. The media lies to us; politicians lie to us; advertisers lie to us. Truth has been compromised, and therefore, we are called upon to verify it with our lives as well as our words.

As Christians in our homes and churches, we must be sure that we are walking our talk, that we are not professing one thing and living another. When we are not diligent about this, we can hurt others and cause them to walk away from God. That's what a life of integrity is all about; it is a life that is consistent everywhere.

MOMENT OF REFLECTION

How well are you walking your talk in your home, your church, and your community?

June 16

Don't Compromise

Daniel resolved not to defile himself with the royal food and wine, and he asked the chief official for permission not to defile himself this way.

DANIEL 1:8

The Bible tells us about an awesome young Jewish man, Daniel, who powerfully impacted the Babylonian culture and society where he lived as an exile. He was not defiled by his culture but instead maintained a strong witness and brought change to it. While all the people around him worshiped foreign gods, Daniel chose to stand by his convictions, even when the punishment for disobedience was death. He never compromised his witness or standards. And God so honored Daniel's faithfulness that he gave him gifts, privileges, and authority that Daniel could never have dreamed of—all because God knew he could trust him.

We should all aspire to live as Daniel did. It is a challenge to stay pure in today's culture, particularly when immorality is all around us on the Internet, television, magazines, and on the big screen. In our effort to be relevant to our culture, we must never compromise biblical standards or truth. Like Daniel, we must set boundaries in our lives.

MOMENT OF REFLECTION

Has any area of your life been compromised by ungodly behaviors? How will you change that?

June 17

Nurture the Seeds of Greatness

As long as the earth endures, seedtime and harvest, cold and heat, summer and winter, day and night will never cease.

GENESIS 8:22

I will never forget the moment that I first saw the thin blue line on the pregnancy test confirming that I was indeed going to have a baby.

Inside of me was a human being. I could not see or feel the child, but that did not change the fact that she was there. At that time, Catherine was smaller than a grain of rice, but her entire genetic code was already set in place. All of her potential was inside her, and my responsibility was to provide the best possible environment to nurture and grow that seed so that she could be and do all that Christ called her to.

Our lives are like a seed. We are born with the potential to fulfill the destiny that has already been established within us, because God always makes us with the end in mind. It's all there in that tiny seed, but what we do with it determines our destiny.

And what, in a nutshell, is potential? It's the unexposed ability, reserved strength, unused success, dormant gifts, and hidden talents that lie within each one of us. It is the person we are still to become, where we can go but still have not been, all we can do but have not yet done, where we can reach but have not yet aimed. It may be in seed form right now, but if we diligently sow, water, and nurture that seed, by faith it will come to fruition.

Let's determine to actualize our potential by bearing much fruit in our lives. In this way, God will be glorified.

MOMENT OF REFLECTION

What are you doing to nurture the seeds of greatness that God has placed within you?

June 18

Don't Be Childish

When I was a child, I talked like a child, I thought like a child, I reasoned like a child. When I became a man, I put the ways of childhood behind me.

1 CORINTHIANS 13:11

My girls did so many things that were cute when they were younger, but would be entirely inappropriate now. When they started using a spoon for the first time, there was more food on the floor than in their mouths, and I must have a hundred different photos of those days.

Nick and I would laugh and clap as Sophia flung baby food across the floor and on the walls. The truth is, if she were still doing that today, I would think there was something terribly wrong. I would hope that after years of eating meals in our home, she had at least learned to use a knife and fork and how to place the entire contents of her meal in her mouth. Not only that, but I now expect my girls to set the table, clear the table, wash and dry the dishes, and put everything away. We have come a long way over the past decade.

In today's Scripture, Paul reminds us that maturity is the goal of the believer. Some things that were okay when we were baby Christians would be considered childish by the time we have walked with Jesus for a while. We cannot expect to be spoon-fed our spiritual diet forever. We must take on our own study of the Scriptures, develop our own intimate relationship with God, and allow the Holy Spirit to change us. Mature people take responsibility for their lives and begin to contribute and give back rather than only take.

Children are the centers of their worlds—everything revolves around them and they rarely care if we are tired, or wonder what is happening in our lives; they just want to be fed, burped, changed, rocked, and entertained. They expect us to always be there for them, catering to their every whim twenty-four hours a day, seven days a week. While they are still babies, we are thrilled to do this, even when we are exhausted. But for the sake of healthy families and healthy children, this routine cannot continue indefinitely. At some point, our children must become responsible and aware enough to realize they are not the only people on the planet and that the earth does not revolve around them.

If we are going to be healthy, functional, mature believers, we must grow up, take responsibility for our lives, stop expecting everyone to do everything for us, and start to contribute kingdom service.

MOMENT OF REFLECTION

Are you taking responsibility for your own spiritual growth by availing yourself of the numerous resources available today?

June 19

Be a God Pleaser

We are not trying to please people but God, who tests our hearts.

1 THESSALONIANS 2:4

After years of full-time Christian ministry, I have found that a major snare for many people is their fear of other people. So many people fail to make decisions or take action because they are overly concerned about what family, friends, workmates, or peers might think about them. Essentially, in such moments they are more concerned about what people think than what God thinks.

We cannot be people pleasers and simultaneously be God pleasers. In order to be obedient to God, we will have to be okay with disappointing some people or making decisions that they do not understand. Our fear of God must become bigger than our fear of man.

No amount of temporal satisfaction or approval from others is worth compromising the destiny for which we have been created. That may mean refusing to join our friends at the school party, risking ostracization and rejection by our family and peer group for our choices, not sleeping with a person and getting dumped for someone else, not going to all the girlfriends' sleepovers because we have promised to serve at church, or not compromising our work ethic in order to gain favor or recognition from the boss.

Until you choose to be a God pleaser above a man pleaser, you will not walk in the fullness of the purpose and destiny that Jesus Christ has for your life. Let's determine to please our Lord more than each other or ourselves.

MOMENT OF REFLECTION

Would you consider yourself primarily a people pleaser or a God pleaser? Whose approval do you seek most?

June 20

Our Destiny in Christ

Give thanks in all circumstances; for this is God's will for you in Christ Jesus.

1 THESSALONIANS 5:18

Regardless of our circumstances, it is God's will for us to remain thankful. That does not mean that we thank God *for everything* —when difficult circumstances confront us, we don't run around wildly thanking God for them like some kind of spiritual masochist —but we thank God *in everything.* In other words, we remain thankful to God for all he has done and is doing for us.

We stay thankful because we know that, even through the difficult circumstances, God has an overarching plan for our lives that will not be diverted. Having an attitude of thanksgiving is like having a disaster insurance policy—it prevents us from being thrown off course by life's mishaps. Thanksgiving has the power to take us into our destiny in Christ.

MOMENT OF REFLECTION

How can you become more like Christ by expressing gratitude?

June 21

Make Room for the New

Lead out those who have eyes but are blind, who have ears but are deaf. All the nations gather together and the peoples assemble. Which of their gods foretold this and proclaimed to us the former things? Let them bring in their witnesses to prove they were right, so that others may hear and say, "It is true."

ISAIAH 43:8–9

It seems as though my Sophia is losing a tooth every other day lately (which can be an expensive exercise when you are the tooth fairy). I must admit she looks very cute as she flashes her toothless grin. She is just as excited when a new tooth starts to come through as she is when an old tooth falls out.

The one thing I do understand is that her new teeth cannot come through and grow unless she makes room for them by losing her old baby teeth. Perhaps in our own lives we sometimes try to hang on for too long to things that are past their expiration date. Baby teeth are fine when you are a baby but not when you are an adult. To be able to eat solid food, you need your big teeth.

I have found that my Christian life is a constant journey of getting rid of the old in order to make room for the new. The longer I try to hold on to something that the Lord is finished with, the more clutter I create and the less room I have for the new thing to take root and operate. We often pray for the new thing but are not prepared to endure a season of a "toothless grin" in order to make room for it.

God wants to do a new and fresh thing in our lives. Let's make sure we are not hindering what he wants to do by hanging on to things we need to let go of.

MOMENT OF REFLECTION

Are you hanging on to things that are cluttering up your life and preventing you from becoming more like Jesus?

June 22

Jesus Asked Questions

After three days they found him in the temple courts, sitting among the teachers, listening to them and asking them questions.

LUKE 2:46

I have always been the type of person who asks questions. In fact, if we were spending time together over a coffee, I would ask you endless questions because I love to learn from everyone. (Some might say that I am just nosey.) I am not sure if it is genetic, but my two daughters have definitely inherited this trait from me; their favorite question at this age seems to be: "Why, Mummy?"

Some questions really are pointless, such as one that I recently found on Catherine's homework paper. "Why when butterflies emerge from the chrysalis do they dry their wings?" or "Why is two the smallest prime number?" I had to look interested for Catherine's sake, but seriously, who cares? (On a side note, I must admit I have never been more grateful for Google than I am now that my children started getting homework.)

Unlike some of their homework questions, the right questions asked at the right time actually have great power. In fact, Jesus made a habit of asking questions daily. If we had met Jesus in person, he was more likely to ask us something than to tell us something, and his questions always penetrated to the core. He asked questions such as: "Who are my mother and brothers?" "Why are you so fearful?" "How is it that you have no faith?" "What do you want me to do for you?" "What will a man give in exchange for his soul?"

Jesus asked questions because the right question at the right time can change the course of one's life. God can move in our situation when we ask the right questions, and act accordingly.

MOMENT OF REFLECTION

In becoming more Christlike, it may surprise us to learn that we have to ask questions. Jesus asked many questions! What questions do you have for Jesus?

June 23

Falling in Love with Jesus

I love those who love me, and those who seek me find me.

PROVERBS 8:17

I love to watch people fall in love. Admittedly, I am a bit of a matchmaker, and like it even more when I happen to get one right. I love to watch the gradual progression from the stage of indifference to a reluctant date, to an eager second date, to the surprise of "I want to go on a third date," and so on all the way to the wedding aisle. It is especially joyful when the couple crosses over from "like" to "love," but one of them has not realized it yet.

You can see it all over their faces. They cannot wait to see each other, and when they finally are together, they cannot take their eyes off each other. When they are apart, they cannot stop talking on the phone or sending text messages. They listen to love songs when they are not talking about the other person, and drive everyone else around them crazy because they can't stop sharing their feelings or telling about the funny things the other person did yesterday.

There is just something about being in love. Nothing is too difficult; you will go out of your way to make the other person happy. The grass looks greener; the sky looks bluer; you can go to bed late and get up early without feeling tired at all. You no longer look at anyone else as a possibility because you have found your love, and he or she is now your priority. You willingly rearrange your life and make all your decisions with the person you love in mind.

I think this is exactly how Jesus wants us to be with him. Not only to love him but to be in love with him.

MOMENT OF REFLECTION

Are you in love with Christ?
If so, how can you tell?

June 24

We Become Like Him

The next day John saw Jesus coming toward him and said, "Look, the Lamb of God, who takes away the sin of the world!"

JOHN 1:29

The longer we are Christians, our love for God should grow, mature, and become more intense. We become what we behold, so as we behold him in love, we become more like him. If we are in love with God, then out of that love relationship will flow a love for humanity and for the world. His heartbeat becomes our heartbeat; his passions become our passions; his priorities become our priorities.

When you are in love, you do not want to sleep but be wide awake, enjoying every moment of every day with your beloved. You want to find out what your beloved is like, who she is, how he ticks—and then you want your life to fall into the rhythm of your beloved's life as together you make a new life.

Love awakens us. That's why I believe that in order to wake up to the purpose of God for our lives and the world around us, we must return to our first love . . . Jesus. If we try to wake up from our slumber out of a sense of obligation, guilt, or shame, then we will quickly jump back into our spiritual bed to avoid these feelings. Slumber anesthetizes the pain. Not wanting to face someone who causes us to feel this way, we close our eyes and look at nothing.

If we really want to wake up, get up, and stay up, then we must passionately fall in love with Jesus. Nothing else will keep us awake. It is love that causes us to behold him, and when we behold him, we enlarge him and become like him. We begin to think how he thinks, say what he would say, and act how he would act.

MOMENT OF REFLECTION

How are you becoming more like Jesus?

June 25

We Are Blessed to Be a Blessing

In everything I did, I showed you that by this kind of hard work we must help the weak, remembering the words the Lord Jesus himself said: "It is more blessed to give than to receive."

ACTS 20:35

God wants to bless us so that we can be a blessing to others. He does not bless us so that we can become self-absorbed or self-indulgent but rather so that we can be more fruitful and effective for him in our lives.

There are so many different ways that God can bless us: marriage, family, degree, satisfying career, nice house and car, great friends, good health, spiritual well-being, and the list goes on. We all enjoy being blessed, but we must remember that we cross a subtle line when these things become ends in themselves, and Jesus becomes the means to these ends.

The end goal of our life as Christ followers is to be conformed and transformed to his image and to live the life he has purposed for us, not to use God to give us what we think we want or need.

When God does indeed bless us, then we must always remember that we are blessed to be a blessing. It is the world of the generous that gets larger and larger, so the more generous that we are with our words, thoughts, deeds, time, and possessions, the larger our sphere of influence and impact becomes.

Let's never be the kind of people who hoard everything for ourselves. Whatever we have, let's give it away.

MOMENT OF REFLECTION

Do you seek to become more Christlike or simply to obtain divine blessings?

June 26

From "Have To" to "Want To"

Walk in the way of love, just as Christ loved us and gave himself up for us as a fragrant offering and sacrifice to God.

EPHESIANS 5:2

I have never found fear, guilt, or condemnation to be effective long-term motivators for change. Ultimately, we all do the things we want to, and so we must *want* to allow God to change us in order to actually change. Sometimes the place to start is by simply saying, "God, I don't want to change. Please help me want to change." I have prayed this prayer on so many different occasions about so many things in my life.

When I was struggling to find the power to forgive those who had perpetrated abuse against me, I prayed for *months* that God would help me to want to forgive them. I knew that his Word said I had to, but I just did not want to. Truthfulness and honesty are great places to start with God; they never take him by surprise.

Whenever I ask Sophia to go to bed, she usually replies, "Do I have to, Mommy?" In fact, when I ask her to do most things, she normally replies with the same response. But every now and then I am stunned when she comes in and says, "Mommy, I want to clean up my room now." (I must admit that in these instances I wonder who swapped my child for the little girl standing in front of me!) On a rare occasion, she will even say, "Mommy, I want to eat all of my broccoli." (Now I need resuscitation.) There is something endearing when a person *wants* to do something, as opposed to *having* to do something.

I have discovered that if I can shift my perspective from a "have to" approach to a "want to" approach, then I can stop procrastination from taking hold in my life. When I think of the fact that I *want to* be fit rather than I *have to* go on a diet, I tend to make the right choices each day. When I *want to* share my faith rather than *have to* give my testimony, it is amazing how many more opportunities open up. Wanting to do something is the first step.

MOMENT OF REFLECTION

As you learn to be like Christ, can you pray that God would help you want to emulate his example?

June 27

Be a Bridge Builder

And are built upon the foundation of the apostles and prophets, Jesus Christ himself being the chief corner stone.

EPHESIANS 2:20 KJV

Admittedly, growing up in one of the most beautiful cities in the world has its perks.

I have walked across, run under, and driven over the Sydney Harbor Bridge dozens of times. I often simply stare at her in awe, captivated by the engineering and beauty. Without a doubt, she is one of the most amazing landmarks in the world, connecting the north and south sides of my beloved city.

I have photos of what Sydney looked like without the bridge, and she seemed somehow incomplete. When the bridge was opened, new opportunities were created for travel, commerce, employment, leisure, and so on. People who once had little or no access to the city suddenly had a way in. What was once impossible was now made possible!

This is what bridges do. They join things together that were once separated, providing connection points, opportunities for community, and new possibilities. I love bridges. They show us that there are things worth exploring on both shores.

We must always remember that Jesus Christ is the ultimate bridge between humanity and God. He made a way where there was no way. In the same way that he made it possible for us to be reconciled to God, he has sent us into our world to build bridges to a lost and broken humanity so that they too can know this great and gracious God. As we strive to become more like Christ, let's ensure that we are building bridges to people.

MOMENT OF REFLECTION

How are you a bridge builder in your life?

June 28

Lord, I Will Follow You

Jesus replied, "No one who puts a hand to the plow and looks back is fit for service in the kingdom of God."

LUKE 9:62

Jesus had an interesting encounter with three men in the book of Luke (9:57–62):

> As they were walking along the road, a man said to him, "I will follow you wherever you go." Jesus replied, "Foxes have dens and birds have nests, but the Son of Man has no place to lay his head."
>
> He said to another man, "Follow me." But he replied, "Lord, first let me go and bury my father." Jesus said to him, "Let the dead bury their own dead, but you go and proclaim the kingdom of God."

Still another said, "I will follow you, Lord; but first let me go back and say goodbye to my family." Jesus replied, "No one who puts a hand to the plow and looks back is fit for service in the kingdom of God."

This text is confusing; it appears that Jesus is making unrealistic, harsh demands on those who want to be his followers. These men are asking what seem to be reasonable questions. In fact, we would think that financial concerns, parental obligations, and family blessings are things we should all consider. We would commend such apparent wisdom.

But notice the word *first* that keeps repeating throughout the passage. Not one of these men said anything about *not* following Jesus; their issue was *when* to follow him. They intended to follow Jesus someday, but not immediately. These men exemplify delayed commitment, but following Jesus must come *before* every other responsibility. The challenge is to set our priorities first and not just follow Jesus when it is convenient. We cannot let our comfort, convenience, or choices distract us from Jesus and his purpose.

MOMENT OF REFLECTION

Do you typically follow Jesus immediately, wherever and whenever he asks?

June 29

Run for It!

By this everyone will know that you are my disciples, if you love one another.

JOHN 13:35

On my morning run one day, I accidentally ran into a triathlon race. I could not get out of the race as I was overtaken by athletes from every side. Up until this moment I thought I was running at a fast pace. It was only when I found myself in the middle of a pack of runners that I realized that I was not running as fast or as smoothly as I thought. While in my own little world, I was doing great, but when I stepped into a bigger, faster, fitter world, I discovered that I had lots of room for improvement and development.

As Christians, it is crucial that we do not become lulled into a false sense of comfort, security, or achievement. We must constantly ensure that we are pushing ahead, determined to lay hold of all that Jesus has prepared for us. We must keep enlarging, placing ourselves in a world that is bigger than our own, so we can keep God's perspective. We may think we are doing great, but let's keep the Word as our mirror and measure to ensure we are always allowing ourselves to be transformed to the image of Jesus.

I loved the fact that the spectators and officials that morning thought I was a participant and were cheering me on and giving me water. Because they believed in me, I increased my pace and found myself running faster! It is amazing what encouragement can do for someone. Let's be the kind of Christians that spur each other on, believe in one another, and are each other's cheerleaders. Jesus taught us that "by this everyone will know that you are my disciples, if you love one another." If a fellow Christian is struggling or falls, let's determine never to kick that person while they are down but to extend the love, grace, mercy, and encouragement of Jesus to them.

We are all here today because someone has done that for us somewhere along our journey (very often, in my case). If we all determine to come alongside one another and encourage one another, many more people will not only start their race but ultimately finish their course.

MOMENT OF REFLECTION

Are you running your race alongside people who spur you on and encourage you to keep improving?

June 30

Humility Is the Key

In your relationships with one another, have the same mindset as Christ Jesus: Who, being in very nature God, did not consider equality with God something to be used to his own advantage; rather, he made himself nothing by taking the very nature of a servant, being made in human likeness. And being found in appearance as a man, he humbled himself by becoming obedient to death—even death on a cross!

PHILIPPIANS 2:5–8

Jesus was God himself, yet Paul reminds us that he assumed a posture of humility while he walked on the earth. Each one of us should aspire to live in the same way each day. We walk out a life of humility by considering others better than ourselves.

This does not mean that we feel bad about ourselves, hate ourselves, or ignore ourselves. *A selfless life is not one where I think that I am less than you; it is one where I simply think of myself less than I think of you.*

What would our days look like if we actually thought about our wants, needs, desires, and rights less and considered the needs of others more? The happy life is achieved when we can get ourselves off our own minds and be consumed with God's heart for others.

Humility is the key to liberty and joy. Concern for others should be the hallmark of our lives as Christians. Our world often depicts humility as weakness, but God through his son Jesus shows us that it is actually the key to living a successful, victorious Christian life.

MOMENT OF REFLECTION

Are there any areas in your life
where you could walk in greater humility?
(I have plenty.)

EMPOWERED

July

PEACE, WHOLENESS, AND FLEXIBILITY

July 1

The Balancing Act

Our lives get in step with God and all others by letting him set the pace.

ROMANS 3:28 MSG

The question I am most frequently asked is how do I balance being a wife, mother, leader, social activist, friend, writer, speaker, and daughter of God. For me, this question has an easy answer: I don't actually strive for a balanced life but for an ordered life. I find that if I live a divinely ordered life, then godly balance comes. That looks different for me than it will for you, but with divine order comes a grace to run our own race and do what we are called to do whatever our season of life.

Order in our household only comes when I come under the mission of my husband. As long as I come under submission in my church and under the mission of my pastor, I will have order as both a leader and a follower. *Submission to a mission brings order that then brings balance that defies logic and reason.* Divine order supersedes natural balance any day of the week.

Now I must not disregard the role that discipline plays in balancing my life. I have to be very disciplined in finding time to exercise, to recharge, and to fulfill my tasks in each of my hats, but I learn to do that through consistency. Like any mother, I've gotten quite good at multitasking—putting in the wash while ironing, or folding laundry while dinner is on the stove.

I also ensure that I set and follow a clear focus, objectives, and priorities. Above all else, I have learned to remain incredibly flexible. It's amazing how peace can come in the midst of seemingly chaotic circumstances when we have our priorities right.

MOMENT OF REFLECTION

Are you living a divinely ordered life or one that is a constant juggle and struggle? What adjustments do you need to make?

July 2

The Whole Person

Those who live according to the flesh have their minds set on what the flesh desires; but those who live in accordance with the Spirit have their minds set on what the Spirit desires. The mind governed by the flesh is death, but the mind governed by the Spirit is life and peace.

ROMANS 8:5–6

Christians cannot afford to live compartmentalized lives. We have one life—and that is the life we have in Christ. That is why it is so important to care for our bodies, souls, *and* spirits, and take a holistic approach to training and discipline that will help us win our race. If we neglect one area, we compromise our race fitness; but if we take a "whole person" approach and realize that all aspects of our lives are interconnected, we begin to run the race of life in a way that is pleasing to God.

God cares about our bodies—he made them to carry his presence; therefore we should ensure that, to the best of our ability, our bodies are operating at maximum capacity. Diet and exercise are both crucial and should not be neglected. If I were not fit and healthy, then I could not possibly sustain the schedule that I do.

We must regularly deal with any soul issues that we face, such as unresolved hurt from the past or persistent negative emotions such as pride, jealousy, or anger. We must not let "soul weakness" hinder our race. I find that a regular "detox" keeps my soul uncluttered.

And, of course, we should each maintain a discipline of feeding our spirits by reading God's Word, praying, worshiping, and meeting with other believers. And we might add to those disciplines other activities that will build us up in the faith (watching or listening to sermons or podcasts, reading Christian books, etc.).

Let's be strong in body, soul, and spirit so that we can be more fruitful for the kingdom. It really does all matter.

MOMENT OF REFLECTION

Which of these three areas (body, soul, and spirit), do you need to work on the most in this season of life?

July 3

Luxury or Necessity?

Remember the Sabbath day by keeping it holy. Six days you shall labor and do all your work, but the seventh day is a Sabbath to the LORD your God. On it you shall not do any work.

EXODUS 20:8 – 10

For a runner, rest and sleep are not luxuries; they are necessities. Sleep plays a vital role in restoring the body because intense running produces inflammation and micro-tears in the muscles. One complete day of rest every week is essential as part of a runner's weekly training schedule. Training day in and day out without a break leaves a runner feeling very stale, weary, and unmotivated because the body needs recreation time.

Recreation is an interesting word. It means precisely what it says: we need time to allow our self-regenerating body to be "re-created." Rest and recreation have been part of God's plan for humanity from the very beginning. He even modeled it for us himself by working on creation for six days and then taking a day off.

As technology continues to advance, a significant trade-off is that our lives get busier and busier. We can communicate with others at any time in any place in the world with amazing speed and clarity, but this has resulted in increased pressure and stress as people are pushed to achieve more and do it quickly! We have to ensure that we don't get caught up in all this frantic activity.

"Remember." This is God's way of saying, "You are likely to forget in the busyness of life, so remember you were designed to need a day of rest." We are created in the image of God, so if God needed a rest day after six days of working hard, how much more do we? The instant nature of our society — our food, our entertainment, our communication, and our travel—can have such a great effect on our lives that we never slow down enough to recover. But spending time with family and friends and taking a break from the pressures of life are exactly what we need to recuperate and restore our energy levels.

MOMENT OF REFLECTION

How do you accommodate the need for rest in your life?

July 4

Vision Sustains Us

You will keep in perfect peace those whose minds are steadfast, because they trust in you.

ISAIAH 26:3

One of the first real challenges I encountered in my own marathon of life came when I made the decision to enroll in Bible school in order to move forward in my calling. This was something no one in my family had ever done, and the wider community of which I was a part generally frowned upon it. I had to stand alone in my decision and remain steadfast in my convictions even though everyone I loved and cared about had removed their support.

During this time, the pressure was so intense that I almost gave up, but the vision that God had placed in my heart sustained me. I knew that God's plan was for me to preach all over the world and see lives transformed by the power of the gospel. It was the presence of long-term vision that helped me endure that very difficult season in life.

Another area in which I had to have long-term vision was dating and marriage. When I was in my late twenties and single, I had a vision for the kind of man I wanted to marry. He had to be passionate about fulfilling the purpose of God, love the house of God, and be a great husband and father. This vision stopped me from settling for just any relationship and enabled me to keep waiting patiently for the "God one." There are so many people who sabotage their destinies in this area by failing to trust God to bring along the right partner. Trapped by fear and desperation, they end up settling for less than God's best.

Yet another area that has required long-term vision is that of health and fitness. I gave birth to my second daughter, Sophia, when I was thirty-nine, knowing I would be sixty at her twenty-first birthday party. It is the vision of me being not only present but fit and healthy at Sophia's twenty-first that keeps me going to the gym every morning. Each time I am tempted to sleep in, my vision enables me to pick my head up off the pillow, keep working out, and maintain a healthy diet. So many of my daily decisions are fueled by my long-term vision.

MOMENT OF REFLECTION

What have you done to keep God's vision before you?

July 5

He Who Promised Is Faithful

And by faith even Sarah, who was past childbearing age, was enabled to bear children because she considered him faithful who had made the promise.

HEBREWS 11:11

I have discovered that God will often wait until a situation is impossible before he works a miracle. Sarah was already "past the age" when she conceived Isaac. It should have already happened. It could not happen biologically. It was simply impossible for a woman over age ninety to have a child. While Sarah tried to make it happen in her own strength, it never did. When Sarah considered her natural limitations and the condition of Abraham's body, it did not happen. It was only when Sarah came to the place of judging the Lord faithful that the miracle occurred.

So often we look at our circumstances, our bank accounts, our education, our physical bodies, our gifts, or our connections and we think that a promise cannot come to pass because it is not naturally possible. We should never limit our infinite God to finite options. If he said it, then he is faithful to perform it, no matter our natural circumstances.

Just because we cannot do something does not mean God cannot. When something is no longer possible and God turns up, then only he can get the glory. The more impossible it seems, the more possible it is that God is just about to show up and show off.

Don't let impossibility quench your faith; rather allow it to fuel your faith. It is those things that are impossible with man that are possible with God. Have you given up on believing God because your situation looks hopeless? I want to encourage you to look beyond your circumstances to a faithful God. If he said it, then he will do it.

MOMENT OF REFLECTION

What are some of the promises God has given you that you have given up on because they seem impossible?

July 6

Vessels for the Spirit

Don't you know that you yourselves are God's temple and that God's Spirit dwells in your midst?

1 CORINTHIANS 3:16

How amazing that God chose the human body as the vessel that would contain his Spirit! What a profound mystery! If our bodies are that important to God, they should be important to us too—important enough for us to take good care of them. We can have the best spiritual intentions but if our bodies cannot function to their full capacity, we will inadvertently cut short our destinies.

The apostle Paul was strongly against any abuse of the body and advised followers of Jesus to avoid sins that could damage their health—such things as sexual immorality, gluttony, and drunkenness. Paul trained his body to be in submission to his spirit-man. Similarly, each one of us has the ability to exercise self-control through the power of the Holy Spirit working in us. We can "subdue" our bodies and make them do what we want, just as Paul did.

Nick and I travel more than 200,000 air miles each year preaching, teaching, and running all of our A21 Campaign offices around the world. We wouldn't be able to physically cope with such a demanding schedule if we weren't fit and healthy. It would be foolish of us to neglect our physical fitness and then pray, "Oh God, make us able to do this!" Why should God answer that prayer if we are not doing our part? Instead, we have to do all that we can do by exercising properly, taking the correct nutrition, and avoiding those things that would damage our health. When we faithfully do what we can do, God will do what only he can do to supernaturally sustain us.

MOMENT OF REFLECTION

What is your approach to physical fitness?

July 7

Soul Survival

Dear friend, I pray that you may enjoy good health and that all may go well with you, even as your soul is getting along well.

3 JOHN 2

There is no doubt that a healthy soul (meaning our mind, will, and emotions) is crucial in order to run to win. Many people with great spiritual gifts and even great health have had their destinies sabotaged simply because they have never learned to manage their emotions, their wills, or their thought lives.

Some Christians make the mistake of thinking that Christianity is all about changing the way we behave (doing certain things because we consider them to be "good" or "righteous" and avoiding other things that we judge to be "bad" or "sinful"). But Christianity far transcends external behavior modification. Christianity is not all about rules and regulations, wearing the right clothes, saying the right things, etc. It is about an internal "heart" transformation. This means that our minds, wills, and emotions have to be submitted to the Holy Spirit so that he can begin to change us from the inside out. We can't give our hearts to Christ and then let our emotions or thought lives run out of control.

In the same way that we apply discipline to our bodies, we also need to exercise discipline in the realm of our souls. We have to face the issues that so often dominate our thoughts and feelings—such as brokenness, unforgiveness, bitterness, rejection, lust, greed, envy, hurt, and anger—and bring them into line with God's Word. Otherwise, we are in danger of sabotaging our destinies.

Many people are not using their spiritual gifts to their full potential because they suffer from unresolved issues in their souls. They constantly let themselves down because their emotional issues are never resolved. This soul-weakness is an Achilles' heel that will eventually take them out of their race. We simply have to learn to deal with unresolved issues in our past in order to ensure a healthy soul life and therefore a healthy future.

MOMENT OF REFLECTION

Are there any unresolved soul issues weighing you down and potentially keeping you from your destiny?

July 8

Strong in Spirit

The child grew and became strong in spirit; and he lived in the wilderness until he appeared publicly to Israel.

LUKE 2:40

How do we become "strong in spirit"? There are many ways, but here are just a few:

- Absorbing God's Word
- Praying
- Fasting
- Reading Christian books
- Being planted in a life-giving local church
- Listening to biblical teaching CDs

- Being a worshiper
- Being in community with other strong believers

We often neglect doing these things because we become too caught up with the frantic pace of everyday life and have little time to give to spiritual concerns. We focus on the finite, temporal aspects of life and lose sight of the infinite, eternal, and spiritual aspects. We need to learn to silence the distractions and voices that daily bombard us in order to make time and space to build our spiritual man (or woman).

If we want to be sure of running a great race, we need to feed our spirits by observing the simple disciplines that will ensure that we have a high level of spiritual health and well-being. We must always remember that although our bodies and souls are important, it is only our spirits that are eternal. We must therefore always prioritize by giving our attention first and foremost to the strengthening of our spirits.

MOMENT OF REFLECTION

How would you describe the difference between the soul and the spirit?

July 9

Rest for God's People

There remains, then, a Sabbath-rest for the people of God.

HEBREWS 4:9

Nick and I are very aware that we lead unbelievably full lives. It is not unusual for us to be in several countries in the space of one month. We travel with our two young children and have many offices and staff to oversee around the world.

We are constantly teaching, preaching, writing books, opening new offices for The A21 Campaign, and dealing with all the issues of running an international ministry. But we have learned that in the midst of all the pressures and demands on our lives and time, we cannot afford *not* to take time out to rest and recuperate.

In order to stay fresh creatively and ensure that we are hearing from God, we need to make time in our lives to simply "do nothing." We are always reminding each other that we need to enjoy the journey, and that if we are going to actually go the distance, rest is essential. To help that process, we schedule times of recreation during our week and ensure that we have restful family vacations.

In my early years of ministry, I rarely if ever took the time to rest and recreate, and the resulting physical and emotional toll on my life almost took me out of the race. I have learned the hard way that if I am going to cross the finish line, I must make time to rest!

Rest is not just a *good* idea but *God's* idea. He showed us the importance of it by modeling it for us himself. Rest is part of God's plan for our lives and if we cooperate with it, we will find that we run with a greater efficiency and purpose. God's desire for us is not that we merely "rest from work," but that we "work from a place of rest," abiding in him and allowing him to recharge our spiritual batteries.

MOMENT OF REFLECTION

Do you allow the pressures of life to drive you?
How are you making rest a priority in your life?

July 10

A Specific "All"

And God is able to bless you abundantly, so that in all things at all times, having all you need, you will abound in every good work.

2 CORINTHIANS 9:8

When I was a teenager, I really wanted to be a basketball player. Then reality hit: the statistical probability of a 5'2" girl making headlines because of her ability to slam-dunk a basketball was next to nothing. If I had chosen to ignore this fact and equated my "all" with being the next WNBA superstar, I would have wasted a lot of years with a relatively futile pursuit. The point is that each one of us has a specific "all" created especially for us, and God enables us to achieve it.

Having it all does not mean we can have anything we want, or that we can have everything simultaneously. Nor should the media, politicians, the feminist movement, culture, history, the popular talk show host, lifestyle magazines, tradition, the latest celebrity, or our flesh dictate our pursuits, dreams, and goals to us. It should be the result of seeking first the kingdom of God.

When it's God who adds the "all" rather than us trying to strive for it on our own, we don't have to be stressed, overworked, or anxious about trying to keep something we cannot obtain on our own anyway. If we simply continue to put God first, he adds it to our life according to his perfect will and his perfect timing. Similarly, the Bible teaches that there are certain things God has created for each one of us to do. If we spend our lives doing the good works God predestined for us, we will always find enough time, energy, and resources to do them. On the other hand, if we try to walk in paths God has not prepared for us, doing works he has not set out for us, we will inevitably end up living stressed, unfulfilled, frustrated, and disappointed lives.

The "all" we should desire to have and do is tied to God himself and his purpose for us. If we always seek him first, it is truly amazing how our crazy, full-to-overflowing lives seem to work.

MOMENT OF REFLECTION

Are you focusing on God's priorities for this season of your life?

July 11

A Heart of Wisdom

Before the mountains were born or you brought forth the whole world, from everlasting to everlasting you are God.

PSALM 90:2

Have you ever found yourself thinking or saying, "If only I had more time, I would pray more, study more, serve more, do more, see more movies, catch up with more friends, read more books, write a book, answer more emails, play with my kids, paint, learn an instrument, see more plays, take a walk along the beach, train for a marathon, etc."? It seems as though we spend the time we do have wishing that we had more time to be doing anything other than what we are doing right then and there!

So often, we miss the moment we are in, the opportunities that we have, and even the time that we have because we are so busy wishing our time away. The truth is that we each have twenty-four hours every day, the exact amount of time we need to fulfill our purpose and destiny. The issue is not whether we have enough time; it is whether or not we are doing enough with the time we have. If we choose to eliminate the things that are wasting our time and replace them with those things we wish we had time to do, we would discover that we actually can accomplish a lot more than we thought possible.

It would be a great tragedy to come to the end of our lives only to discover that we never truly lived. With so many options, distractions, and incessant noise around us screaming for our attention, let's determine to put first things first and not waste our time wasting time. We only have one life; this is not a dress rehearsal for the real thing. Let's make every second count!

MOMENT OF REFLECTION

Are you aware of things that are time wasters in your life? Make a list of them and commit to stop wasting time.

July 12

"All" Begins with Jesus

Commit to the LORD whatever you do, and he will establish your plans.

PROVERBS 16:3

Simultaneously, I am a mother, a wife, a daughter, a sister, a friend, an activist, a pastor, a preacher, an author, and all of the other roles that make me me. Every "ingredient" of my life is interconnected. I don't stop being a mother when I'm preaching, nor do I stop being a wife when I am bathing the children, just as I don't stop being a Christian when I'm having a "discussion" with my husband. I'm all of these all of the time, and they all work together to make me who I am. My life begins to spiral out of control when I try to separate, isolate, and compartmentalize these areas rather than keeping them interconnected. I need to allow all of the components to work synergistically to create the God-life I'm called to live.

I used to wrongly think that as a good Christian woman, my priorities in life had to be in the following order:

1. God
2. Family
3. Church
4. Career/Work
5. Ministry/Service
6. Friends
7. Leisure
8. Health/Fitness

It's not that there's anything wrong with these priorities or the order I chose to put them in, but instead of seeing my life as an interconnected whole, I had set things up in competition with each other.

God never intended for life to be a juggling act, nor for us to feel that if we nurture one aspect of our lives, it will be at the expense of another. The different aspects of our lives are not supposed to compete against each other because each is valid and necessary, and together, make us who we are.

The essential key is that we place Christ in the center and then every aspect of our lives is held together by him.

MOMENT OF REFLECTION

Do you feel like different areas of your life are in competition with each other? What will you do about it?

July 13

Separate and Distinct

Daughters of kings are among your honored women; at your right hand is the royal bride in gold of Ophir.

PSALM 45:9

When we women going for God's "all" stop a moment to dissect our lives, we discover the number of different roles we can play on any given day is remarkable: wife, mom, sister, grandparent, friend, neighbor, employee, mentor, counselor, and on it goes. Just like an actress/friend of mine, who had to make thirty-four costume changes in a single play, we can race around on the stage of life trying to make sure we've got all our props and costumes worked out for each "audience" and unending "performance."

As I thought about it, I began to realize that more challenging than costume changes for that actress was the fact that she had to keep each of her roles separate and distinct. How was it that she never came on stage in the right scene, but as the wrong character?

When I asked her how she did it, she told me something that I believe is a key for us too. She could completely shake off the last character by bringing herself back to the awareness of who she really was—a working actress living in St. Louis—before she moved into the next character. She always remembered to come from that clean perspective of her own identity, and by doing so, she could keep each character unique.

With so many roles to fulfill on any given day (and they can change at any moment!), it is little wonder that at times we feel like we are suffering from a multiple personality disorder; we can be pulled in all different directions based on the demands of people around us and their expectations or needs of us. But as we remain secure in our primary identity as children of the King, everything else we do will flow from this secure place.

MOMENT OF REFLECTION

What do you intentionally do to remind yourself of who you really are?

July 14

Your Do Is Not Your Who

I have redeemed you; I have summoned you by name; you are mine.

ISAIAH 43:1

It was my mother's seventieth birthday party. Within a span of hours, I was characterized by different people in a variety of ways. To one, I was my mom's only daughter; to another I was Nick's wife; to another, I was Catherine and Sophia's mom; to another, I was George's sister; and to my niece, I was "the cool aunt who buys all the great presents." Some old friends considered me the "weird one" who had "got religion," and conversely, friends from church thought I was a great Bible teacher and author.

While it's true that the way each of the partygoers identified me is a legitimate aspect of the various roles I fulfill in life, none of these roles is who I really am. People often identify us based on what we do (the role we play) rather than who we are.

The only way I'm able to "morph" from role to role and not end up mixing them all up is to make sure I have a constant awareness of who I really am, aside from all the different things I do. If I allow myself to be defined by my roles instead of allowing who I truly am in Christ to define my roles, I'm going to get all messed up.

No one role completely defines us. In other words: *Who you are is not determined by what you do, that is, your do is not your who!* Add to this the fact that if we try to get our identity, significance, and security from the roles we play, ultimately our lives become focused upon mere functionality and doing more, rather than something deeper. This will likely lead to feelings of frustration, dissatisfaction, and emptiness.

So the question we need to ask ourselves is: When no one is calling us mommy, wife, sister, mentor, boss, or friend, who's left?

MOMENT OF REFLECTION

When all your roles are stripped away,
do you still feel valued and confident on the inside?

July 15

Just Two Commandments

He answered, " 'Love the Lord your God with all your heart and with all your soul and with all your strength and with all your mind'; and, 'Love your neighbor as yourself.' "

LUKE 10:27

If we're to fulfill our God-given purpose, we need to master the art of simplifying our lives. When Jesus began his ministry here on earth, he brought a message of life, liberty, and simplification to people who were bound by the complexity of overdemanding laws and regulations.

The Jewish law, which originally consisted of the ten simple commandments given to Moses, had evolved into a list of 613 commandments by the time Jesus walked the earth. Can you imagine going through each day trying to obey (let alone remember) 613 laws about every detail of life? There were strict rules about how to clean certain dishes, how to wash your hands, how to eat your food, how to deal in business, how to tithe to God, how to interact in society, and the list goes on. I wouldn't have been able to make it out my door every morning without breaking at least eighteen of them.

Jesus felt compassion for people who were bound by these unnecessary yokes and burdens of religion because God never intended such complexity for our lives. In fact, in a single exchange with the Pharisees, he whittled down the 613 Mosaic laws to just two. For those of us who struggle with mathematics, let me make this as clear as possible. In three verses of Scripture, 613 laws became two. Now that is simplification at its best!

MOMENT OF REFLECTION

Are you complicating what should actually be simplified?

July 16

Season of Preparation

As long as the earth endures, seedtime and harvest, cold and heat, summer and winter, day and night will never cease.

GENESIS 8:22

We must realize that God strategically gives us our "all" in layers, in seasons, each one according to his perfect time frame which, by the way, usually takes a lot longer than we want! This can be frustrating because we would love for our "all" to just drop out of the sky and into our laps . . . today! Rather than appreciating every part of our lives as a God-given season of preparation and molding, we can grow impatient and dissatisfied, especially when that particular season feels mundane, difficult, or frustrating.

The truth is that every single season—the school years, singlehood, career building, marriage, parenthood, grandparenthood—is a gift from God. It's not a means to our "all," but rather part of it. That means every single one of us is living in a slice of our "all" at this very moment. When we grasp this thought, it will not only enable us to see the opportunities for learning and growth in this season but also help us to embrace the exciting things that are going on right now. We need to learn to love the season we're in while simultaneously keeping a fresh and expectant attitude about all that lies ahead.

I know it certainly doesn't feel like a gift when we're changing our fourteenth diaper of the day, or when we've tediously been finishing those term papers and studying for exams, or when we're working our tails off at an entry-level job, or attending yet another wedding feeling like we are the only single person left on the planet. It's very easy to become discouraged and forget we're actually moving forward in our destiny. We begin to think, "Is all this stuff I am doing really getting me anywhere in life?" We wonder if we somehow slipped off God's radar and got stuck doing laps in a proverbial desert. But you see, it's the seemingly insignificant and mundane moments of life—when we feel we are amounting to nothing—that God is using to get us ready for the next season. God is so faithful to bring to fulfillment the dreams he has placed in our hearts!

MOMENT OF REFLECTION

What season of life and ministry are you currently experiencing?

July 17

Weights and Burdens

Do you see what this means—all these pioneers who blazed the way, all these veterans cheering us on? It means we'd better get on with it. Strip down, start running—and never quit! No extra spiritual fat, no parasitic sins. Keep your eyes on Jesus, who both began and finished this race we're in.

HEBREWS 12:1 MSG

I'm sure you've experienced that frustrating moment when you've arrived at the checkout counter, reached into your purse to pay, but it's so full you can't even find your wallet. You begin to frantically dump the contents of the bag onto the counter only to discover antiquities dating back almost to the Dark Ages—half-eaten mints, movie stubs from last year, a pacifier (and your youngest just turned thirteen), that earring you've been looking for, and enough coins to buy your next car.

Sometimes our lives can look just like an overstuffed handbag. We find ourselves carrying so many needless weights and burdens. And just as all the unnecessary contents in our purses can keep us from finding our wallets, these internal weights and burdens will hinder us from having and doing all God has for us. But in an age of lightning-fast technology, worldwide interconnectedness, mass media saturation, endless noise, and over-programmed schedules, unless we intentionally take steps to lose the weights, it's never going to happen. I know—like we wanted to become aware of another kind of weight problem!

Seriously though, what woman at some point of her life has not been obsessed with losing weight? The thing is, we need to lose "weight" in the spiritual realm as well! The Bible makes it clear that we all need to strip off every weight that would slow us down and hinder us on our journey. I think some of the weights that the writer to the Hebrews is referring to are internal ones: jealousy, comparison, anger, worry, anxiety, fear, insecurity, unforgiveness, bitterness, offense, lust, greed, envy ... and the list goes on.

Every one of us needs to do a regular inventory of every area of our lives in order to identify and drop any unnecessary baggage we've inevitably picked up along the way. In the same way those extra pounds can begin to creep on when we're not consciously eating right and exercising regularly, so it is with our internal world.

MOMENT OF REFLECTION

What are the weights that
are dragging you down?

July 18

Breathe

He says, "Be still, and know that I am God; I will be exalted among the nations, I will be exalted in the earth."

PSALM 46:10

Just as I go to the gym regularly to maintain my fitness, I also intentionally do certain things on a regular basis to ensure my spiritual fitness. One of those is simply to "breathe."

Busy, busy, busy ... we are always so busy. Many of us are driven by the urgency of our schedules because we have wasted so much time on relatively purposeless activity. We need to evaluate: What things in my life can I replace with time for me, in order to recharge and breathe?

I have found that the greatest gift I can give Nick and the girls is a healthy me, and the only way I am able to be the best me is if I have taken the time to recharge my soul and spirit. If I allow all my personal time to be eaten up by activities that do not enrich or inspire me, then it's not long before I'm feeling frazzled. I have to be very disciplined to actually set aside time for just me, and use that precious time wisely!

For some, this looks like sitting in a comfy chair, sipping coffee, and reading a good book; for others, it's putting on the running shoes and going for a jog in the park. It can be listening to inspirational music, gardening, cooking, or simply sitting on the porch watching the sunset.

An essential by-product of stopping to breathe and stilling our spirits and minds is that it gives God time to get a word in edgewise and speak to us! So much of our mental confusion, emotional outbursts, and physical exhaustion would greatly dissipate if we would simply take the time to stop, breathe, and lean into the presence of God.

MOMENT OF REFLECTION

Where in your schedule can
you find time to breathe?

July 19

Finding Rest

The LORD replied, "My Presence will go with you, and I will give you rest."

EXODUS 33:14

It's funny how fast life can get away from you, isn't it? A few years ago, I realized I had somehow managed to let my life get away from me. Nick and I were running like crazy to keep up with the growth of the ministry. We knew that if we didn't take time to stop and really replenish our bodies and souls, it was not going to be good for our marriage, kids, or ministry. We learned the importance of making sure to schedule times and even seasons of rest and rejuvenation between the seasons of busyness. It's the only way we will have the ability to have and do all God has for us!

Sometimes we find navigating a particular season difficult simply because we're just plain tired! Here's some advice: Take a nap. Go and get a pedicure. Make all the kids have "quiet time," and then lock yourself in your bedroom and read a great book. Get out from your cubicle and fluorescent lights and take a walk outside on your lunch break. Meet a friend for coffee. Be spontaneous and leave the dishes until tomorrow morning.

Do something today to find some personal refreshment, whatever that might be for you. Make sure that as you're taking care of everything and everybody else, you're also taking care of yourself!

MOMENT OF REFLECTION

Do you feel you need rest, or that your life is getting away from you? What will you do to give yourself a break?

July 20

Set Your Mind on the Right Things

Finally, brothers and sisters, whatever is true, whatever is noble, whatever is right, whatever is pure, whatever is lovely, whatever is admirable—if anything is excellent or praiseworthy—think about such things.

PHILIPPIANS 4:8

We women have the ability to fix our minds on twenty different things at a time; it's a God-given mechanism for juggling the zillion daily tasks at hand. It's actually quite an art when you think about it. We can be talking on the phone, solving the problems of the world, expertly changing a poopy diaper with only one wipe, performing the Heimlich maneuver on our other child who just swallowed a Lego, and still notice the internal alarm sounding in our brain to take the tuna casserole out of the oven before it's scorched. On the flipside of this superpower, multitasking mind-set is the fact that we can worry about eighty-seven different things in thirteen seconds flat!

"My son just failed his alphabet quiz in kindergarten; how is he ever going to make it through college? I must not be parenting him well enough." Or, "I just saw a cute guy at Starbucks, and I wasn't wearing any makeup ... what if the day I meet my husband I make the same mistake, or what if I have spinach in my teeth, or what if that day I have a terrible panty line? There is just no hope; I'm never going to get married!" And on and on it goes.

Ultimately, our thoughts govern our actions, and our actions play a role in creating or shaping our environment. If we are constantly thinking about how we'll never find a husband, how our kids will never obey us, how we never have enough money, or how we'll never lose those extra pounds, we'll begin to act as though it's true, and before long these negative thoughts will become our reality.

The good news is that we can decide what our mind-set is going to be! We don't have to meditate on whatever thoughts and images happen to drop into our heads each day; we can choose our thought life by "setting our minds" on the right things. If it weren't possible, then God wouldn't have put it in his Word.

MOMENT OF REFLECTION

Can you describe your internal mind-set?

July 21

Forever Young

But my fellow Israelites who went up with me made the hearts of the people melt in fear. I, however, followed the LORD my God wholeheartedly.

JOSHUA 14:8

One of my personal Bible heroes is Caleb. The older I get, the more inspired I am by his fervor, tenacity, faithfulness, and relentless pursuit of the purposes of God until his dying breath.

When the spies were sent into Canaan, it was Caleb who came

back with a spirit of faith and told Moses that the Israelites were well able to take the land. He was forty years old at this stage, and committed passionately to having and doing God's "all" for his life. Though he was surrounded with negativity and fear, he never lost sight of his "all." Even when Caleb was forced into the wilderness for forty years because of the murmuring, grumbling, and complaining of the children of Israel, his fire or enthusiasm wasn't quenched. After entering the Promised Land, Caleb could have settled into retirement, and lived a quiet, safe, risk-free, and peaceful life. But Caleb had a different spirit in him. He kept pursuing God.

A fundamental key to having and doing all God has for us is to continually pursue that destiny throughout our lives. It's precisely the spirit and heart attitude that Caleb demonstrated that we require in order to run our race and finish our course. Later in Joshua we read that when Caleb was eighty-five years old, he was just as vigorous and ready for battle as when Moses first sent him out. Age had not managed to diminish the godly man's youth and stamina.

MOMENT OF REFLECTION

What do you think made it possible for Caleb to keep his youthfulness to old age?

July 22

Loss of Energy, Strength, and Speed

He gives strength to the weary and increases the power of the weak.

ISAIAH 40:29

As I travel through airports, it is inevitable that every time I have to make a tight connection, Murphy's Law kicks in. I always seem to get stuck behind a company of slow people with a group tour blocking the entire terminal, causing a human maze for anyone wishing to navigate through—which isn't helped by the fact they are all wearing matching tour T-shirts! And then, once I ever-so-politely weave my way through the crowd, and begin to race down the moving walkways, I'm stopped by another distracted group of women chatting excitedly about their cruise to Bora Bora. In my haste, I want to shout, "Can you not see the signs requesting that standers move to the right so the sprinters can get through on the left?"

I'm sure if we could see the world from God's perspective, we would see many people spiritually ambling through life, or getting distracted and stopping altogether. Some of these people may have at one time or another been speeding along in the fast lane, but along the way they decided to take the scenic route to eternity!

Often, when we begin pursuit of our God-given purpose, we're full of passion, energy, and enthusiasm. We run full-steam ahead. But several months or years later, we start to burn out. We feel empty, frustrated, weary, on the verge of a meltdown, ready to give up. There are many reasons for this, but I believe it boils down to trying to do in our own strength what only God can do.

There's nothing wrong with pacing ourselves—but there's a big difference between taking time to rest or refuel and feeling weary in our soul because we've been doing things in our own strength.

Only God can complete what he started in us. Our strength and source of completion is not found in other people, things, positions, or titles. It's only to be found in Christ—the author and finisher of our faith.

MOMENT OF REFLECTION

What are you trying to accomplish in your own strength?

July 23

The Power of Being

The LORD is my shepherd, I lack nothing.

PSALM 23:1

When a back injury left me confined to the couch, barely moving to avoid the pain, I felt as though the very breath of my Christianity had been sucked out of my lungs. I had no choice but to literally stop all my Christian activity and *be.* Stripped of my ability to act, I lay there feeling like I had nothing left to offer God.

As I struggled with this newfound stillness, I realized that for the first time in my life, I stopped drowning out the voice of my soul with the sound of relentless activity.

Then I heard a whisper in my heart: "Chris, your soul is not prospering."

I was dumbstruck. "God, what do you mean, my soul isn't prospering? Look at everything I'm doing and achieving for you! How could I *not* be prospering? The ministry is growing, my calendar is full, and we are having great success. I don't understand how I could prosper any *more* for you."

God's response was shockingly clear: "Yes, Chris, I'm aware of everything that you are doing, and so is your body—which is why you're lying there on the couch. I tried to get your attention numerous times to warn you about the path you were on, but you were too busy to listen."

I had been expecting sympathy from God, but instead he was convicting me (albeit very lovingly) that there was a problem in my soul—apparently one that had been there for a long time.

As I lay there day in and day out, I eventually did receive a revelation about my soul. I began to realize that if God wanted to restore my soul, then it must have been injured somehow. Only things that have been damaged, faded, or defiled needed to be restored. And only then would my activities bring me the joy and fulfillment I so badly needed.

MOMENT OF REFLECTION

Is your soul at peace? What markers do you see in your life that let you know your soul is prospering or not prospering?

July 24

Renegotiate Regularly

I commend the enjoyment of life, because there is nothing better for a person under the sun than to eat and drink and be glad. Then joy will accompany them in their toil all the days of the life God has given them under the sun.

ECCLESIASTES 8:15

Don't you wish there were a perfect formula for becoming all that God purposes for each of us? A handbook to tell us how to navigate each season, how long it will last, what to expect next? It would be so easy to stay focused if that were the case! Alas, there's no magic formula, but I can give you a key to ensure you won't get stuck in a season: renegotiate your life on a regular basis.

People, circumstances, and seasons are continually changing; to have and do God's "all," we must learn to change with them. What we did yesterday to succeed in a particular season will not necessarily work for us today or tomorrow.

For instance, it would be unwise of me to think I could run as hard now as I did when I was in my early twenties. Having a husband and family to consider, I've had to refocus my priorities, removing certain things and adding others. As my children grow, new doors open, and we move into new seasons, we will have to adjust accordingly.

Having and doing all God wants for us is a constant process of change—a continual ebb and flow from one season to the next. That's why we must remain malleable, flexible, open to what God wants to do in and through us in every season.

MOMENT OF REFLECTION

Do you see yourself as flexible enough
to renegotiate your situation regularly?
In what areas are you least flexible?

July 25

Working Out

Physical training is of some value, but godliness has value for all things, holding promise for both the present life and the life to come.

1 TIMOTHY 4:8

The apostle Paul advised that physical training is of some value, but godliness has value for all things. I have heard Christians use this verse as an excuse for not looking after their bodies. They say things like, "It's having a heart right with God that counts." That is true. But this verse does not say that exercise doesn't profit one at all! The physical dimension of life cannot be ignored just because "God is more interested in the state of our hearts."

Christians, more than any other group of people, have reason to look after their bodies, for we are responsible for working with God to bring about his will on earth as it is in heaven. We have more reason to stay fit than any gym junkie. After all, it's not about how good we can make ourselves look or how many muscles we can develop. It is about being effective carriers of God's Spirit.

We know our bodies are going to wear out and expire eventually, but we don't have to let them wear out prematurely. The sad fact is that some people will simply not fulfill their destinies because their bodies cannot take them there. We can have the best spiritual intentions, but if our bodies cannot function to their full capacity, we will inadvertently cut short our destinies.

A wealth of information is available today to advise us on how best to look after our bodies. It is an issue that we should take seriously. We should, to the best of our ability, ensure that we exercise reguarly, eat well, get enough sleep, and stay away from destructive habits in order to function at our peak.

MOMENT OF REFLECTION

What are you doing to promote your body's health and fitness? What are you not doing that you should be doing?

July 26

God's Yoke

Come to me, all you who are weary and burdened, and I will give you rest. Take my yoke upon you and learn from me, for I am gentle and humble in heart, and you will find rest for your souls. For my yoke is easy and my burden is light.

MATTHEW 11:28–30

By nature, I'm a very complex person. I love to analyze ... well, everything! People, situations, conversations, spiritual concepts—you name it, I've analyzed it. And then after I've completed my analysis, I feel the need to reanalyze the post-analysis of my pre-analysis! Nick laughs at me because he can't comprehend how (or why) any person would choose to dissect anything on as many levels as I do. He gets exhausted just trying to follow one pathway of my intricate multidimensional web of analysis.

The truth is, we women sometimes have a tendency to make things more complicated than they need to be! We can put unnecessary pressure on ourselves to achieve and do so much more than God asks or even expects of us. This often results in feelings of inadequacy, stress, anxiety, and being stuck on a self-imposed performance treadmill. Subsequently, our lives are full of activity, but with little forward progress. Inevitably, our friends, families, colleagues, and often God himself bear the brunt of our overcommitted lifestyles. No wonder we feel overwhelmed; we were not meant to do life like this.

A life of having and doing it all should not be burdensome or full of stress and anxiety—not if we learn to find rest in Christ. A yoke is a wooden beam that connects two animals such as oxen to assist with pulling a load; it also refers to a length of wood carried over the shoulders to balance two equal weights. In both cases, the yoke provides for a more even distribution of the weight. By yoking ourselves with God, we are able to go beyond our own natural limitations.

MOMENT OF REFLECTION

What burdens are you presently carrying that are weighing you down?
Are you willing to be yoked together with God?

July 27

Ask and You Will Receive

May you be strengthened with all power, according to his glorious might, for all endurance and patience with joy.

COLOSSIANS 1:11 ESV

Do you remember when you asked God to enlarge and stretch your life so that you could be more effective for his kingdom? Perhaps you prayed for a spouse, children, a more challenging job, a geographical change, a new ministry opportunity, a chance to serve on a mission team, or more business to come through the doors.

The good news is that God answered your prayer and with that resounding yes came something else. Increased responsibility and accountability. Now your previously perfectly balanced and manageable life has suddenly become crazy and chaotic.

It is so easy to forget the prayers we prayed when we are feeling overwhelmed. We begin to resent the very things we once asked God to give us, simply because these things have required us to increase our capacity.

In order to regain perspective, it is good to get into the habit of reminding ourselves that there was a time when we would have walked over hot coals to have the opportunities we have now. So stop. Ponder. Inhale. Exhale. Smile. Pray. And keep on going. You will grow into the place you need to go.

MOMENT OF REFLECTION

Are there any areas in your life you have come to resent that you once prayed for God to give you? Start to give him thanks right now.

July 28

A Little Time Out Ensures a Long Time In

"Martha, Martha," the Lord answered, "you are worried and upset about many things, but few things are needed—or indeed only one. Mary has chosen what is better, and it will not be taken away from her."

LUKE 10:41–42

Busy seems to be a badge of honor that many people wear. Somehow we have been duped into thinking that the busier we are, the more productive we are—and perhaps even the more important we are. The truth is that a lifestyle of being constantly busy simply makes us feel overwhelmed, inadequate, and exhausted.

If we are to enjoy the journey, then we must ensure that *before* we get to the overload stage, we take time to rejuvenate. This might mean watching a sunset, walking along the beach, enjoying a hobby, joining a friend for lunch, watching a fun movie, celebrating a holiday—whatever it is that replenishes us. When we do this, we will find that our physical, spiritual, and emotional batteries are recharged, helping us to operate at a higher capacity. Then we can make better choices and lead with greater clarity, grace, and wisdom.

If we are constantly depleted, we will have no reserves to fall back on when challenges or trials come. (We only ever feel like quitting when we have nothing more to give.) The more we have in reserve, the longer we will be able to go.

Don't ever see time off or time out as time wasted. It is time *invested* so that you will be able to persevere to the end, not restricted by physical, mental, or emotional fatigue. No one can always travel at full throttle. Jesus took time away from the crowds and ministry to refresh himself. If he needed to do this, how much more do you?

MOMENT OF REFLECTION

Where would you say your fuel gauges are right now?
In what areas of your life do you need replenishing?

July 29

You Possess Authority over Your Heart

Do not let your hearts be troubled. You believe in God; believe also in me.

JOHN 14:1

We all experience storms and trials in our lives, but we do not need to be overwhelmed by these circumstances. Jesus is with us in every situation and has already prepared a path through whatever storm we may encounter. We need never collapse or become anxious in the midst of our storm because we know that he will never leave nor forsake us.

We must learn not to lose our peace over something that we can do nothing about. If the enemy takes our peace, then he has our heart. Through prayer we can still our hearts in turbulent times. We can learn to say, "Lord, even if I do not see you, I trust you."

When you know deep down that no weapon formed against you can prosper, you can ignore the storm. Just because everything in your life is going crazy does not mean you have to. There are some problems that we cannot solve or fix, but we can take them to the One who does. He is our very present help in time of need. Whatever is happening in your life today, let not your heart be troubled.

MOMENT OF REFLECTION

Are you in the midst of a storm at the moment?
Can you trust Jesus in the midst of your circumstances?

July 30

Quest for Eternal Youth

I am still as strong today as the day Moses sent me out; I'm just as vigorous to go out to battle now as I was then.

JOSHUA 14:11

The quest for eternal youth has become an addiction in today's society. We all want to hold on to the energy, agility, and sense of adventure we felt in our younger years. Who can blame us? Sadly, so many of us have bought into the lie that we can achieve this by *looking* younger; but true youthfulness is determined not by our outward appearance but by our internal spirit.

If our spiritual condition is vibrant, energetic, and healthy, then we'll have the internal fortitude to fulfill our purpose and go the distance. As we already know, the "having and doing it all" life is not a moment in time, but rather a lifelong journey of having all God has for us in order to do all God has purposed for us. This is going to take longevity, which is going to require stamina, which in turn can only come from a strong and youthful spirit.

Staying young ultimately has very little to do with the number of wrinkles on our skin and everything to do with our attitude and heart. Do we still have a glint in our eye and a spring in our step, or are we weary? Do we still expect God to do miracles, or are we living in unbelief? Are we believing God for more or have we settled where we are? Are we still thrilled by his Word or is reading it nothing more than an obligation? Do we still long to worship him? Do we love to serve the generations? Are we inspired by young people doing mighty exploits for the kingdom? Do we have fresh stories of all that God is doing? Are we talking more about the future than the past? Are we still hope-filled and not cynical? We can stay as young as we want to stay if we maintain a healthy spirit.

MOMENT OF REFLECTION

What does your spiritual fitness regimen look like?

July 31

Real Contentment

I am not saying this because I am in need, for I have learned to be content whatever the circumstances. I know what it is to be in need, and I know what it is to have plenty. I have learned the secret of being content in any and every situation, whether well fed or hungry, whether living in plenty or in want.

PHILIPPIANS 4:11–12

Since I spend so much time flying across the globe, I am often awake at unusual hours and find myself watching late-night infomercials. I have seen the most amazing products on these shows that I never even knew I needed. I knew I was over the edge the day I found myself ordering an EZ Egg cracker because I wondered how I could ever continue to crack open eggs with my own hands now that I knew this device existed. I had been content cracking eggs for my morning omelet by hand until I saw that infomercial.

Life is a little like that, isn't it? We never seem to be content until we have the next gadget, update, house, car, or thing that will make us just a little happier than we are right now. In fact, every marketing campaign out there is designed to make me discontent. It tells me that I will not be happy until I have a little more of something else.

Paul reminds us that while in prison he has learned to be content. The fact that it is something we must learn shows me that contentment is not something we are born with. If you have children, you know that to be true. Real contentment can never be found *out there*; it can only be found *in Christ*.

The grass is not greener somewhere else; it's greenest wherever we water it. If you nurture and water your relationship with Jesus Christ on a daily basis, you will find that you will be content regardless of your current circumstances. Things and people can change on a daily basis, but Jesus is the same yesterday, today, and forever.

Let's determine to know the secret of contentment. His name is Jesus.

MOMENT OF REFLECTION

Are you discontent with the circumstances of your life?
What or who are you looking to for your contentment?

August

THE SPIRIT-FILLED LIFE

August 1

Simple Truths

Make a tree good and its fruit will be good, or make a tree bad and its fruit will be bad, for a tree is recognized by its fruit.

MATTHEW 12:33

We human beings tend to overlook the simple truths of life and forget that the profound is usually revealed in the simple. For example, we can *act* out what we are not (at least for a little while), but this will not produce long-term fruit in our lives. In other words, an apple can only reproduce apples, because that's what it is at its core (pun intended). Similarly, if we have an issue with anger, then no matter how kind and demure we try to act, eventually a challenging situation will arise and we'll blow! As long as that anger goes unchecked and unhealed in our souls, we will continue to produce the fruit of anger. The same holds true for fear, jealousy, depression, low self-esteem, and so much more.

Many of us miss out on the abundant life that Jesus has for us because we haven't taken an honest look at our spiritual core and recognized that our souls need some work. Forced to examine the fruit of my own life, I realized that I lacked any real deep joy and was only happy when things were going my way. Instead of having any peace, I was constantly striving for perfection and approval. I only had one speed—and that was supercharged. I don't think I even knew how to spell the word *patience*. I wanted everything yesterday.

I realize that this is not rocket science, but so often we tend to overlook the simple truths of life and forget that the profound is usually revealed in the simple. Remember Jesus' lesson from the fruit tree: we'll only produce on the outside what we are growing inside.

MOMENT OF REFLECTION

Which fruit of God's Holy Spirit do you see growing in the orchard of your life? Are any missing? Which ones?

August 2

Gifts and Fruit

This is to my Father's glory, that you bear much fruit, showing yourselves to be my disciples.

JOHN 15:8

It was sobering to realize that the fruit of the Spirit did not include how well I could preach or how effective I was at giving altar calls. Nowhere in the Bible could I find a Scripture that said, "By their *gifts* you will know them" (trust me, I searched the whole Bible). I realized that there could be no doubt that I had been examined by the Lord and found lacking. Deep within me, I came to accept the fact that I had a long way to go in my spiritual walk. I needed some time to deal with my issues and to strengthen my inner person so that my gift would not take me to a place that my character would not keep me.

I had obvious gifts in my life—and I put them to good use in a growing church. Now that's not necessarily a bad thing, as the gifts of the Spirit are given by God to strengthen the church. But when we seek them at the expense of the deep and often unseen internal work of God, it becomes a problem. In my case, although externally I was moving in the gifts of the Holy Spirit, my soul couldn't sustain me. The fruit of the Spirit was not growing as quickly in my life, and that can be a dangerous cocktail.

Sadly, all too often I hear of destinies that have been sabotaged because Christians have focused on developing the gifts of the Holy Spirit in their lives rather than seeking the fruit. They have mistaken a gift given to them by God, which they have done absolutely nothing to merit, as evidence of spiritual maturity. They have convinced themselves that the manifestation of the gift is an accurate measure of their success as a Christian. They could not be more wrong.

When the gifts of the Spirit *on* a person's life are greater than the fruit of the Spirit *in* a person's life, that life will begin to crumble. Let's ensure that we are not only seeking spiritual gifts but that we are also producing the fruit of the Holy Spirit.

MOMENT OF REFLECTION

What gifts of the Holy Spirit have been manifested in your life? How can you tell if they are well balanced by the fruit of the Holy Spirit in your life?

August 3

Good Fruit

The fruit of the Spirit is love, joy, peace, forbearance, kindness, goodness, faithfulness, gentleness and self-control. Against such things there is no law.

GALATIANS 5:22–23

No amount of Christian *activity* compensates for the failure to be an authentic Christian. Our authenticity (or lack thereof) is made evident by the fruit that our lives are bearing. If we're to be recognized as Christ's followers, we need to be producing the fruit of his Holy Spirit.

Going to church or praying a prayer doesn't automatically result in the fruit of the Spirit being produced in our lives. Rather, the condition of our souls strongly influences the fruit that comes out of our lives. Quite simply, if there are areas of our souls that have been damaged in some way, we will inevitably produce bad fruit in those areas. And keep in mind that bad fruit doesn't necessarily point to a horrific past or abuse—it can simply mean that certain areas of the soul are still not Christlike (and we all have these).

We can identify these areas by examining our responses to the people and events in our lives. For example, when we hear that a coworker has received another promotion, do we exhibit the fruit of kindness and rejoicing, or do we talk about why someone else could do a better job? When we see a grim report on the news, do we freak out, sell our stock portfolio to buy gold, and fill our cellars with a six-month supply of imperishable food? Or do we respond with a strong peace in our hearts, knowing that God will take care of us?

If we want to bear good fruit, working on our soul muscle is imperative, regardless of whether or not our past looks like a train wreck (like mine). The goal for all of us is to develop the kind of prosperous soul from which flows the qualities Paul mentions in Galatians 5. This fruit cannot be manufactured or externally generated; it results only from soul transformation and an authentic relationship with Jesus.

MOMENT OF REFLECTION

What fruit of God's Spirit do you see growing in your life?
How is that fruit expressed?

August 4

Not of This World

My prayer is not that you take them out of the world but that you protect them from the evil one. They are not of the world, even as I am not of it.

JOHN 17:15–16

At university, I thought I was a strong Christian simply because I didn't do what many of my college friends did—things like getting drunk, taking drugs, or sleeping around. I was defining my Christianity by what I *was not* doing rather than what I *should be* doing. The goal of my university years should have been not only to abstain from "bad" behaviors but also to bear witness to the abundant life of God living in me.

When Jesus said that people would see our good works and give glory to the Father in heaven, he was not talking about making religious behavior modifications but rather about displaying the fruit of an authentic Christian life. These actions flow from the fruit of the Holy Spirit working in our lives and are characterized by kindness, mercy, justice, love, and compassion.

Instead of being intimidated by the darkness, I should have been the catalyst for some honest, deep communication. Then perhaps I might have influenced the choices some of my friends were making. I needed to be *in* their world but not *of* their world so that through me, God could bring lasting change to their lives.

Jesus specifically said he did not ask that his followers be taken out of the world. Quite the contrary, he said that he is sending us *into* the world. In the twenty-first century, this world is filled with immorality, iniquity, crime, violence, greed, chauvinism, gossip, sexism, slander, racism, and the list goes on. The world that Jesus has sent us into is not a distant, far-off land in the remote regions of the earth but the place in which all of us conduct our everyday lives: our homes, neighborhoods, schools, colleges, and workplaces.

If we are personally transformed by God's Spirit and build a strong spiritual core, our light will shine forth brightly from a place of strength, while we remain holy in the midst of the darkness. We do not need to fear the darkness, but rather allow the light of Christ in us to dispel the darkness around us.

MOMENT OF REFLECTION

How do you feel you are influencing the choices of those you encounter in your world?

August 5

What's Mine Is Yours

Keep on loving one another as brothers and sisters. Do not forget to show hospitality to strangers, for by so doing some people have shown hospitality to angels without knowing it.

HEBREWS 13:1–2

When my daughter Catherine was about two, she had many words she was able to communicate, but whenever we would have another toddler over to play at the house, there seemed to be only one word in her vocabulary: "Mine!" The guest could have ventured to the very bottom of the toy chest and picked out something Catherine had not played with for months, but as soon as she saw it in another child's hands ... well, you know: "Mine!"

All children go through this phase, and it takes another year or two for them to sincerely want to share their toys. With the right direction, they begin to grasp the concept that they are not the center of the universe—that every other human being has *not* been placed here for their pleasure and convenience.

When many of us became saved, we had so much negative junk in our souls that we needed to spend that first season as Christians focused on healing and renewing our spiritual core. This isn't a bad thing at all, unless we get comfortable and stay there. There comes a time when we must begin to reach out to the world around us. Becoming a Christian does not mean we join a private and exclusive club. On the contrary, Jesus invites us to be part of an inclusive community in which we love our neighbors as we love ourselves.

Christianity is loving God *and* loving other people. It would be ridiculous to think about a person standing in front of her church, guarding the front doors, and yelling, "Mine!" to any new person trying to enter; we would think something was seriously wrong with that person. But if we are brutally honest, don't we sometimes think this way? The church does not exist to satisfy each and every one of our selfish pursuits and ambitions, but rather it is a place where we can serve the needs of others.

MOMENT OF REFLECTION

How do you feel when new people come to your church?
How about those who seem irregular or disruptive?

August 6

Bearing Fruit

Remain in me, as I also remain in you. No branch can bear fruit by itself; it must remain in the vine. Neither can you bear fruit unless you remain in me.

JOHN 15:4

Remember in grade school when we played sports at recess? Two kids would be appointed as captains for each team, and the rest of us nervously stood there, hoping that we wouldn't be the last one picked. I think that was when most of us first began to notice that popularity was closely linked to the kinds of gifts and talents we possess. We learned that if we had all the "right stuff " (looks, charisma, talent, and so on), we would be able to be part of the "in" crowd—and if we didn't, we were banished to the geek table at lunch.

You just need to turn on the TV or buy a magazine to see that we live in a society that celebrates and exalts people who are gifted and talented. Our media bombards us with images of the greatest athletes, actors, and rock stars whom they deem to be the most beautiful, famous, and intelligent. The public will even excuse shortcomings these "idols" might have, such as a string of failed marriages, immoral behavior, substance abuse, lack of self-control, and pride. Despite their failings, these people are still considered role models.

As Christians, we cannot allow ourselves to fall into the trap of being enamored by someone purely on the basis of his or her gift or talent. A person's spiritual gifting does not define who that person is. We need to examine the *fruit* of a person's life to truly determine his or her character. Certainly, every one of us is unique and special to God and has God-given gifts and talents, but it is the fruit in our lives that truly reveals the depth of our intimacy with the Father. It is when we are in his presence that we are changed into his likeness and consequently produce the fruits of his Holy Spirit.

Let's resolve to focus on developing the fruits of love, joy, peace, patience, kindness, goodness, faithfulness, gentleness, and self-control. These are the measure of our Christlikeness.

MOMENT OF REFLECTION

What fruit of God's Spirit would you like to see growing in your life?

August 7

Found Lacking

In those days Israel had no king; everyone did as they saw fit.

JUDGES 17:6

Self-control is not something we hear a lot about. Our culture has become increasingly liberal, and we have made every effort to cast off all restraint in the name of "freedom of choice" and the "rights of the individual." Yet the Bible insists that self-control is both the hallmark of a real Christian and a natural by-product of living righteously for God.

Self-control is mentioned as part of the "fruit of the Spirit." The list—love, joy, peace, patience, kindness, goodness, faithfulness, gentleness, and self-control—is a sharp contrast to the characteristics of a person who is not surrendered to God, identified by the apostle Paul earlier in Galatians 5: sexual immorality, impurity, jealousy, selfishness, and many more.

What connects these negative characteristics more than anything else is a lack of self-control. Without this vital spiritual resource, people are liable to do whatever they like whenever they feel like it. Without self-control, we are easily led astray by our emotions and our own selfish desires. When this happens, we tend to get off track with our God-given destinies. In order to fulfill our purpose, we must exercise self-control. In order to honor Jesus, we must exercise self-control. In order to achieve any measure of lasting success, we must exercise self-control. Self-control does not limit or contain us; it's for our benefit, allowing us to flourish.

MOMENT OF REFLECTION

In what areas of your life do you lack self-control?

August 8

Self-Control

Make every effort to add to your faith goodness; and to goodness, knowledge; and to knowledge, self-control; and to self-control, perseverance; and to perseverance, godliness; and to godliness, mutual affection; and to mutual affection, love.

2 PETER 1:5–7

I was talking to a neighbor a little while ago who told me that her husband had walked out on her and left her to look after their two children alone, one aged five and the other seven. On one occasion, she spoke to him on the phone and demanded, "How can you do this to our kids? Even if your feelings toward me have dried up, what about our kids?" Surprised, he responded, "No one else has ever asked me that. Everyone says, 'What about you? How do you feel? You need to be true to your feelings and do what you want to do.' Therefore, I haven't really thought about how this would affect them."

We are immersed in a culture that thrives on pleasing "self," but we need to go against the flow and set Christ as our goal rather than self-fulfillment. When we do this, the fruit of his Spirit will be evident in us, and we will not sabotage our destinies by making bad decisions. Society's answer is always, "Do what feels right for you; go with your feelings; do what your heart is telling you to do." But this is just an excuse that enables us to abdicate our personal responsibility and forget about the consequences to our lives and the lives of others. If we want to find God's best for our lives and truly maximize our potential, we must choose to live a different way. We need to learn to love self-control.

Remember that it is a consistent commitment to doing the "basics" of the Christian life, combined with a constant "refilling" of the Holy Spirit, that will produce the right fruit in our lives.

MOMENT OF REFLECTION

In what areas of your life is the fruit of the Spirit growing abundantly?

August 9

Attitude of Gratitude

Give thanks to the LORD, for he is good. His love endures forever.

PSALM 136:1

It is amazing how thankful we are when we first become Christians. We step out of one world and into another and suddenly everything looks great! When I first got saved, every day was an adventure with God, and I was grateful for every blessing he sent along. Most new Christians would be the same. They think, "Wow! God is awesome, the church is awesome, the music at church is awesome, and so are the people there!"

But it doesn't seem to take long before all those things that were "awesome" lose their gloss, and cynicism and criticism set in. Why does this happen? Because we quickly forget to be thankful. If we are going to run our race and finish our course, we must keep "an attitude of gratitude" that permeates everything we do. We must ensure that we don't become overly familiar with the goodness of God or develop a sense of familiarity or entitlement which will cause us to lose sight of the finish line. When we get off track in life, a lack of gratitude is often the root cause.

This often happens in marriage. When people first get married, they usually act as though their partner is the missing fourth member of the Trinity (especially if they were single for a long time)! But it is amazing how after only a few months, they can become a bit dissatisfied with the very person they prayed so hard for. It's easy to go from gratitude to familiarity, and from familiarity to disappointment.

It is vital to keep nurturing that spirit of thankfulness and allow it to infuse everything we do. I've discovered that ongoing gratitude makes us whole and keeps our journey fresh.

You might say, "But, Chris, I've got nothing to be grateful for!" If you know Jesus Christ, then at the very least, you can be grateful for the fact that you're going to heaven. If we look hard enough, we will find that there is always something we can be grateful for every day. The choice is ours.

MOMENT OF REFLECTION

Why is it so important to be thankful?

August 10

Best of Friends

The righteous choose their friends carefully.
PROVERBS 12:26

When it comes to relationships, the first thing we must remember is that they must be life-giving rather than life-depleting. Some of us struggle because we have allowed relationships to flourish that are full of toxic emotions such as negativity, criticism, comparison, jealousy, insecurity, and fear. We can't pursue God's purpose for our lives if we are constantly weighed down by negative relationships.

We must proactively build those relationships that are a friend to our purpose and destiny. We must determine which ones have the biggest influence on us, which ones help and which ones hinder. If we find relationships that are not producing the fruit of the Spirit in us—love, joy, peace, patience, kindness, goodness, faithfulness, gentleness, and self-control—then we need to reevaluate what place they have in our lives.

One of the major reasons why I have been able to have and do it all is because of the great friends I have in my life—friends who support, love, inspire, encourage, and when necessary, challenge me. These friends are all different from each other in personality, interests, and vocation, but singularly passionate in their desire for God's best. I spend a lot of time and energy investing into these specific friendships because I realize what a significant part they play in helping me to accomplish my destiny (and vice versa).

I can't help but smile when I think of how dynamic and unique each one of my friends is. Some of these girlfriends really step in and help me with my children. Others are there when I need to process certain issues, let off some steam, or get a different perspective. Others challenge me to step it up and press in. And some love to shop and catch a movie with me. There are some friends with whom I could honestly just sit for hours and do nothing but laugh. There are so many wonderful rewards that come from fostering strong, healthy friendships — who would possibly want to have and do it all if the adventure didn't include great friends!

MOMENT OF REFLECTION

Do you have any toxic relationships in your life?
How will you change that?

August 11

What Do You Have?

"How many loaves do you have?" he asked. "Go and see." When they found out, they said, "Five — and two fish."

MARK 6:38

I have always loved the story of the fish and the loaves. It delights my heart to think that God always uses the least likely to achieve the unimaginable. Who would have thought that a little boy who was not even included in the counting of the five thousand men would provide the ingredients for a miracle that counted so much we are still talking about it today?

When Jesus was preparing to perform a miracle and feed the multitudes, he began by asking the disciples what they had. Like most of us, the disciples saw the enormity of the challenge and the lack of their own resources and thought nothing could be done. Jesus made them examine what they had in their midst because, whether we initially see it or not, the ingredients for a miracle are always within our reach in seed form.

Miracles always begin with recognition of what we *do* have. We must stop listing all of the things that we do not have as if God is not aware of our limitations. Jesus does not ask what we don't have; he asks us to recognize what we do have. Jesus does not multiply what we do not recognize.

God had the ingredients for the miracle stored up in the lunchbox of a child. We must remember that miracles are often produced from the things we might not count as useful to God. The miracle in this story began with a packed lunch. Never underestimate what God can and will use in your life if you allow him. Don't withhold anything from him.

MOMENT OF REFLECTION

What do you have in your life that you may have never considered God could use?

August 12

Are Your Words Bringing Life?

But what comes out of the mouth proceeds from the heart, and this defiles a person.

MATTHEW 15:18 ESV

We women sure do know how to talk. With all these words flying out of our mouths, do we ever stop to think what exactly it is we're saying? Are our words bringing life to our world or are they bringing death? Words contain great power, and when an unexpected storm rises up to confront us, how well we endure it is often determined by the words we speak.

A few years ago, I was in the USA during hurricane season, and I was watching the news as a huge storm was about to make landfall. A reporter was standing outside in full rain gear, practically being blown over as the winds grew stronger and stronger. The winds were so intense that he gripped onto a nearby pole for dear life. "Now that guy is committed!" I thought. "If only every Christian would be as dedicated to God's Word during a crisis as this man is to reporting the news."

This is a perfect picture of the posture we must have when the storms of life rise against us. Just as this reporter held on for dear life, we must hold fast to our confession of faith when "bad weather" hurtles toward us. This is not the time to pick up the phone and call Auntie Merriwether so you can whine and complain about your husband or lack thereof, or bemoan the impossibility of your financial struggles, or talk about how serious your health issues are and how you will probably die. I understand that sometimes fear, doubt, and uncertainty can feel overwhelming, but this is certainly not the time to use your word quota to reinforce those negative thoughts.

Let's be careful to watch over our words and to choose wisely that which we allow to come out of our mouths. Instead of giving power to our fears, let's speak life over our situation, our finances, our family, our marriage, and our relationships. Our words are a creative force and through words of faith, we can speak life into every circumstance.

MOMENT OF REFLECTION

What kind of words are you speaking over your life?

August 13

Understand and Know

Day after day men came to help David, until he had a great army, like the army of God . . . from Issachar, men who understood the times and knew what Israel should do—200 chiefs, with all their relatives under their command.

1 CHRONICLES 12:22, 32

We are definitely living in uncertain times—unprecedented political, social, moral, educational, environmental, and spiritual change characterize our world today. I like to say that the spiritual tectonic plates of the earth have shifted and they are never going back to how they once were. We are living in a new day and, in order to remain steadfast and immovable, we must be empowered by the Holy Spirit and follow his leading.

If we are going to live victoriously in our times, we must not only understand our world but we must also know what to do. In uncertain times there are certain things that remain certain, and these are the things we must continue to do. Just because everyone and everything around us is going crazy does not mean that we have to.

One of the things we must do is stay close to Jesus, focused on him and his Word. He will give us comfort, wisdom, insight, and discernment to navigate the daily challenges that are an inevitable part of life. When we simply do not know what to do, he does; we can go to him for counsel, direction, and guidance. His truth is timeless and eternal.

We also need to be part of an active local community of believers and continue to stir one another to good works. We must encourage one another to keep going and not give up, to get back up if we stumble or fall. We will not make it as lone rangers; the battle is fierce and things are just heating up. God has made us into a body so that we are, by necessity, utterly dependent upon one another. Let's be for each other and not against each other.

We must also commit to praying at all times because prayer moves God and when God is moved, he moves mountains. Let's spend more time talking to God than we do talking to other people about our problems and the condition of the world. God is able to do what no human being can do and, despite what we may see or think, he is sovereign and is ultimately in control. In order to trust him we must know him, and we know him by communicating with him.

Don't be anxious about the shifting landscape of this world. Set your mind on things above and trust the One who holds the whole world in his hands.

MOMENT OF REFLECTION

Are you anxious about the state of our world?
If so, are you taking your concerns to God and being encouraged
by his people, or are you listening to the world's voices?

August 14

Who Shrunk God?

Who among the gods is like you, LORD? Who is like you—majestic in holiness, awesome in glory, working wonders?

EXODUS 15:11

In 1989, Walt Disney Pictures released a comedy called *Honey, I Shrunk the Kids*, the story of a professor who accidentally shrinks his and his neighbors' kids to a quarter-inch high with his electromagnetic Shrink Ray Machine, and then sets them outside along with the trash. The backyard, relatively small when the kids were normal size, now seemed like a jungle to them, one it would take hours to cross to the safety of the house. Insects and plants were now towering giants that could potentially destroy them.

I know that was only a movie, but I have often wondered if we have not done exactly the same thing to God. Have we not taken a God who holds the entire universe in his hands and shrunk him to a distant, irrelevant, impotent grandfather figure somewhere up there in the sky? A God who is largely unconcerned with, and even overwhelmed by, huge global injustices such as poverty, disease, famine, terror, HIV/AIDS, racism, crime, human trafficking, violence, and war? A God who is remote, disinterested in our pain, heartache, and longings? Have we not made him into a God who is small in love, small in grace, small in favor, small in mercy, small in forgiveness? Are we not increasingly overwhelmed by circumstances and events over which we should have dominion and victory? I have been known to ask the question, "Honey, who shrunk God?"

MOMENT OF REFLECTION

As you endeavor to live a more Spirit-filled life,
how can your view of God be expanded
so that God's power is more real to you?

August 15

Thanksgiving and Wholeness

Jesus asked, "Were not all ten cleansed? Where are the other nine? Has no one returned to give praise to God except this foreigner?" Then he said to him, "Rise and go; your faith has made you well."

LUKE 17:17–19

In Luke's gospel we read the amazing story of ten lepers who were miraculously healed by Jesus. These men were the least of the least, but Jesus in his love, compassion, and mercy cured them all. After the miracle, the men departed to report to the priest—the only person who could legally declare them "clean," thus allowing them to be reintegrated into society. Later, just one of the men returned to thank Jesus for what he had done. I often wonder what happened to the other nine. So did Jesus.

Like nine out of the ten lepers in this story, often we can go about our lives having been cleansed by God, but still very much wrapped up in ourselves. We are not living with a sense of awe and wonder at the greatness of God; we're just going our own way, doing our own thing, unaware of just how much God has blessed us.

There is a higher state of living than this! One leper in this story was not content simply to return to his former life, cleansed as he was. Immediately he pursued Jesus in order to thank him. What I find striking is that when the man returned to Jesus and thanked him, he received a further blessing. The American Standard Version (ASV) translates Jesus' words to him as, "Thy faith hath made thee *whole*."

There is a direct link between thanksgiving and wholeness in the Christian life. Many Christians live *cleansed* because God has saved them, but they don't live *whole* because they don't understand the value of thanksgiving. Being cleansed is essential, but I don't just want to be a "survivor" in the Christian life; I want to harness the power of thanksgiving and be more than a conqueror—someone who can begin to contribute to God's kingdom through a now-whole life.

MOMENT OF REFLECTION

What is the connection between thanksgiving and Christian wholeness?

August 16

Your Answer Is on Its Way

Jesus looked at them and said, "With man this is impossible, but not with God; all things are possible with God."

MARK 10:27

Maybe you feel you have prayed and prayed and yet the heavens are like brass. Perhaps you feel that God is ignoring you, that he hasn't heard your prayer. No—God is not ignoring you! He never ignores his children. The fact is, we have no idea what God is doing on our behalf in the heavenlies.

Think of it like this: we may ask God for one thing, but he has to rearrange ten thousand other things in order for our one thing to come to pass. You may have prayed for one person you know to get saved. You've been praying that prayer for several years now and ... nothing ... apparently. Meanwhile, unbeknownst to you, God is moving all heaven and earth so that person *will* get saved. God is working on your behalf, organizing a Christian from another town to move to yours and begin working for the same company as your unsaved friend, so that one day they might have a significant conversation by the coffee machine. Elsewhere, God is arranging for a particular Christian band to come and play in that person's town and is organizing someone else to offer her a free ticket to the gig.

All this activity is going on behind the scenes and you don't even know what God is doing, but your answer is on its way!

MOMENT OF REFLECTION

Are there any prayers that you are still waiting for God to answer? Take a moment to ask him again right now.

August 17

What You Look for You Will Find

Through him then let us continually offer up a sacrifice of praise to God, that is, the fruit of lips that acknowledge his name.

HEBREWS 13:15 ESV

So often we focus on what we do not have, who we are not, and where we have not yet arrived. I have found that if we are simply grateful for all we do have, all we are in Christ, and where we are right now, all of the "nots" in our lives pale into insignificance. It may take more effort to focus on what we do have, but it is well worth the effort. What you look for you will find, so keep looking for all the things that you do have and you will surprise yourself.

Today make a list of all that you have to be grateful for, and as you appreciate what you have right where you are, you will be enveloped by God's grace, peace, and contentment. I have cultivated the habit daily of giving thanks to God for all that is happening in my life—the blessings, the opportunities, the good things—*before* I go to him with all of my needs. It is definitely not my natural inclination. Just like everyone else, if I did not make the decision to focus on the good things ahead of time, all I would see are lack and limitations. I have had to retrain my spiritual eyes.

When we are in such a hurry to get to where we are going, we often neglect to enjoy the journey. Life is as much about the journey as it is about the destination, so don't miss your life while you are waiting for your life to happen. We have so much to be grateful for, and gratitude opens the door to opportunities!

MOMENT OF REFLECTION

Do you naturally see limitations or opportunities?

August 18

Exceedingly Magnificent

David said, "My son Solomon is young and inexperienced, and the house to be built for the LORD should be of great magnificence and fame and splendor in the sight of all the nations. Therefore I will make preparations for it." So David made extensive preparations before his death.

1 CHRONICLES 22:5

This verse has to be one of my favorite in the entire Bible. I love the fact that David makes no apologies about the kind of house that must be built for the Lord. This was not going to be a second-rate temple, but one that the nations would look at and be in awe of the God who was worshiped there. It was to be of "great magnificence and fame and splendor," one that exceeded every expectation and would reflect some of the glory, wonder, and majesty of our King.

I believe that is exactly how we should see the church of Jesus Christ today. Everything about our lives should bring glory to God. We should be living lives that make people stop and wonder, "How is this possible?"

If the same Spirit that raised Jesus Christ from the dead lives on inside of you and me, how could we live lives that are any less?

Our God lives in us.

We are the temple of the Holy Spirit, and we should not shrink back from all that God has called us to do. The church is not peripheral to the world; the world is peripheral to the church. You and I are central to God's plan and purpose on this planet in this time. It is our job to ensure that we present a glorious, relevant, hope-filled, life-giving church to a lost and dying world. When we understand the purpose, potential, and power of the body of Christ, I think it will change our entire approach to the house of God and the way we live our everyday, ordinary, seemingly insignificant lives. There is nothing everyday, ordinary, or insignificant about the life of any believer. We all carry the Spirit of God himself within us, and there is nothing ordinary about that. It is magnificent. Splendid. Grand. Glorious.

The world would love to keep the church small, on the fringes, broken, irrelevant, and archaic, but God has called his bride to be great. Let's not be afraid of loving God's house, serving there, and building exceedingly magnificent lives that bring glory to the One who lives within us. The more we allow the fruit of the Spirit to be developed in our lives, the more like him we become and the more splendid our lives become.

Believe for big things, dream extravagantly, expect God to do great things, and let's make his name famous across this earth.

MOMENT OF REFLECTION

Do you think God's church should be magnificent, famous, and splendid? If not, why not?

August 19

All That We Are in Christ

I can do all this through him who gives me strength.

PHILIPPIANS 4:13

I fell into bed completely exhausted after another long day of meetings. All I could think about was everything I still had left on my to-do list, including laundry sitting on the kitchen table waiting for the angels to fold it, kids' uniforms that were not washed for school the next day, an unreturned phone call from my mother (I was going to be in serious trouble), and an inbox so full it had stopped receiving any more emails.

Have you noticed that we spend a huge proportion of our lives thinking about all the things we have not done, what we do not have time for, and who we are not? We never seem to have enough time or get enough sleep, rest, or exercise. We never feel rich, thin, attractive, or educated enough. Before our feet hit the ground in the morning, we already feel we are behind, lacking, or losing—and we go to bed at night feeling we never did quite enough.

If we only focus on what we do not have or devalue the little we do have, we will surely despair. We need to arise, change our posture and perspective, and begin to see all that we have in Christ, all that we are in Christ, and all that we can do through Christ.

MOMENT OF REFLECTION

Do you sometimes feel exhausted by all the demands of your life? How can you change your focus from the things you don't have time for and value instead all that you are in Christ?

August 20

The Voice of the Holy Spirit

But as for me, I am filled with power, with the Spirit of the LORD.

MICAH 3:8

I don't have a compartmentalized life; I have an interconnected life. There are not enough hours in a twenty-four-hour day to fulfill a supernatural destiny. Therefore, I have to draw on supernatural empowerment from a supernatural God to fulfill a supernatural destiny and walk in peace and love.

I see my life as a wheel and all parts of my life spoke from the hub in the middle of that wheel. I find that as long as I aim for that hub that is Jesus every day, the wheel will keep turning. The oil that keeps the wheel spinning smoothly is the Holy Spirit. As I keep my ear inclined to the Spirit, he will tell me which spoke needs more attention on any given day. He will keep the wheel spinning; I do not have to spend my time paying attention to every detail but simply be obedient. I ask, "God, where do I need to focus my time?"

If I am in the right place in my spirit, it is amazing how much I will hear God tell me about what is going on and what I need to pay attention to. I need the voice of the Holy Spirit speaking in my heart. Jesus does not expect us to try to live a supernatural destiny using natural means. He gave us the Holy Spirit as our helper to do just that . . . help us.

MOMENT OF REFLECTION

Have you heard the voice of the Holy Spirit speaking in your heart today?

August 21

Fear Not!

So do not fear, for I am with you; do not be dismayed, for I am your God. I will strengthen you and help you; I will uphold you with my righteous right hand.

ISAIAH 41:10

Without a doubt, I think fear is the thing that cripples and immobilizes people more than anything else. In fact, while researching the topic of fear, I learned about literally hundreds of different phobias, including acrophobia (the fear of heights), arachnophobia (the fear of spiders), claustrophobia (the fear of being closed in), pyrophobia (the fear of fire), and anthropophobia (the fear of people). It saddens me to think of all the people who struggle with these types of phobias and the degree to which these fears must hinder their everyday lives.

Fear is not a respecter of persons, and the truth is that we all have things that we are afraid of. If we are to truly step into our destiny, then we must decide that we will not allow fear to rule us. Fear paralyzes us, thus destroying our effectiveness. Every day I am faced with the choice of whether to let fear stop me from moving forward or to let faith propel me into the future.

We must stay firmly rooted in Christ and grounded in the truth of his Word in order to remain fearless and faithful in pursuit of our destiny.

MOMENT OF REFLECTION

As you move toward a Spirit-filled life,
what fears might be holding you back?

August 22

More Than Enough

Go at once to Zarephath in the region of Sidon and stay there. I have directed a widow there to supply you with food.

1 KINGS 17:9

God had commanded a widow to provide food for the prophet Elijah, but all she could see was what she did not have and what she could not do. When Elijah asked her to bring him a morsel of bread, she replied, "I don't have any bread, only a handful of flour in a jar, and a little olive oil in a jug. I am gathering a few sticks to take home and make a meal for myself and my son, that we may eat it—and die" (1 Kings 17:12). The widow's immediate response, when asked for bread, was to say, "I do not have." This is a natural response, but our big God was looking for an opportunity to perform a miracle. He knew what she did and did not have, but he is never limited by our lack, only by our unwillingness to give him the little that we do have.

How often do we do this same thing in our own lives? God asks us to do something and our immediate response is, "But, Lord, I do not have the time; I do not have the resources; I do not have the flexibility; I do not have the qualifications, talents, gifts, or ability."

Instead of offering what we do have, we become paralyzed by what we do not have. Faith is exercised when we trust God with our limitations, not when we trust our own abilities. If we choose to put our little in the hands of a very big God, then we will find that somehow we will always have more than enough.

MOMENT OF REFLECTION

Do you trust God with your limitations?

August 23

Deny the Petty Things

For our light and momentary troubles are achieving for us an eternal glory that far outweighs them all. So we fix our eyes not on what is seen, but on what is unseen, since what is seen is temporary, but what is unseen is eternal.

2 CORINTHIANS 4:17–18

Your God is bigger than any challenge you are confronting. Our problems that seem so overwhelming will grow small in the light of his greatness. Sometimes we just need to stop and *backdrop our problems against eternity*. If we can remind ourselves that God is bigger than any opposition, disease, crisis, question, struggle, frustration, hurt, or offense, then we will not spend one more minute magnifying the enemy and his plans. The last time I checked, the devil was small enough to fit under my feet, and God is big enough to fill the heavens and earth.

In life we can miss so much of God and his greater plan and purpose because we exhaust our energy on the little things. We need discretion about what we think about, listen to, speak about, and give our attention to.

We must learn to deny the petty things in life, the things that scream at us for our attention, and instead focus on God and his promises. Our God is well able to do all things.

MOMENT OF REFLECTION

What are the petty things in your life that are dragging you away from God's promises of a Spirit-filled faith journey?

✾ *August 24* ✾

Death Has Been Defeated

Where, O death, is your victory? Where, O death, is your sting?
1 CORINTHIANS 15:55

We can eat healthily, take vitamins, exercise regularly, apply anti-aging creams, and even have surgery in an attempt to look younger, but there is no way anyone can avoid the inevitable. We are all going to die one day. We must determine that we will not spend our lives in fear, sidestepping any risks simply because something potentially bad could happen and we might die.

When I was in college, we studied many of the works of George Bernard Shaw, who once wrote, "Death is the ultimate statistic; one out of one will die." We live in a world that likes to avoid talking about death, and instead offers us twenty steps to stop the aging process. We somehow believe that by ignoring death, it will not happen to us. The truth is that every person has been appointed to die once and then face the judgment. We all will die and stand before God to give an account of what we did with this one and only life that he has given us.

Of all people, Christians should be the most untamed, wild risk takers for the sake of the gospel because we believe that death has been defeated by Christ's victory at Calvary! Let's determine to live the kind of life that shows we do not fear death.

MOMENT OF REFLECTION

A life empowered by the Spirit is one
that acknowledges the stark reality of death—
and the unshakable truth of Christ's victory over it.
Praise God for this today!

August 25

The Least

The LORD turned to him and said, "Go in the strength you have and save Israel out of Midian's hand. Am I not sending you?"

JUDGES 6:14

In the book of Judges, the Lord had selected Gideon to save Israel and to defeat the Midian army. One would think that Gideon would be full of courage and strength, knowing that the Lord was on his side and had chosen him for such a crucial assignment. Yet, once again we see an example of someone looking at his own limitations instead of looking to the One who has promised him victory.

Gideon responded to God, "O my Lord, how can I save Israel? Indeed my clan is the weakest in Manasseh, and I am the least in my father's house" (Judges 6:15 NKJV). Instead of looking to a big God who was going to work on his behalf, he kept his gaze on his own limitations. He focused on what *he* was not rather than on who God was. We often think we are simply being realistic when we list the facts of our own limitations, but actually we are being prideful. If we focus on what we cannot do, or who we are not, we are really saying to God, "My limitations are greater than your supernatural power and strength." Now that is a sobering thought.

Like Gideon and so many others in the Scriptures, at times we all feel inadequate to perform the assignment that God has for us. We must learn to trust God despite our limitations, and believe that he is faithful to do the very thing he has purposed to do in and through our lives.

MOMENT OF REFLECTION

What makes you feel inadequate? How can you turn to God's promises to help you feel strong in his Spirit?

August 26

Imagine

Therefore God exalted him to the highest place and gave him the name that is above every name, that at the name of Jesus every knee should bow, in heaven and on earth and under the earth, and every tongue acknowledge that Jesus Christ is Lord, to the glory of God the Father.

PHILIPPIANS 2:9 – 11

After a number of years ministering in America, I finally had the opportunity to go to a college football game—LSU versus Georgia. It was one of the most incredible events I have ever attended! Not only did I gather with more than 93,000 extremely LOUD fans to watch the game, I also discovered something called "tailgating." People arrive at the stadium at 8:00 a.m., park their car, set up their barbeque, and watch the game right there in their parking spot. It was all very amazing!

I watched the enthusiasm of the fans, the encouragement of the cheerleaders, the commitment of the players and coaches, and thought, "If all of this could happen at a football game, how much more should we be passionate, engaging, and cheering one another on when it comes to the gospel!"

Imagine if we brought that deafening roar to church, declaring the praises and greatness of God! Imagine standing alongside other believers in the journey of life, cheering them on, inspiring them to greatness.

Imagine coming to church already stirred up, fired up, and ready to participate, not just to passively watch.

Imagine if we all moved forward in one accord, each playing a part and knowing that together the team can win.

Imagine listening to God as our coach and simply obeying what he tells us ... we would actually get the ball over the goal line in our spiritual lives more often.

Imagine if all our dreaming, scheming, conversations, endeavors, aspirations, and labor were directed to the primary purpose of the evangelization of earth before the second coming of Jesus Christ ... we might just get the job done with that kind of focus.

MOMENT OF REFLECTION

When you think of church, what do you imagine?

August 27

It's Time to Arise

And He said, "Young man, I say to you, arise."

LUKE 7:14 NKJV

You and I are the church of Jesus Christ on the earth today, the visible representation of an invisible God. We have the Holy Spirit living within us and have been commissioned to shine his love in the midst of a dark world. Have you ever wondered what the church should look like to the world around us? What does it mean to "arise" and shine in this day and this hour?

Perhaps this is a glimpse of what God intends:

- We are a church whose heart beats for what his heart beats ... the world.
- We are fearless, proactive, and strategic.
- We run into the darkness and dispel it with the light of Christ.
- We offer hope where there is despair, love where there is hatred, peace where there is turmoil, and kindness where there is anger.
- We provide food, clothing, and shelter when there is need.
- We cultivate community and family where there is loneliness.
- We bring forgiveness and grace where there is judgment and condemnation, protection where there is danger.
- We are a voice for those who have been silenced.
- We are more concerned with pleasing God than people.
- We are biblically correct rather than politically correct.
- We are the first to respond to crisis and disaster.
- We open our arms to the poor.
- We are the first to foster or adopt orphans.

- We dwell in the ghettos of our own cities.
- We give value, worth, dignity, identity, and significance to every single human being.
- We are the hands and feet of Jesus on this planet.
- We are quick to forgive and rich in mercy, love, and grace.
- We are full of hope, life, and joy.

Perhaps the world will know that Jesus Christ is alive if we simply live as though it were true.

MOMENT OF REFLECTION

As you ponder the list above, in what areas do you need to ask God to help you grow?

August 28

Love Thy Neighbor

The second is this: "Love your neighbor as yourself." There is no commandment greater than these.

MARK 12:31

The inner, personal work of the grace of Jesus Christ is meant to show itself in the public lives of those who are Christ's disciples. Yet most Christian literature today has little to do with our public lives but is focused on how to make our own lives better, easier, and happier. Jesus told us to love our neighbor as we love ourselves; therefore, should we not also desire to make other people's lives better, easier, and happier?

A sign that we are living the true Spirit-filled life is that we increasingly demonstrate Christ's love and compassion to the broken, marginalized, and hurting. As his character is formed within us, so are his priorities, values, and concerns. We cannot be like Christ and remain disconnected from the needs of the people he so desperately loves.

Injustice and suffering go untended because we are so often distracted with ourselves. Our hearts may not will us to do injustice, but they are not strong or healthy enough to drive us to seek justice. We want prosperity, education, comfort, and safety for ourselves and those we love, but we do not always stand in the gap for those who do not have such access.

Most of us never think about whether we are going to eat today; instead we struggle to make a choice about what and where we will eat. We don't worry about having shelter but about how many extra rooms we are going to add to our homes. We don't worry about having water; we just want to make sure the hot water heater is working. We don't worry about having electricity; we just flip a switch and expect it. We don't worry about not having an education; we simply try to choose between private or public. We don't worry about protection because we can dial 911. And yet, multitudes do not have access to any of these things.

What about them? Don't they matter to God too? Did he not send us into the world to be his hands and feet to these very people?

I have discovered that loving my neighbor is very dangerous to my own self-absorption. When good people do nothing, injustice thrives. It is as simple as that.

MOMENT OF REFLECTION

Do you consider the needs of others to be as important as your own?

August 29

The Faith Adventure

When I am afraid, I put my trust in you.

PSALM 56:3

There is so much uncertainty in accepting the call of God, but that is exactly what makes it the faith adventure. It is the faith adventure that compelled the Galilean fishermen to drop their nets and exchange a life of certainty for a very uncertain future. Likewise, if we truly want to walk in God's purposes for our lives, then we cannot wait until we have the entire blueprint before we get up and start to move. We need to embrace the uncertainty, trust him, and step into the future.

Abraham went forth, not knowing where he was going. Following Jesus means giving up ultimate control over the direction of our lives and choosing to walk by faith and not by sight. This kind of faith does not reduce or deny the uncertainty that comes with stepping out. Instead, it simply embraces it by trusting that God is in control and that he is good.

A key factor of walking by faith is having the ability to trust God. But we cannot do this if we remain chained by fear, because fear negates our ability to trust him. When we are afraid, we cannot fully trust. When we cannot fully trust, we cannot walk in faith. And without faith it is impossible to truly please God.

MOMENT OF REFLECTION

Do you see faith as a great adventure or a fearful ride?

August 30

The Art of Gratefulness

And whatever you do, whether in word or deed, do it all in the name of the Lord Jesus, giving thanks to God the Father through him.

COLOSSIANS 3:17

Thanksgiving is not something that comes naturally to us; it has to be cultivated. If anything has taught me that thankfulness is not part of the Adamic nature we are born with, it has been parenting two small daughters. If I give one of the girls a lollipop, she won't instantly say, "Thank you!" In fact, she is more likely to say, "I want two lollipops!" Or, if I give both girls a lollipop at the same time, one will inevitably squawk in protest, "Hers is bigger than mine!" Greed comes pretty naturally to us; thankfulness does not—we have to work to develop it.

I am trying to cultivate a grateful-hearted attitude in our girls by teaching them to give thanks every night when they go to bed. Each night as we pray together I get them to think of all the things they can thank God for (people, situations, answered prayers). The funny thing is, when the girls don't want to go to sleep, they will go on and on dreaming up things to be grateful for, thanking God for everything on the entire planet! In other words, their level of gratitude is determined by how much they want to go to sleep!

So many people in our world are cynical, sarcastic, complaining, and ungrateful. Let's determine instead to be full of joy and gratitude. We, who were once dead in our sins but are now alive in Christ, have so much to be grateful for.

MOMENT OF REFLECTION

Make a list of everything you are grateful for.

August 31

Tomorrow Is Now

I tell you, now is the time of God's favor, now is the day of salvation.

2 CORINTHIANS 6:2

When talking about the subject of procrastination, I realize I could fill an entire book. There are so many things we accept as inevitable, that are just a part of who we are, or are too hard to change. Then, when we read the Word, we get a glimpse of our big God and all that we can be in him. We may get excited after listening to a particularly inspiring sermon, reading a great book, or seeing a wonderful movie, but when the moment comes to actually do something, many times we say, "Tomorrow."

You will start that diet ... tomorrow.
You will deal with your attitude ... tomorrow.
You will give up that habit ... tomorrow.
You will start a Bible reading plan ... tomorrow.
You will deal with the wounds of your past ... tomorrow.
You will volunteer at church ... tomorrow.

You will write that check . . . tomorrow.
You will submit your resume . . . tomorrow.
You will confess your sin . . . tomorrow.
You will apologize . . . tomorrow.
You will sponsor a child . . . tomorrow.
You will call that friend (or your mother) . . . tomorrow.

When we continuously do not do the things we know to do when we should do them, we are left with feelings of stress, guilt, disorganization, and fear—which can ultimately sabotage our destiny. We need to trust and obey God in our today, because those decisions and actions today determine our pathway to our tomorrow.

MOMENT OF REFLECTION

Is there something you have put off doing that you know God wants you to do?

September

UNDAUNTED!

September 1

Start Right Now!

For the LORD your God is God of gods and Lord of lords, the great God, mighty and awesome, who shows no partiality and accepts no bribes.

DEUTERONOMY 10:17

Recently I went home to Sydney and spent the afternoon visiting my mum (and eating lots of Greek food). I walked into the bedroom I had occupied in my mum's house for almost thirty years and was amazed at how small it actually was. In that bedroom I not only slept but somehow managed to fit a study desk that, when combined with my bed, took up every available square inch of space.

I smiled as I reflected on the fact that it was in that room I studied for my high school exams, my university exams, and my Bible college exams. It was there I wrote the first six years of sermons I ever preached. (Admittedly, they were so bad I am glad there is no evidence of them anywhere.) I marveled at how a global ministry started in a room where I could literally almost touch opposing walls if I stretched out my arms.

I realized that it is not the size of the room but the size of our God that determines our destiny. Sometimes we want to wait until everything is perfect before we start to do anything, but I have found that if we simply start where we are, with what we have, when we can, then God in his bigness is well able to compensate for any of our smallness.

We never start where we want to end up. We can only start at the beginning and then grow to where we want to go!

MOMENT OF REFLECTION

Are there any areas in your life where you have focused more on the size of your circumstances or resources than the size of your God?

September 2

We Are the Church

You will know how people ought to conduct themselves in God's household, which is the church of the living God, the pillar and foundation of the truth.

1 TIMOTHY 3:15

When I was in school, we studied the play *Shirley Valentine* by Willy Russell. It was the story of a wisecracking, completely unpredictable English housewife whose suburban life had become one boring cycle of getting her husband off to work and helping her kids through school. During the day she would methodically complete her list of tasks—grocery shopping, cooking, ironing, and cleaning—only to go to bed, get up, and begin the same routine all over again.

One of Shirley's most notable quirks consisted of her conversations with the kitchen wall. A large part of the play is, in fact, a monologue of her talking to the wall—seemingly her only real companion. At one point she says, "Most of us are dead before we die, and the thing that kills us is all of this unused life we carry around with us."

So many lives are literally like this: We get up and go through our well-rehearsed motions of existence; we check off all the tasks on our lists and go to bed; we arise the next day and do it all over again. As Christians, we know that such a mundane existence falls far short of the abundant life Jesus came to give us. God did not create all of us with such creativity, cultural diversity, unique gifts, and talents simply to go through the motions of a boring religious life.

As Christians, with the power of the Creator of the universe inside us, we should be living the most exciting, exhilarating lives on the planet! In the same way, a church that is going through the motions of "doing church" has missed the point of what God created her to be. God never intended for his church to be filled with empty ritual, boring and irrelevant teaching, uninspiring music, or a lack of creativity. The church of Jesus Christ ought to be dynamic, vibrant, life-giving—a place of hope, healing, and destiny.

MOMENT OF REFLECTION

How are you making the church you attend a place of hope for others?

September 3

A Life That Proclaims

You will receive power when the Holy Spirit comes on you; and you will be my witnesses.

ACTS 1:8

Right now you might be thinking, "I have my hands full just getting the kids out the door for school, planning something that resembles a healthy dinner, reading that report before work in the morning, and getting the laundry done. When do I have time to preach the gospel to the poor and release the captives? I can't find the car keys, let alone the keys to the prisoners' cell door!" If so, you're not alone. Most of us simply don't compute how we can play any role in God's grand scheme for the world.

The good news is that we don't have to do this all alone. Jesus said that the Holy Spirit gives us the power to be his witnesses throughout the earth. I hope you noticed that Jesus did not say he would give us the power to *do* the witnessing but rather to *be* witnesses. This is because the power that we need to effectively witness to others essentially flows from being an authentic witness ourselves. We must *be* before we *do*. I am in no way suggesting that we do not proactively proclaim the gospel to our friends, neighbors, and other people with whom we come into contact, but I sincerely believe that we need not only to preach the gospel but also live in the power of the gospel.

To be a witness for Christ, we must be bearing witness to the truth of his Word. If I were still broken, wounded, and rejected, I would have no power to preach good news to the poor. If I had not found freedom, how could I shine a light for others to find theirs? If

I were still brokenhearted because of my past, how could I help to heal someone else's broken heart? And if I were still in captivity, how could I possibly proclaim liberty to others? More than any words, program, or doctrine, our lives become a platform from which to proclaim the love of God to others.

MOMENT OF REFLECTION

What areas of your life need to be shored up before they can be used to proclaim the love of God to those around you? How will you begin?

September 4

Staying Focused

I will instruct you and teach you in the way you should go; I will counsel you with my loving eye on you.

PSALM 32:8

It was a typical evening in the Caine household: Nick was taking a moment to catch up on sports on ESPN; Catherine was upstairs tidying her room before dinner (she was not allowed to watch *Dora the Explorer* for the zillionth time until she completed this task); Sophia was contentedly playing in her room; and I was in the kitchen attempting to accomplish five things at once (as I said, perfectly typical).

I was trying to keep an ear out for what the kids were up to, cook dinner, set the table, talk on the phone, all the while making last-minute changes to a manuscript, when I noticed a strange silence upstairs—the kind that registers on a mother's radar.

I scurried upstairs to take a peek in Catherine's room, and there she was, sitting on the floor painting Sophia's nails. Noting Sophia's moussed hair, blue eyelids, and rouged cheeks, I could see my eldest was simply adding her finishing touches to my baby's total makeover.

In my best "mummy discipline" voice, I said, "Catherine Bobbie, what are you doing? I told you to clean your room before dinner." To this, she answered innocently, "But Mummy, I didn't turn on *Dora*."

Catie knew what she was *not* supposed to do—I'll give her that—but she definitely didn't clue in to what she was *supposed* to be doing. So many of us Christians live our lives just like Catherine did that day. We know exactly what we aren't supposed to be doing, but we forget that we *should be* focused on the abundant, purpose-driven, passionate life adventure we have been called to live. If we maintain this focus, we will not find ourselves getting off track, doing things that we should not be doing. Instead our lives will move forward in the direction of God's most perfect plan.

MOMENT OF REFLECTION

Do you think you focus on activities you are refraining from rather than on the things you should be participating in? If so, why?

September 5

Living Fearlessly

There is no fear in love. But perfect love drives out fear, because fear has to do with punishment. The one who fears is not made perfect in love.

1 JOHN 4:18

For years, I yearned for deliverance from my fears—but I wanted something more than the Lord's simple instructions to keep my eyes on him. "Why won't you just take this fear from me?" I demanded.

God in his tender mercy sent me back to his Word. There I read that perfect love casts out fear. I realized that fear will not get us through danger. But love can. God's love resides in us, but we're not always confident of that because we can't see it. We do see the dangers—being too high off the ground, perhaps, or staring into the cold face of an enemy. So we doubt, we question—and we let fear take over.

God knew that we would be afraid. That's why he tells us again and again in the Bible, "Fear not." Three hundred and fifty times he tells us. Fear not. Fear not. Fear not. Fear not. When angels appeared to characters in the Bible, the first words they spoke were usually, "Fear not."

It's like a mother instinctively reaching for her child who is crying in the storm, wrapping her arms around the trembling heart, and soothing over and over, "It's okay. I'm here with you. Don't be afraid."

God works in us to help us confront our fears and take a risk. He's there with us—before, during, and after.

MOMENT OF REFLECTION

Think back to a time when you were fearful,
but you took a risk and now you are glad you did.
How did that victory make you feel?

September 6

Wind and Waves

Then Peter got down out of the boat, walked on the water and came toward Jesus. But when he saw the wind, he was afraid and, beginning to sink, cried out, "Lord, save me!" Immediately Jesus reached out his hand and caught him. "You of little faith," he said, "why did you doubt?"

MATTHEW 14:29–31

When a storm came up on the Sea of Galilee, Peter, a fisherman used to choppy waters, faced the choice of giving in to fear or stepping out in faith. He knew how to navigate through a storm. He practically lived on the water. But he also knew his limitations. All his fears were whispering in his head, as they were in the heads of his companions: "The winds are too fierce, the waves too high, the boat too fragile for us to survive this gale." Everyone in the boat began to cower in fear, their concentration fixed on the dangers of the storm.

Just as Peter was about to give up, he looked out on the water and saw Jesus *w*alking through the storm toward their boat! Jesus called to Peter, asking him to step out of the boat and onto the water, to step into the danger and out of fear, to take a step of faith.

So, believing that with Jesus he could do anything, Peter took that step of faith, his eyes fixed on the Lord. One step—and just like that, he was walking through the storm, undaunted by danger, defying it even, doing the miraculous.

And then an especially large gust of wind swept over Peter, spray whipped his face, and his attention was back on the storm. "The waves are too high," he must have thought, "the wind too fierce, Jesus too far away." Peter's vision was suddenly clouded by the storm. His sight was deceiving him. Jesus was never far away. He was with Peter in the storm, right there when the greatest gale blew.

Why *do* we doubt?

Jesus beckons us to come. If we stay focused on him, we will be able to go anywhere and do whatever is required of us. If we take our eyes off him and stare at the storm, at the danger, we will surely sink. We will never go to the millions trapped in the darkness suffering abuse, disease, famine, injustice, loneliness, or hopelessness.

To get to them, we may have to walk on water.

MOMENT OF REFLECTION

Has God asked you to step out of your comfort zone and do something amazing? How do you plan to answer his call?

September 7

Ambition That Destroys

Do nothing out of selfish ambition or vain conceit. Rather, in humility value others above yourselves.

PHILIPPIANS 2:3

Ambition is that grit in the soul that makes us dissatisfied with the ordinary and dares us to dream. It helps us to keep focused and disciplined, and to make right choices. I encourage Catherine and Sophia to dream big dreams. I most certainly do not want them to live aimless lives but to fufill their God-given purpose. For that reason, I encourage them to grow in godly ambition, but I also remind them frequently of another type of ambition that our world celebrates but does not bring glory to God.

The selfish ambition that Paul describes always looks out for one's own interests above the interests of anyone else. This type of ambition is what our world applauds and promotes, but it is very destructive. This is self-promotion that steps on others to exalt oneself. It will trade loyalty, friendship, and integrity for self-advancement. It will lie, cheat, and use people to get ahead. It delights in another's failure and sacrifices relationships just to get to the top.

Jesus calls us to a life that is the opposite of selfish ambition. We are to love, serve, prefer, and honor others before ourselves. Doing good for others should be our focus. Remember, when we finally stand before God, the main point of his evaluation will not be how much we accomplished for ourselves but how well we loved.

MOMENT OF REFLECTION

Are you an ambitious person?
If so, is your ambition godly or selfish?
In what areas can you become more ambitious for the glory of God?

September 8

The Joy of Obedience

If they obey and serve him, they will spend the rest of their days in prosperity and their years in contentment.

JOB 36:11

As we were hurriedly being shuttled from one airport terminal in Frankfurt to the other, I looked across the crowded bus and noticed one particular elderly couple. They looked fearful—I knew that they must be worried that they were not going to make their flight. Our plane had arrived very late, and it was likely that many of us on the bus would miss our connecting flights. I noticed that the couple could not speak English or German, and I saw their boarding pass was for Istanbul. "They are Turkish," I thought to myself, "and they have no idea what's going on."

As I looked back at Nick and the girls to see how they were faring on this squished and bumpy bus, I heard God's still, small voice within me say, "You need to help that couple." I almost answered out loud, "God, how can I help them? Their plane leaves from another terminal—I will miss my plane, and I have to preach in Stockholm tonight. What about Nick and the girls?" His only response was, "Help that couple get to their plane." I only had a split second to decide.

"Nick," I said, "you take the girls and go—give me my passport and pray that I make it."

I walked over to the couple, who must have been in their eighties, at least. I gently took them by the hand and walked them to their gate. The woman was so thankful that she began to sob as we walked. When we arrived at their gate, she looked at me, patted my face, and kissed me, thanking Allah for sending me to them.

Suddenly, I got the full picture of what God was doing. In that instant, I was able to look into her eyes, smile, and whisper, "Jesus Christ loves you." She looked at me, began to cry some more, and then disappeared onto the plane.

I felt so humbled and honored to be a part of God's beautiful invitation for this couple to know him. What seemed at first like a hassle to me became a once-in-a-lifetime moment to sow a seed. Imagine the opportunity I would have missed had I not been obedient.

MOMENT OF REFLECTION

How would you respond if God asked you to do something completely unexpected?

September 9

Things Have Changed

As the body without the spirit is dead, so faith without deeds is dead.

JAMES 2:26

I have always been passionate about my work as an evangelist. I loved teaching and preaching, bringing the good news of Christ to people. But as I grew as a Christian, I felt that God was drawing me deeper still, stirring something within me that I had intuitively known but never understood. There is no distinction between preaching and doing for Jesus. They are the wings on the same plane of faith.

I had always envisioned those who fought for justice as the heroes written about in books—other people in other countries, living in different days. Though I'd studied about the Holocaust and other horrific events, those events seemed distant in time and place. Other atrocities did too: the Rwandan genocide in 1994, during which an estimated eight hundred thousand people were mass murdered in just one hundred days; the Cambodian genocide, during which almost two million people died through political executions, starvation, and forced labor. But the day I visited Auschwitz, the Nazi extermination camp, I was aware of the need to fight for justice in a way I had not been before. I sensed that something new would be required of me—not someone else. Something had awakened within me that internally shifted the emphasis from *we* to *me.* God seemed to be saying: "This new love and this new sense of purpose I've put within you are for a reason. Rise up. Get ready. I have more for you to do."

God wanted me to rise, ready to go, as Jesus had gone on my behalf—out of love, walking wide awake through this world, seeing one prisoner yearning to be free, and then another, and another. God did not want me staying in bed, resting while a battle rages around me, fought by others. He wanted me to go—and he wanted me to go undaunted. I never knew then that a simple step of obedience would result in what has become The A21 Campaign, an organization committed to fighting the injustice of human trafficking around the earth. (A21 stands for "abolishing injustice in the twenty-first century.")

There are so many daunting things in the world that we must overcome: daunting needs, daunting enemies, daunting obstacles. Only the undaunted in Christ will be able to triumph over them.

This is what he wants for me. And he wants the same for you.

MOMENT OF REFLECTION

Where has God called you to go?
Do you feel daunted by the task ahead?

September 10

I Know I Can

Moses answered God, "But why me? What makes you think that I could ever go to Pharaoh and lead the children of Israel out of Egypt?"

EXODUS 3:11 MSG

When God asked me to start The A21 Campaign, he was actually interrupting my ministry schedule so that I could do something even more impactful. He had prepared even more good works for me to do, if I were willing—and I was. In fact, I was excited. I wanted to do this. I, who had been rescued from a dark place and restored, could help set others free.

And no sooner was I inspired to go than I immediately began to think of a hundred reasons I was unable—a hundred reasons to be *daunted*. Isn't that human nature? We're roused to do something, and then we immediately forget the one reason that we are capable of doing anything at all. When I initially discovered the magnitude of the problem of human trafficking across the earth, I, like most other people, was so overwhelmed that I began to compile a list for God of all the reasons I, a forty-year-old mother of two living on the other side of the world, could not possibly do anything to significantly change the statistics. I don't know what your "but God" list might be. Are these items on it?

But God, I don't know enough about the issue.
But God, I'm not educated enough to get involved.
But God, I'm not skilled enough.
But God, I already have enough on my plate.
But God, I have a family.
But God, it's too dangerous.
But God, I'm too old to start something new.
But God, I'm too young to be taken seriously.
But God, this will tip the scales of balance in my life.

But God—the list goes on. Does it sound familiar? This is the same kind of daunting self-doubt (or just plain excuses) we all stub our toes on.

MOMENT OF REFLECTION

What are the "but God" excuses in your life?

September 11

Small Gifts

You, dear children, are from God and have overcome them, because the one who is in you is greater than the one who is in the world.

1 JOHN 4:4

When God invites us to leave our comfort zones and help others, he never asks us to go alone. He goes along. He goes ahead. He's by our side. We know this because he has promised to never leave us nor forsake us. The wonderful (but easily overlooked) reason we can stride into our destiny confident and undaunted is not that we are so great—*but that the God who is within us is so great!*

What does this mean for us? It means that while we may think we don't have enough time, money, resources, or know-how for the task, God will use what we do have. It's important to remember this, because otherwise we may be so convinced that our contribution will be so small, insignificant, even inconsequential, that we decide to do nothing.

Jesus has always used small things to make a big difference. He used a young boy's lunch to feed five thousand people. I'm sure that if you'd asked the boy that morning if he had brought enough food to feed the whole crowd, he'd have laughed—"With five little loaves of bread and two fishes? There are thousands of people here! We'd be lucky to each get a piece the size of a pebble." If you had asked him what he was doing, then, offering his lunch to Jesus, he might well have said, "He might be hungry—and even though I don't have enough lunch for everyone, I have enough for one person. I'll let him eat my lunch."

But once he'd given that small gift to Jesus, Jesus used it to do something far beyond what that boy might have imagined or expected. And that's exactly what he does with our small gifts.

MOMENT OF REFLECTION

Is there a gift in your life that God has been asking you to share, but you feel it is too small and insignificant to matter? What can you do to change your thinking?

September 12

Gate A21

In this world you will have trouble. But take heart! I have overcome the world.

JOHN 16:33

I once prayed that God would help us overcome the challenges we were facing as we launched The A21 Campaign in Greece. In fact, I was on my way there and had just said *amen* when an announcement came over the loudspeaker. "All passengers on Aegean Airlines flight to Thessaloniki, Greece, we are now boarding. Those on Aegean Airlines to Thessaloniki, Greece, board at gate A21."

Gate A21. Sometimes God has to shout over the crowds and the clamor for us to understand that, although there will always be difficulties in this world, the One who created the universe can overcome them.

This was one of those times.

By choosing, at the exact time A21 was under fire, to have my flight leave from the gate that bore the same name as our campaign, God was subtly reminding me of who was in charge: "Yes," he was saying, "the odds are stacked against you. Overwhelmingly, in fact. Yes, every bit of reason and all the advice you've paid for says to stop before you've even started. Yes, the giants you're facing can make you think there's no way forward. But none of those things can stop me, and when you do my will, they can't stop you, either."

There's so much temptation to think otherwise. We're asked

to speak to a group but think, "I can't! I'm too shy." We want to volunteer at a local shelter, but our schedule will tell us that we're too busy and cannot add one more thing. We want to make a career change to follow what we know is our calling, yet our confidence will mutter, "Stay where you are. There are too many unknowns! It makes no sense to give up a job other people would kill for just to try for some ephemeral sense of happiness." We must remember that God is always with us and always making a way for us to do his will, to bring his hope and change into this world.

MOMENT OF REFLECTION

Do you feel like the odds are stacked against you?
How will you overcome the odds and accomplish God's purpose?

September 13

Nothing My God Cannot Do

We live by faith, not by sight.
2 CORINTHIANS 5:7

How misleading our perspective is for the things God calls us to do. We see problems. He sees possibilities. We see difficulty. He sees destiny.

There is no promise too hard for God to fulfill. When our consultants told Nick and me that A21, our campaign to rescue victims of human trafficking, would never work in Eastern Europe, that it needed much more than a wing and a prayer to fly, we took only part of their advice.

The prayer part.

Now we have offices all over the world. A21 works to raise awareness of human trafficking, establish prevention programs in schools and orphanages, represent victims as legal advocates, give them refuge in safe houses, and then restoration in transition homes.

God didn't remove all the difficulties from our path. Difficulty is part of this world. But God is bigger than any difficulty. He sees above and beyond any obstacle. He leads us a step at a time over the mountains into the valleys he wants us to possess because no prayer is too big for him to answer, no problem too large for him to solve. There is no disease he cannot heal or heart he cannot mend. There is no bondage God cannot break, need he cannot meet, enemy he cannot defeat, or mountain he cannot move.

There is nothing our God cannot do.

MOMENT OF REFLECTION

How big is the God you serve?
Is he big enough to help you do what he's called you to do?

September 14

My God Is So Big

I will show my greatness and my holiness, and I will make myself known in the sight of many nations.

EZEKIEL 38:23

I will never forget the day my daughter Catherine came home from children's church with that song, "My God Is So Big," on her lips. As most children do, she kept singing the song over and over as if it were stuck on "repeat" in the CD player: "My God is so big, so strong and so mighty/There's nothing my God cannot do."

Eventually, the endless repetition began to get on my nerves. I was just about to tell my daughter, "Catie, Mommy needs some quiet time—alone." Then I stopped. "What if this is all Catherine ever knows and believes about God?" I thought. "What if the truth in these simple lyrics is woven into the very fabric of her heart and every fiber of her being? Imagine what she could do, if she truly believed that no difficulty, obstacle, or hurdle could defeat God's plan for her life. Imagine the difficulties she could overcome without a second thought or glance."

How I wanted that kind of faith.

"My God is so big," I began to sing along with her.

I still face giants, but I'm determined not to be stopped by them.

"Go into all the world," God told us.

He didn't say how. He didn't say if. He just said: "Go and look for the lost. Find the missing. Bring them into this land where hope is plentiful. Start where you are, with what you have, however you can."

God has set before each of us an exciting and world-changing mission. He wants to work *in* us, to equip and empower and qualify us, so that he can work *through* us. Many of us are daunted either by the mission he calls us to or the prospect of turning our lives over to him so that he can prepare us. But to live truly *un*daunted, to ask others to have faith, we must summon our own faith in God. After all, God can move mountains.

MOMENT OF REFLECTION

How big is your God?
Do you believe he can still move mountains in your life?

September 15

Wonder Woman

If the Spirit of him who raised Jesus from the dead is living in you, he who raised Christ from the dead will also give life to your mortal bodies because of his Spirit who lives in you.

ROMANS 8:11

I always dreamed of being Wonder Woman. As a girl I tried jumping off my garage roof a few times, complete with a cape and my underwear on the outside of my pants, only to get to the roof and realize I've always been scared of heights. I thought Wonder Woman could do anything; and if I'd had a pair of those gold wristbands I could have achieved the impossible!

My aspirations of becoming a superhero came to naught, as countless other little girls' dreams have, but aren't there days in our lives when we feel like we have to be a superwoman if we're going to get through it alive? Sometimes it can seem like everybody wants a piece of us: our kids want lunch or to be driven to sports training, our boss needs that report, our mom says we never visit, our friend is on the phone because her marriage is in crisis, we have bills to pay, dinner to cook, and when we finally think the day is over and climb under the covers, our husband wants to make love!

God's "all" for your life is right before you, ready to be seized, enjoyed; ready to bring you tremendous fulfillment and stretch you to your limits. You absolutely can have and do it all—live the life you've dreamed of—if you understand that your "all" will be a journey of a lifetime, and that sometimes your "all" can shift and morph when you least expect it.

The "secret" I'm about to reveal won't eliminate these kinds of days, but it will take the stress out of living through them. The secret (drum roll, please) is: we don't have to be superwomen, we just need to be supernatural!

No matter where you are in life, where you've come from, or what you may have experienced, God has an "all" designed specifically for you so you can become a force—supernaturally empowered by the Holy Spirit—that can change your world!

MOMENT OF REFLECTION

What do you think it means to be supernaturally empowered by the Holy Spirit?

September 16

Consider Moses

The angel of the LORD appeared to him in flames of fire from within a bush. Moses saw that though the bush was on fire it did not burn up.

EXODUS 3:2

I wonder if Moses ever thought of giving up. He's a perfect example of how God uses every season to prepare us for our biggest moments —at least, if we let him. Moses was a Hebrew baby who was adopted by the Egyptian Pharaoh's daughter. He spent the first forty years of his life in Pharaoh's palace, where he was educated by the finest teachers and trained for leadership by the best in the land. Then, an inner call stirred him to help his people who had been living as slaves to the Egyptians for more than four hundred years.

Rather than wait for his opportunity, however, Moses took his destiny into his own hands. One day, he saw an Egyptian mercilessly beating a Hebrew slave, and his anger flared. As retribution, he killed the Egyptian and hid his body in the sand. When Pharaoh heard of his crime, he sought to kill Moses, but Moses fled into the desert to the land of Midian, where he married, had children, became a shepherd, and remained for four long decades until God confronted him in the burning bush.

Moses spent 14,600 days on the backside of a desert. There must have been at least a few occasions when, sitting on a rock, sand in his sandals, watching over his flock, he wondered, "How in the world did I wind up here?" Moses could have devalued that season and written off all those days as meaningless. Although the Bible doesn't say much about what Moses did during those forty years, it's clear he spent the season honoring God because when God "suddenly" showed up on day 14,601 in a burning bush, Moses was ready to respond, and in so doing, changed the course of history for the then-known world!

What if Moses had given up? The people of Israel would have remained oppressed, perhaps for generations, until God could raise up another person to complete the task destined for Moses.

MOMENT OF REFLECTION

What are you waiting for? Have you given up?
Or are you waiting for God to confront you?

September 17

Loss of Flexibility

There is far more at stake here than religion. If you had any idea what this Scripture meant — "I prefer a flexible heart to an inflexible ritual" — you wouldn't be nitpicking like this. The Son of Man is no lackey to the Sabbath; he's in charge.

MATTHEW 12:6 – 7 MSG

While it's easy to stand in front of a mirror and see the obvious ways our skin and bodies are aging, it's much more difficult to recognize when we are getting older, duller, and just plain worn out spiritually. One indication that we are not pressing on and serving the Lord at full throttle is when we start to stiffen and refuse to continue to stretch so that we can keep enlarging our personal capacity. We settle at our current level and no longer lean into the challenge and discomfort of stretching.

I'm constantly amazed at the contortions our girls can accomplish with their little bodies. They are incredibly malleable as they sink into the splits and then strike poses with their legs behind their heads. And then they ask Mummy and Daddy if we want to try! While I consider myself to be in pretty good physical shape, I would never dream of getting on the floor with them to attempt some of their pretzel postures. Although my body may not be quite as flexible as it was when I was a child, I endeavor to keep my inner self extremely flexible through regular spiritual stretching. We have to keep stretching and expanding on the inside; otherwise God will never be able to use us to do bigger and better things.

For those of us who have had babies, think labor! Just when you think you have nothing left to stretch, the Holy Spirit serves as our midwife and whispers, "Just a little longer, and just a bit more."

If we allow ourselves to get too comfortable and stiff, never wanting to stretch into new levels of life, we will hinder so much of what God has planned for us. He has great exploits for us to accomplish, but it's up to us to keep growing, changing, and enlarging if we want to see these plans come to pass.

MOMENT OF REFLECTION

In what areas of your spiritual being do you feel God stretching you?

September 18

Passion Draws People

The Lord added to their number daily those who were being saved.

ACTS 2:47

As the apostles began to openly proclaim Jesus as Lord and Savior following the day of Pentecost, people marveled at their zeal. Passion gets people's attention. People want to follow people who are passionate and living for a cause.

As Christians, we are fighting for the greatest cause known to humanity: the evangelization of planet Earth before the second coming of Jesus Christ. For this reason, we should passionately put all that we have into what we are doing for the kingdom. After all, our cause has eternal consequences—we are offering people eternal life and hope through Jesus Christ.

Our aim should be to live so filled with passion for Christ that, just like in the early church, people will not be able to ignore it and will want what we have. Passion attracts, inspires, motivates, challenges, and changes people. In fact, it was Jesus' passion for the will of the Father that enabled him to lay down his life for humanity.

Christians ought to be the most passionate people on earth. We know the Creator of the universe. We are saved, delivered, healed; full of life, purpose, and hope. Every day is an adventure as we follow Jesus into all the world. In a world full of bad news we have good news to proclaim. If we really believed what we profess to believe, then no one would have to try to convince us to live a radical life of faith; it would be a natural response to our internal hope. Jesus did not die to give us a life of rules and regulations but a passionate, purpose-driven, abundant life. If we maintain an eternal perspective, then we will live this temporal life with passion.

Imagine what our passion for the cause of Christ could ignite in the world.

MOMENT OF REFLECTION

Is Jesus and his cause your greatest passion?

September 19

Supernatural Woman

She is clothed with strength and dignity; she can laugh at the days to come.

PROVERBS 31:25

In Proverbs 31, we see a picture of a supernatural woman. This woman was an excellent wife and mother; she worked diligently, provided food for her family, rose early, was an entrepreneur; she dressed immaculately, helped the poor and the needy, was wise, kind, strong, and dignified. The fact that this woman exists in the Bible—long before cell phones, computers, and dishwashers—shows us that we can have and do it all in life without having a nervous breakdown.

I understand that for some of us, simply reading about this Proverbs 31 woman can make us feel tired, weary, and stretched to capacity. Rather than motivating us, she only serves to remind us of how much we are *not* doing. However, I see this woman not as a superhero but as one who sets the standard for every Christian woman. In the midst of a normal life, she discovered a secret—the God factor—and came to realize she didn't need to be superhuman at all, but supernaturally empowered by the Holy Spirit. Through his strength, wisdom, and endurance, she was able to have and do her "all." As a result, within the context of her family and her world, she enlarged her capacity to live the abundant life God wanted her to live.

And this abundant "Proverbs 31" life is exactly what God deeply desires for every one of his girls. He wants us to learn how to tap into the supernatural empowerment of the Holy Spirit because this is the only way we will be able to fulfill our God-purpose and destiny without burning out or giving up along the way. The Holy Spirit is the helper Jesus promised would be with us always, who will enable us to live the supernatural life. With him and through him, we really can be like the Proverbs 31 woman, able to have and do it all, despite the screaming children, traffic jams, work deadlines, sleep deprivation, laundry piles, date nights . . . and so on.

MOMENT OF REFLECTION

In what area of your life do you most need God's supernatural power?

September 20

Walking by Faith

Without faith it is impossible to please God, because anyone who comes to him must believe that he exists and that he rewards those who earnestly seek him.

HEBREWS 11:6

Our faith is what pleases God. We must resolve never to get so experienced at what we do that we actually omit the faith element from our lives. If there is not a supernatural gap in our vision, which only God can fill, then it requires no faith, just natural planning and ability. We must be careful that we do not try to so control every aspect of our lives that there is no room for God to interrupt us and disturb our plans for his cause.

It is only when we live in the faith realm that we begin to do the extraordinary. If our vision were achievable *without* God, I would have to question whether it is *from* God. Faith needs to be the driving force in everything we do for God. Faith keeps us on the edge and prevents us from becoming stagnant.

We will always need more finances, staff, venues, resources, leaders, and ideas. We will always need wisdom beyond our own to raise our families, have healthy marriages, and grow great relationships. We will always be required to step out into the unknown, overcome our fears, and take great risks to advance the cause of the gospel. We will always need faith to make a stand for our faith among family members, friends, neighbors, and coworkers who need Jesus.

Faith is the currency of heaven.

That's why no matter what God has called us to do—whether great or small, public or private, on the world scene or on the local scene—we must learn to tap into the supernatural realm. We walk by faith, and not by sight.

MOMENT OF REFLECTION

What are you earnestly seeking God for?

September 21

We Slumber

As you sent me into the world, I have sent them.

JOHN 17:18

Jesus owned the cross so that he could make a way across the nightmarish abyss, enabling us to walk through the gap too, bringing his love and hope and change to a world engulfed by the dark, screaming in fear. He loves us, chooses us, and makes us whole not only for his pleasure but so that we might join him in reaching a world otherwise lost. He is passionate to save the world and gave his life for that very reason. God "did not send his Son into the world to condemn the world, but to save the world through him" (John 3:17). Jesus commissioned us to go into that same world and shine his light in the darkness so that others may be rescued and set free.

And yet we slumber. We sleep.

When Jesus said to go into all the world, he didn't mean to wait until morning, or until you get the right job, or find the perfect spouse, or have finished raising the kids, or have your house in order, or find a spare weekend. Christ brought us light in the darkness so that we can reach everyone living a nightmare *now.* He longs to shake us awake so that we can shout out the truth—that humankind is made for eternity but trapped in time, and time is running out. He means for us to be a lantern in the darkness. He means for us to find and rescue others because we know what it is to be lost and then found, hurting and then healed.

He means for us to walk into the gap where he's thrown down the cross, to walk like him, to walk with him.

Unwilling to stay asleep.

Unafraid of the dark.

Unflinching in the face of disappointment.

Unstoppable in the face of difficulty.

Undaunted.

MOMENT OF REFLECTION

Where will you go for God?
What will you do — undaunted?

September 22

His Awesome Power

The Spirit of the Lord is on me, because he has anointed me to proclaim good news to the poor. He has sent me to proclaim freedom for the prisoners and recovery of sight for the blind, to set the oppressed free.

LUKE 4:18

When it comes to computers and technology, Nick is the super whiz of the family. With his computer, he can do all kinds of neat things with photos, videos, PowerPoint, music—you name it. I'm honestly excited to see the computer do everything that Nick says it can do, but when he starts explaining how I can do the same, everything starts to go fuzzy. So here we have a girl (that would be me) who has a computer that has the capacity to do all that she needs done, but she does not take the time to learn the programs.

You may laugh at my computer illiteracy, but think about Nick's frustration with me in terms of how God must feel about us at times. He has not only saved us but has also given us his Holy Spirit so that we can achieve his mission on the earth. Yet so many of us are not aware of the reasons why God has given us his Spirit, nor do we do all that we could with the power of the Holy Spirit working in us.

Jesus clearly tells us *why* we have the power of the Holy Spirit working in our lives: The Spirit of the Lord is upon us to enable us to reach out beyond ourselves and help others. God has not empowered us with his Holy Spirit just so that we can have a peaceful Christian lifestyle. He has not given us his Spirit just so that we can go to church, avoid the world, prophesy, and pray in tongues. Don't get me wrong, all of that is great, but if we stop there, the Holy Spirit inside us is a little like my computer in my hands.

Just as my computer barely scratches the surface of all it was designed to do, so too the Holy Spirit is able to unleash awesome power within us, making us more like Jesus and bringing hope and life and liberty to a lost, sick, and brokenhearted humanity.

MOMENT OF REFLECTION

What are some of the ways the Holy Spirit has been able to unleash God's awesome power within you? How have you seen it affect those around you?

September 23

The Right Train of Thought

When I said, "My foot is slipping," your unfailing love, LORD, supported me. When anxiety was great within me, your consolation brought me joy.

PSALM 94:18–19

"Honey, don't you worry about a thing; everyone is going to adore you." Yet even as I said this to Catherine, I could tell she was not the least bit concerned. It was her first day at school, and I was taking her to class by the hand, quite pleased about how calm I felt. "This is going to be a breeze," I thought.

As we approached the door, however, I had this strange unsettling feeling inside me, and when it came time for me to let go of

Catherine's hand, I couldn't seem to uncurl my fingers. I had the thought, "Maybe this wasn't such a good idea. Maybe Catherine isn't ready." Then Catherine said, "Mummy, you will be okay. I will be home this afternoon, and now I want to go and play with my friends. Goodbye."

Without waiting for me to reply, my five-year-old let go of my hand and did not even look back as she went to the playground to find some new friends. I watched her skip off and the "what ifs" began: "What if she doesn't get along with the other girls? What if she can't do the schoolwork? What if she needs me in the middle of the day and I'm not here?" And so it went for about ten minutes as I played out different scenarios in my mind.

As absurd as my story sounds, I'm sure you have experienced something like it. At times we have all allowed our thoughts to travel down a random track and end up concluding ridiculously negative scenarios that will never actually happen. Just as I had to do, standing on the playground, we must "come to our senses," take control of our thoughts, and begin to think as God would think! If we resolve to keep getting on the *right* train of thought, we will always get off at the right destination.

MOMENT OF REFLECTION

In what areas of your life do you struggle to keep your worries under control? Your children? Finances? Relationships?

September 24

Guiding Principles

Keep my commands and follow them. I am the LORD.

LEVITICUS 22:31

We will never reach our full potential while a disparity exists between what we know and what we put into practice. If you want to live a passionate, purpose-driven, victorious, overcoming Christian life, you have to do what God says. You can't have the results you want without obeying the rules. Remember that God's rules are not intended to contain or limit us, frustrate or hinder us, but rather to release us to fulfill our God-given potential.

Over the years, I have learned certain principles pivotal in helping me to keep running strong and avoid disqualification. Most of these principles are simple yet profound—spiritual common sense, as it were—but incredibly effective if applied consistently to our lives. No matter how gifted or anointed we are, we cannot disobey God's fundamental rules for living and expect to run to win. Here are the principles I've come to appreciate and live by:

- Winners obey God's laws.
- Winners fix their eyes on Jesus.
- Winners learn to love self-control.
- Winners stay passionate.
- Winners deal with the past.
- Winners live generously.
- Winners remain grateful.
- Winners always get back up.

The apostle Paul reminded us that we are to run to win. Winning does not mean that we cross the line first; it simply means that we actually complete what we started. We fight the good fight, finish our course, keep the faith.

Let's determine to keep doing the basics well each and every day and then believe God for the miraculous in our lives.

MOMENT OF REFLECTION

Which of these eight principles do you need to work on today?

September 25

God's Unfolding Vision

Very truly I tell you, whoever believes in me will do the works I have been doing, and they will do even greater things than these, because I am going to the Father. And I will do whatever you ask in my name, so that the Father may be glorified in the Son. You may ask me for anything in my name, and I will do it.

JOHN 14:12–14

It is a great tragedy to have the ability to see but to lack vision. Vision is the fuel that keeps us pursuing our dreams and destiny. The ability to see the future as a current reality is crucial because without a future hope we would all despair. God has given us spiritual eyes to see ahead so that we do not get stuck where we have been or where we are. If what we see now is all we *can* see, then we will never see all there is to see. There's always more ahead if we would only look up.

Make no mistake, when the enemy wants to discourage us, he will always blur our vision. Sight is a function of the eyes, but vision is a function of the heart. It is vision that makes the unseen visible and the unknown possible. It generates hope in the midst of despair and provides endurance in tribulation. Vision is the energy of our entire God-given progress.

When there is no revelation of the future, people throw off self-control, personal discipline, and restraint. It is the vision of what God has ahead that enables us to live undaunted in the present. When we know what is beyond the wall, we can believe for the wall to come down. When we know there is dry land on the other side, we can believe for the sea to part. When we believe that there is a Promised Land, we can believe for provision in the wilderness. Believing that there is something greater ahead allows us to stay faithful now.

So today, stop looking at your current circumstances and start looking at the promises God has stored up for you in the future. There is more ahead for you than there is behind you. God's hope, plan, provision, and purpose are before you. All you need to do is to keep taking one step at a time and watch the vision unfold before your eyes.

MOMENT OF REFLECTION

Are you still full of vision or
has your sight replaced your vision?

September 26

Bold in Prayer

Truly I tell you, if you have faith as small as a mustard seed, you can say to this mountain, "Move from here to there," and it will move. Nothing will be impossible for you.

MATTHEW 17:20

Once, when visiting North Carolina, I read in the local press about a well-established church that was outraged when they learned a pornography store would be opening right across the road from their building. In response, the church called a special Friday night prayer meeting, the purpose of which was to pray against the store. One week later, a freak bolt of lightning struck the store and the whole thing burned to the ground. The article I was reading concerned the court case that followed. The proprietor of the store had somehow learned that the church wanted to "pray him out of the area," so he blamed the church for the decimation of his store due to their prayers! The church, however, protested saying that it was not their fault; this was an "act of God" (in the insurance sense, not the spiritual!). The bit of this story I love is the comment made by the judge in his summation: "I have a dilemma. In front of me I have the proprietor of a pornography shop who believes in prayer and a church that evidently doesn't!"

How effective do we believe our prayers are? Do we ask God for something and then dare to believe him for the answer? Can we rise to the challenge of holding on and believing him for the answer even when we don't see a bolt of lightning after only a week?

MOMENT OF REFLECTION

Have you ever prayed for something truly audacious—and gotten results? If so, how did you respond?

September 27

Run to God First

They will do such things because they have not known the Father or me.

JOHN 16:3

Life is full of challenges, and although we cannot avoid these trials, we do have a choice as to how we react to them. Often, the way we choose to respond (or not respond) will determine whether we are simply going through the motions and allowing life to "happen," or if we are standing on God's Word and allowing him to work in our lives. It is in the midst of a trial that our faith is tested. Do we truly believe that prayer can affect everything? Do we truly trust that God is with us in the midst of our storm? Will we remain faithful despite our circumstances? It is all a theory until it is tested, and nothing is tested until it is tested in the heat of the battle.

As Christians, we must be committed to growing—increasing our capacity—in order to move into the new things God has for us. We must be committed to closing the gap between our theology and our reality. When trials and tribulations come (and they will come!), we must decide to run to God *first* and allow him to speak to us about how to handle these situations. Instead of panicking, having a breakdown, running to friends, or indulging in various substances or habits that we have turned to in the past, we must run straight into the arms of our ever gracious, loving God.

In the midst of our trials, our confidence lies in the fact that Jesus had already won ultimate victory at Calvary. He has overcome the world, and no weapon formed against us will prosper! We face our challenges from a place of victory; we wait for what has already been won.

When trials come, be sure you run to God, not away from him.

MOMENT OF REFLECTION

When trials come, do you run to God first?
How can God's strength help you overcome your fear?

September 28

"God, I Will Do Whatever"

Whatever your hand finds to do, do it with all your might.
ECCLESIASTES 9:10

My dream was to travel the globe and win souls for Christ. But I had prayed a simple prayer—"God, I will do whatever"—and whatever came in the form of pioneering a youth center in our city. I had turned up to a cleaning day at the church and the assistant youth pastor asked if I would help serve at a brand-new community youth center we were starting at church.

I had never envisioned serving youth; I did not know what a youth center was or did; and I felt totally inadequate for the task. Still, I had said "God, I will do whatever," and my pastor had preached, "If you are faithful with what God puts in your hand, he will give you what you desire in your heart." Serving at a youth center was in my hand and nations were in my heart. I could either work with what I had or wait forever for what might never be.

That was the beginning of seven incredibly fruitful years where I learned so much about working with government, communities, the education department, other non-government organizations, and combined churches. I learned how to communicate with unchurched teenagers and saw God provide in miraculous ways, open supernatural doors of favor, and influence and train me in communication and leadership.

Only God knew that two decades later he would call me to start an international anti-human trafficking organization, and that every single one of the lessons I learned at the youth center would be used to build The A21 Campaign.

God is intentional and never wastes anything. Imagine if I had thrown in the towel, explaining that I didn't feel like God's call on my life was to work with teenagers. Or if, out of duty, I had halfheartedly done a few things for the youth center, all the while waiting for my "real" destiny to kick in (as if destinies just "kick in").

In my heart, I knew God wanted me to take ownership of the task he had placed before me. Looking back, I truly believe it was my receptive and obedient spirit that helped launch me into one of the most defining and stretching seasons of my life—one that internally prepared and equipped me for so many of the seasons that have followed.

Whatever your whatever is right now, do it with all your might. If you don't start right where you are with what you have, you will never end up where you are supposed to be with what God has.

MOMENT OF REFLECTION

Have you been asked to do something outside what you believe you are called to do? How did you respond?

September 29

Defeating Giants

David said to the Philistine, "You come against me with sword and spear and javelin, but I come against you in the name of the LORD Almighty, the God of the armies of Israel, whom you have defied."

1 SAMUEL 17:45

Fear is the opposite of faith, so it is impossible to be operating simultaneously in both. Faith helps us conquer the giants in our lives and go on to take the land. The story of David and Goliath is a great example of what one person's faith in God can achieve. The whole army of Israel was immobilized because of fear, but one young man mobilized by faith stepped forward and defeated a giant.

We cannot live our lives victoriously if we are ruled by fear. I call this the "what if" factor: "What if no one comes; what if there is not enough money; what if something bad happens? What if I fail; what if we lose everything; what if my friends walk away?" And so the list continues endlessly. Many people live their Christian lives constantly thinking about what might not work if they step out in faith and they never actually find out what could happen if they actually took the step.

Imagine if we changed our "what ifs" to possibilities instead of potential obstacles? "What if we were approved for the loan; what if hundreds of young people came to the event and surrendered their lives to Christ; what if my coworker said yes to coming to church? What if that business deal worked; what's the worst that could happen if I didn't get that promotion? What if that invention was patented; what if I got a degree; what if I said yes to the marriage proposal?"

Instead of allowing that "what if" question to hold you back, let it become the launching pad for endless possibilities. What if, just for today, you choose to believe God and his promises?

MOMENT OF REFLECTION

What is God asking you to step into,
but you have resisted thus far because of your "what if"?

September 30

Don't Settle for Lentil Soup

Then Jacob gave Esau some bread and some lentil stew. He ate and drank, and then got up and left. So Esau despised his birthright.

GENESIS 25:34

Whenever I am home in Sydney, I always drop in to chat with my mother for hours on end and, of course, to eat. No one cooks like my momma, and no one mothers me like my momma.

While eating a bowl of lentil soup (did I mention how yummy it was?), I thought about the moment when Esau sold his birthright to Jacob over one meal of lentil stew and bread.

In ancient times the birthright was very important and sacred. Esau took something holy and good and treated it with contempt;

he profaned it. He had a lack of reverence and respect for the things of God. He so devalued his birthright that he sold his inheritance to gratify a temporary hunger.

I wonder how many times in our own lives we give up our spiritual inheritance because we want some short-term gratification? Are there areas in our own lives where we are not willing to wait, obey, pray, yield, sacrifice, commit, serve, forgive, and love? Instead, for the equivalent of a bowl of lentil stew, do we compromise, disobey, succumb, rush, and react?

I pray today that we choose a hunger for God over a hunger for the things of this world. Our destiny and inheritance is worth so much more than temporary carnal pleasures.

DO NOT settle for anything less than God's best. Do not sell out!

MOMENT OF REFLECTION

Can you identify any areas in your life where you are selling out to short-term gratification because you have been unwilling to wait for God to come through?

COMMISSIONED

October

YOU ARE CALLED

October 1

Called to Rescue

Moses said to the LORD, "Pardon your servant, Lord. I have never been eloquent, neither in the past nor since you have spoken to your servant. I am slow of speech and tongue." The LORD said to him, "Who gave human beings their mouths? Who makes them deaf or mute? Who gives them sight or makes them blind? Is it not I, the LORD? Now go; I will help you speak and will teach you what to say."

EXODUS 4:10–12

There is only one rescuer with the power to free us from the darkest prison. That rescuer is the God who loves us so much he left everything to come for us, to free us. He is the one who made us, each of us, for a unique purpose and a magnificent destiny. His plans are for good, not for evil. His ways are straight and merciful. He came to give me a hope and a future—and to give you one too. His promises are true. His love is full of forgiveness and peace, joy and kindness, grace. He is the true rescuer. He saves us from any prison, whether physical or emotional or spiritual, the ones we're forced into and the ones we fall into on our own. He chooses us.

Our God loves us without condition, unrelentingly, forever. He loves us broken, and he loves making us whole again. And he asks those of us who love him to love others the same way. To choose them. To be agents of his hope, his forgiveness, his grace. He asks us to join him in rescuing others.

So why don't we?

There are reasons why when we hear God's call, when we feel that gentle urging of God's Spirit for us to make a bold step, take a risk, serve others, save a life, commit—we so often hold back.

It may be because we don't feel qualified.

We think we lack the courage, the strength, the wisdom, the money, the experience, the education, the organization, the backing.

We feel like Moses when, from out of the burning bush, God called him to speak for him before Pharaoh. "Not me, God. I'm afraid. Weak. Poor. Stupid. Unqualified. Daunted."

Not long ago, that is exactly how I would have responded. But it has never been my desire to be *daunted*, to be afraid, to be unable to respond to God's call. Just as God gave Moses exactly what he needed to accomplish great things, he will equip us in the same way. If he calls us to slay giants, he will make us into giant slayers.

God doesn't call the qualified. He qualifies the called.

MOMENT OF REFLECTION

Has God called you to take a bold step toward serving others? For what reasons do you feel you are qualified or unqualified for the job?

October 2

Qualified by God

There are different kinds of gifts, but the same Spirit distributes them. There are different kinds of service, but the same Lord. There are different kinds of working, but in all of them and in everyone it is the same God at work.

1 CORINTHIANS 12:4–6

Throughout Scripture and history, it seems God has chosen the most unlikely and unqualified people to fulfill his plan and purpose on the earth. Most often, the response of those people has been to insist on their own unworthiness. And if they don't—the people around them may do so, loudly and shrilly. And therein lies a danger: If we allow other people to tell us what we are and are not qualified to do, we will limit what God wants to do through us. We may never get to those who truly need our help.

What is impossible with people is possible with God. We have to believe that God has called us to go into the world in his name, and not listen to the crippling labels and limitations imposed on us by others. Whom God calls, he qualifies—and he chooses everybody to do something specific, something that is part of his design.

I am profoundly aware of how unqualified I am to do what God has called me to do. Yet I have found that God continues to call me out deeper and deeper, to trust and obey him. In fact, I am so far out in the deep that I have lost sight of the shore. I must keep my eyes on Jesus or I will sink.

Some of the things I am doing, one actually could not get qualified to do—because the job profile does not exist! If we are going to forge new paths, unleash new ideas, and create new pipelines, then we must trust God to qualify us for the purpose to which he has called us. Make no mistake, I am a diligent student, but no matter how hard I study or how much I learn, God continually calls me out of my comfort zone, knowledge zone, and ability zone into his supernatural zone.

Don't limit your future by your ability; ask God to give you his.

MOMENT OF REFLECTION

When has someone told you what
you were and were not qualified to do?
How did you respond?

October 3

No Excuses, Please

Each of you should use whatever gift you have received to serve others, as faithful stewards of God's grace in its various forms.

1 PETER 4:10

I'll never forget receiving a letter from the dean of the school of social work at a prestigious university, implying that I was unqualified to work with young people. At the time I was directing a thriving youth program. To work long-term in youth services, though, the dean said I needed formal training.

"Sure, she's right," I thought. "I'm technically unqualified to do the very thing I'm doing." I considered submitting my resignation. Yet something inside me said, "No, don't quit." And for fourteen years after receiving that letter, I worked full-time with youth, and now I work to rescue young people from the injustice of human trafficking. To the world, I looked unqualified. But God cared more about my willingness than my qualifications. He saw something in me that others did not and called something forth from me that others could not.

There are many roles in God's kingdom for which one must be uniquely gifted. Music, medicine, law, science, accounting, and art are some examples. We should be sensitive to the possibility, if we lack those gifts, that God may be leading us in a different direction. But once we *find* that direction, we must not allow ourselves to be deterred. Consider these biblical examples of those who God chose despite characteristics that should have disqualified them:

- Noah got drunk (Genesis 9:20–27).
- Sarah was impatient (Genesis 16).
- Abraham was old (Genesis 17:1; 24:1).
- Jacob was a cheater (Genesis 25–27).
- Miriam was a gossiper (Numbers 12:1–2).
- David had an affair (2 Samuel 11–12).
- Elijah was moody—one minute bold and courageous, the next fearful and on the run (1 Kings 18–19).
- Jonah ran away (Jonah 1:3).
- Peter had a temper (John 18:10).
- Paul was a persecutor (Acts 8:3; 9:1–2).
- Martha was a worrier (Luke 10:40–41).
- Thomas doubted (John 20:24–26).
- Zacchaeus was short (Luke 19:3).
- Lazarus was dead (John 11:14–44).

God had a purpose for each of these people. He chose them. He qualified them. He called them, just as he is calling you and me—to go and do in his name. Don't limit yourself because of your own limitations. Lean into a limitless God and see where he takes you. I suggest that you strap yourself into the roller coaster for the ride of your life.

MOMENT OF REFLECTION

God chose each of the individuals above despite a critical shortcoming. Which one do you most closely relate to? Be sure to read that person's story.

October 4

House of Worship

God placed all things under [Christ's] feet and appointed him to be head over everything for the church, which is his body, the fullness of him who fills everything in every way.

EPHESIANS 1:22–23

The word *church* comes from the Greek word *ecclesia*, which is defined as "an assembly" or "called out ones." The root meaning of "church" doesn't pertain to a building but rather to a people. That's you and me! The apostle Paul called it the body of Christ. This would suggest life and activity.

This concept came alive to me when Nick and I were visiting a two-hundred-year-old European cathedral, one of the most majestic ever constructed. A sign erected for tourists told us that it had once been the center of community life. It had served not only as a house of worship but also as the major social justice agency, the main relief organization, and the primary center for medical and aged care. This church had not been limited to the four walls of a cathedral. Her influence had reached far beyond the confines of the bricks and mortar that constituted her physical structure.

Back then, the congregants had been living from the inside out—not only loving God with all their hearts, souls, and minds but also loving their neighbors as themselves. But where had all those believers gone? There was no sign of that living, active body of Christ. How does something that starts out as a dynamic, living organism end up as a dead monument, nothing more than a tourist attraction? And if this church was no longer a living church, who was actually loving the people who lived in this neighborhood?

I have discovered that a church loses its life and effectiveness at the point it stops *being* the church that God created her to be and starts going through the motions of *doing* church. What is true for the individual Christian remains true for the corporate body of Christ. As long as a local church is actively involved in the lives of those who live in the community, it remains alive, dynamic, vibrant, and healthy. This kind of church—the kind the cathedral once was—is, at its core, what God created it to be.

MOMENT OF REFLECTION

What comes to your mind when you hear the word "church"? As you explore your own sense of being called to heal the world, how will you do that with other Christians?

October 5

Salt of the Earth

Let me tell you why you are here. You're here to be salt-seasoning that brings out the God-flavors of this earth. If you lose your saltiness, how will people taste godliness? You've lost your usefulness and will end up in the garbage.

MATTHEW 5:13 MSG

Jesus clearly states that our role as Christians on the earth is a transformational one. We are called the "salt of the earth," and salt essentially does three things: it adds flavor, preserves, and heals. So our task is to bring flavor, preservation, and healing to the world around us. This is why it is imperative that we be personally transformed from the inside out. If we have not been changed, we cannot bring out the "God-flavors" of this earth.

In the same way that salt was never designed to remain in the shaker, the church was never created to remain insular. We are called to live from the inside out both personally and corporately. God's love flows from within us out into a hurting world. The church is to be a caring, gracious, and inclusive community. Our mandate is to love others as we love ourselves; it's the only way that we can keep our "saltiness" and remain effective Christ followers.

"Salty" churches are wonderful places—actively preaching the good news; responding to human needs through loving service; transforming areas of injustice; and teaching, baptizing, and nurturing new believers. They have a revelation of why the church is here—that they serve as God's hands and feet on the earth, called to reach a lost and broken world.

Every aspect of our church experience should actually empower us to "go into all the world and preach the gospel to every creature" (Mark 16:15 NKJV). We cannot afford to simply do church on Sunday—we must *be* the church seven days a week, leaving a beautiful flavor and aftertaste wherever we go.

MOMENT OF REFLECTION

How does this concept of church change your day-to-day life?

October 6

Fishers of People

"Come, follow me," Jesus said, "and I will send you out to fish for people."

MATTHEW 4:19

Not every one of us is called to stand on a platform and preach (I can almost hear sighs of relief) or sign up for the church evangelism team, but we are *all* called to live a life that bears witness to his truth.

I love the way Jesus did not complicate his commission but made it attainable for us all. Whatever our personalities, gifts, and talents, Jesus will take them and make of us "fishers of people." The word *make* actually means "to shape, to frame, to form, to construct." In other words, Jesus will take us as we are and literally transform us. This is not a gift or a calling; it is what each of us is becoming as we continue to follow Christ. As we are transformed, becoming more Christlike, we will naturally draw other people to Jesus. Regardless of our past, disposition, or personality type, a true sign that we are followers of Christ is that we are becoming fishers of people.

Can you imagine how quickly we could fulfill Christ's mission on the earth if each of us took up the challenge to be a witness to the world? Statistics vary, but let's just assume that there are two billion Christians on earth today. If every one of us took seriously our mandate to transform our communities by being salt and light, we could achieve in one week what the greatest preaching evangelist could not possibly achieve in a lifetime. Can you see why we must stop acting like Christians and start *being* Christians? It will take each and every one of us doing our individual part in order for the church as a whole to fulfill her mandate. You count and your contribution matters. Don't devalue the vital part you play in helping share the gospel to your generation.

MOMENT OF REFLECTION

What do you think it means to be a fisher of people?
How are you uniquely called to do that?

October 7

Still Grateful

Let the peace of Christ rule in your hearts, since as members of one body you were called to peace. And be thankful.

COLOSSIANS 3:15

I clearly remember the first Sunday night I walked into our church and my breath was taken away. The warehouse was jam-packed with people praising God; I could see the passion and devotion in their faces. None of the teenagers resembled how I had approached church at their age: trying to find any excuse not to be there. I had never heard such amazing music, as I came from a church that had no time for instruments or congregational singing amid all the chanting and incense burning. I could not believe that the message preached was (1) from the Bible, (2) in a language I could actually understand, (3) made sense, and (4) could be applied to my life!

As I can never do anything halfway, I immediately signed up to become a part of a small group, to volunteer in the youth group, to attend the 6:00 a.m. prayer meeting, to be on the evangelism team —I wanted to live this life of worship to the fullest.

I was so grateful to God that such an awesome church—so full of life, vibrancy, and hope—even *existed*. Now, almost decades later, I have to say I am *still* grateful. I am grateful to God that I am saved, that he has brought an amazing husband into my life, and that he has given me awesome children, friends, church, and a purpose. Each time I get on a plane to go to a conference, I still give thanks for the opportunity to preach the gospel. I have determined that I will never take my family, friends, or church for granted.

Often the longer we walk with God, the more familiar we become with him and his Word. If we are not careful, before we know it, we are no longer grateful—and if we are not *being* Christians from the overflow of grateful hearts, *acting* like Christians is just around the corner.

MOMENT OF REFLECTION

Are you up to a challenge?
Refresh your attitude of gratitude by writing down
twenty-five things you are grateful for.

October 8

Being a Samaritan

A man was going down from Jerusalem to Jericho, when he was attacked by robbers. They stripped him of his clothes, beat him and went away, leaving him half dead.

LUKE 10:30

In the story of the Good Samaritan, Jesus goes on to say that a priest and then a Levite passed by the injured man, but did nothing to help him. Then a Samaritan man came by. Though the Jews and the Samaritans were not friendly to one another, he helped the man, bandaged his wounds, and carried him on a donkey to an inn to rest and heal. He paid for the man's care and promised to reimburse the innkeeper for any additional expenses.

So why didn't the priest or the Levite stop to help? Maybe they were thinking "but God" thoughts like these: "This is way too big for me. I'm not strong enough to lift this fellow. I can't carry him. I need to stay focused on what I already know God wants me to do."

It's understandable—right? We see a rise in teen pregnancy, but we think: "What do I know about teenagers anyway? How could I ever help them when I can't even keep up with my own responsibilities, let alone find homes or resources for teen moms and their babies?"

We see a TV commercial highlighting the plight of starving children in Africa and wonder, "What difference could I possibly make on the other side of the world? I'm just trying to keep my own kids on track!"

How often we pray for God to use us for his purpose—and then when he interrupts our lives to answer our prayer, we list all our inadequacies. I protested, "How can I alone reach twenty-seven million people victimized by human trafficking?" But all along, God was simply asking, "Will you cross the street and reach out to one?"

He does not ask us to cross the street because we actually have the capacity in and of ourselves to rescue hurting people. He asks because *he* does.

He does not ask, "Are you capable?" He asks, "Are you willing?"

MOMENT OF REFLECTION

Are you willing to stop and cross the street to help someone else today?

October 9

Interruption or Distraction?

My sheep listen to my voice; I know them, and they follow me. I give them eternal life, and they shall never perish; no one will snatch them out of my hand.

JOHN 10:27–28

It's important to know whether something is a God-interruption or a distraction from the good works we're on the road to completing. It's not always easy. But we can discern the difference more easily if we are sensitive to the Spirit of God.

Listen to what God keeps bringing to your attention, what he interrupts your thoughts and your days with. In those things, you will recognize his leading. There's no formula for confirming that when you feel such a leading, it's God's voice you're hearing. But if a need presents itself to you that you can easily do something about, then by all means do it! If the interruption is more significant—one that is potentially life-altering for you—then seek the counsel of your pastor, a spiritual leader, or a trusted friend.

You'll find that the one you are supposed to help is often along the way you're already going. God didn't stop me from being a wife, mother, or speaker in order to reach out to the victims of human trafficking; he asked whether I would allow myself to be interrupted—and then expanded my capacity and enlarged my sphere of influence.

I truly believe a direct correlation exists between our willingness to be inconvenienced (interrupted) and the degree to which God can use us to outwork his purposes on the earth. We all have more time, resources, and capacity than we think, but in order to release these, we must rearrange our priorities and disrupt our comfortable, convenient lifestyles. Perhaps we need to create more room in our lives by forsaking some leisure activities, watching less television, or spending less time socializing. We always make time for what we want to do; we tend to find the resources to purchase what we like; and we often use our gifts when we please. If we gave all of these to God to do with as he pleased, we would find that we each could serve many more people than we currently do.

Let's make room in our lives to be able to respond to God-interruptions.

MOMENT OF REFLECTION

What has God been saying to you as you pray and study his Word?

October 10

The Lord's Harvest

[Jesus] told them, "The harvest is plentiful, but the workers are few. Ask the Lord of the harvest, therefore, to send out workers into his harvest field."

LUKE 10:2

It always challenges me when I read what Jesus told his disciples about the harvest of souls. He does not say that the *Christians* are few but rather that the *laborers* are few. We can get the job done if we all choose to participate in Christ's mission instead of just sitting on the sidelines at Christian events. It is a labor to bring in the harvest—one that requires all hands on deck.

It's a common misconception that a laborer in the harvest must be one of the gifted few in the church who have been given some kind of special holy ordinance from heaven to talk to someone about Jesus. Many of us believe there are special units in God's heavenly army that are outfitted from head to toe with all the latest life-saving gadgets so that they—and only they—can swoop in with their stealth helicopters to grab the unsaved from the jaws of spiritual death. Well, sorry to disappoint, but we are all members of God's special-forces team. We are the people Jesus was talking about when he said "You are the light" and "You are the salt." He has no plan B, no designated reinforcements about to drop out of the sky.

Of course, evangelists have a place in the body of Christ. Some are called to proclaim God's truth to large crowds, but their primary task is to train and equip the rest of us to be witnesses to those we interact with every day.

We must never shy away from the proclamation of the gospel of Jesus Christ, "for it is the power of God to salvation for everyone who believes" (Romans 1:16 NKJV). And even though we know that not everyone will respond to the gospel in a positive way, we still are responsible for its proclamation.

MOMENT OF REFLECTION

How are you called to be a "laborer" in preaching the gospel?

October 11

Loosen Up

The LORD makes firm the steps of the one who delights in him.

PSALM 37:23

I always say, "Blessed are the flexible, for they shall not be snapped in two." Flexibility will enable you to keep stretching and reaching out to those who need a helping hand. That means loosening up your life enough to be ready for God-interruptions.

It's easy to book our calendars so full that we run from one activity to another, leaving only Wednesday evening Bible study and Sunday morning church as our times for meeting God. That's not what he wants. He longs to walk beside us into each moment throughout the day, loving us, leading us, guiding us—and yes, gently interrupting us. And that's what we should want too.

I'd thought God led me to Thessaloniki to speak at a conference and strengthen the church there. But he used my momentarily lost luggage and a little lost sleep to show me where he needed me next. He was interrupting not just my day but the whole direction of my ministry. He was asking me to think of how to reach the missing girls and young women on those posters on the wall in the airport. That was the seed that led to the conception of The A21 Campaign.

The ones we're asked to go to are not always across the street or around the globe. Sometimes they're right under our noses and just at our elbows. And the moment we don't think we have to give? God takes even what we may offer reluctantly at first, and he uses it, in spite of time, on what's eternal—the thing each of us wants most of all—hope.

MOMENT OF REFLECTION

How do you think you would respond if God
asked you to go way out of your way,
to take a daring risk for someone who needs your help?

October 12

A Unique Purpose

"For I know the plans I have for you," declares the LORD, "plans to prosper you and not to harm you, plans to give you hope and a future."

JEREMIAH 29:11

Okay, so let me be brutally honest with you for a second. If you haven't figured out already, I'm not exactly what you would call a domestic goddess . . . or at least not as the world defines one. Nor does my unique "all" qualify me as a worship leader (I'm completely tone deaf), a WWF wrestler (I'm pretty sure I would just die), or a WNBA player (I'm barely 5'2"). The funny thing is, for split seconds of my life, I've wanted to pursue each one of these careers, even though they are totally contrary to the way I am wired.

There is very little more frustrating than trying to force yourself into doing and becoming something you were never created for. The truth is that finding your unique God-given purpose is not really as complex as you may think. You'll find it's normally aligned with your gifts, talents, and heart's desires. Moving in the direction of these abilities and interests is like following a road map to discovering your unique life-print.

For me, I can distinctly remember a season when I was desperately trying to work out my particular purpose in life. I would talk and talk and talk and talk and talk about it . . . and then talk some more. It wasn't until one of my mentors said, "Uh, Christine, as immense a word quota as you seem to have, don't you think you're probably called to be a communicator?" I remember thinking, "What? Doesn't everyone talk this fast and furious? Isn't everyone as passionate to talk about the Word for hours upon hours?"

Slowly it became clear to me that the very things I was both passionate about and naturally gifted for were directly tied into the unique life-print with which God had created me. Did I step into the specifics immediately? Absolutely not! It was definitely a process (and still is). With each season of obedience, different aspects of my unique life-print become more defined. I think this is one of the most exciting qualities of our individual call; it's an unfolding adventure.

MOMENT OF REFLECTION

What is your unique purpose?
Are you working to understand what it might be?

October 13

Different Gifts

We have different gifts, according to the grace given to each of us.

ROMANS 12:6

If you have been struggling with uncertainty about what unique gifts you bring to the table of life, here are fifteen questions to ask yourself to help you sift through all the desires in your heart and separate the God-given dreams from the "that would be kinda cool" fantasies. Ask yourself:

1. What is it that I've been good at since an early age?
2. What do others look at me doing that would be hard for them but seems effortless to me?
3. What is it that I consistently find myself sharing about or helping others with?
4. Why do I think God created me?
5. What am I most passionate about?
6. What things enrage me, and what problems in the world do I have a passion, over and above all others, to solve?
7. What subjects could I talk about for hours and days without a loss of momentum?
8. What scriptural truths and subjects have been those that most bear witness to me and speak life to me?
9. What have been the biggest struggles I have encountered in life?
10. What have been my biggest victories and breakthroughs? Why?
11. What subjects or topics do I enjoy learning about?

12. What would I be doing if money wasn't an issue?
13. What type of people do I connect with easily or have compassion for?
14. What were my favorite subjects in high school or college?
15. What part of the globe or cultures do I have a passion for?

I believe that as you meditate upon your answers—even discuss them with strong and mature Christians around you—you will find greater clarity. Afterward, ask yourself what "next steps" you need to take in order to nurture and develop these passions and interests. Commit to a lifetime of learning and growing.

God did not give you gifts and talents so that you could bury them, but so that you would use them to bring glory to his name. Make a decision to use every last ounce of giftedness he has given you for his purpose. It will matter for all eternity.

MOMENT OF REFLECTION

Take some quality time to answer the questions above.

October 14

My "All"

If your gift is prophesying, then prophesy in accordance with your faith; if it is serving, then serve; if it is teaching, then teach; if it is to encourage, then give encouragement; if it is giving, then give generously; if it is to lead, do it diligently; if it is to show mercy, do it cheerfully.

ROMANS 12:6–8

Once we discover our unique "all," our lives become even richer and more exciting as we quickly learn that having and doing it all is not just about us; it's about helping and serving others. We begin to clearly see how our specific destiny is a God-ordained puzzle piece that fits perfectly into his strategy for reaching the lost and the hurting during this moment in time. We have the awesome responsibility of recognizing and developing our gifts because they were given to us by God to impact the world around us.

We need to ask ourselves: If I do not step up and run my race, who may not end up hearing about Jesus? Who may remain hungry? Who may remain enslaved, impoverished, or forsaken . . . or who may miss out on simply discovering that they too have a unique "all"?

Let's determine in our hearts to seek to discover our unique purpose. There's nothing more exciting than living each day having and doing all that we were perfectly designed to do, and there's no use wasting even a second of our time trying to jam our foot into someone else's glass slipper . . . we have a world to change!

MOMENT OF REFLECTION

How do you plan to pursue your unique purpose and calling?

October 15

Live by Design, Not Default

And God said, "Let there be lights in the vault of the sky to separate the day from the night, and let them serve as signs to mark sacred times, and days and years."

GENESIS 1:14

Have you ever stopped to think, "Why am I doing everything I'm doing? Is it God's plan for my life, or is it just what I think I'm supposed to do? Is my family involved in something simply because I'm afraid of what others will think of us if we're not? Is there anything I do only because it's what my mom or dad did?"

The frustration we often feel during certain seasons of life is due to the fact that we've never stopped to ask ourselves these kinds of questions. As a result, we live by default instead of by God's design.

If we live by default, then we will mechanically go through our lives feeling unsatisfied and uninspired. That is not God's plan. If we're simply doing what everyone else is doing, rarely (if ever) stopping to consider what it is God is asking us to do, we will inevitably be tempted to rush through certain seasons, or worse still, try to bypass them altogether.

When we enter every season of life understanding that it has been carefully designed by God as a vital step on our journey and part of our "all," we can then live each one with purpose and passion, whether we fully understand God's plan or not.

Sometimes God is doing a deeper work in us than it seems, maybe simply preparing us for the season that follows. In some seasons we are plowing; during others we are sowing; in still others we are watering; and sometimes we are part of the harvesting team.

Some seasons are more enjoyable than others; some more difficult; some dry and some abundant; but all are necessary. Don't despise the season you are in; instead step into all that God is doing in and through you during that season.

MOMENT OF REFLECTION

What season of life are you in currently?
In that season are you living by design or default?

October 16

One Small Part

Neither the one who plants nor the one who waters is anything, but only God, who makes things grow.

1 CORINTHIANS 3:7

My very dear friend, Lisa Bevere, wrote me the words, "One small part of a very big picture," after speaking at a women's conference. "You have sown so well and so deeply into the life of this church," she said. "I pray I watered well what you've planted so carefully." I was so overwhelmed by her words for so many reasons—especially because such a seasoned, international speaker and great mother in the faith did not need to write this to me. When she wrote these words, she wasn't simply "patting me on the back," but rather acknowledging that we are all in this together.

The more I travel and teach around the world, the more aware I am that what Nick and I do is just a small part of a much bigger eternal plan. It concerns me when I hear of people who think *they* or *their gift* is what everyone needs, or what will cause a spiritual breakthrough. When people believe they themselves are the solution, they will overstep the boundaries within which God has placed them into another's field.

We are called to *co*labor, and if God chooses to use us, then it is an honor and a privilege. We are definitely not the whole puzzle, rather just a small piece. God does not call us to compare or compete but to complement and serve one another.

It is important for any of us who serve in someone else's field to remember that whatever platform we are given actually existed before we ever arrived and will continue long after we are gone. It's the faithfulness of those who have gone before us and those who will come after us that is key. The steadfast labor of those in the trenches, day in and day out, is what produces the fruit, not the guest appearance of a gift.

Never forget that we are each a small part of a very big picture, but nonetheless a very important part without which the big picture will never be complete.

MOMENT OF REFLECTION

What part of the puzzle do you think you are?

October 17

The Next Big Thing

When pride comes, then comes disgrace, but with humility comes wisdom.

PROVERBS 11:2

It is wisdom to remember the purpose for which we have been called. Thinking we are "the next big thing" or the "only thing" is actually very arrogant and prideful, and rarely produces any fruit that will remain.

There is only *one* big thing, and that is *God*.

In order for there to be sustainable, long-term, effective ministry, we must remember that it is God who gives us our gifts and talents;

they are not for our own benefit, but to serve *his* purposes, build *his* body, and give *him* glory.

If we all faithfully do our part, then it is *God* who will give the increase. It is not about how big a crowd we draw, how many follow us on Twitter or Facebook, or what conference we are invited to speak at—it is about God's purposes being outworked on earth and his kingdom advancing.

We must remember that any strength we have is for service, not status. The fact that God would even allow us to play a part in his purpose is mind-boggling to me! It is a good thing to be confident in our gifts and calling as long as we remember that it actually has a whole lot less to do with us than we think.

Anything we have has been given to us by God and is to be used for the glory of God.

MOMENT OF REFLECTION

What gifts has God given you?
Have you looked at them in the light of his purpose?

October 18

It's All about the Dream

> *And afterward, I will pour out my Spirit on all people. Your sons and daughters will prophesy, your old men will dream dreams, your young men will see visions.*
>
> JOEL 2:28

Anyone whose life has impacted the world started with a dream. Martin Luther King Jr. had a dream that fueled an end to the segregation of African Americans. Nelson Mandela had a dream that brought an end to apartheid in South Africa. Mother Teresa had a dream that helped give dignity to thousands of India's poor and marginalized. Bill Gates, the founder of Microsoft, had a dream that continues to revolutionize the way the world communicates and does business.

When we started our youth ministry, we had a dream to reach unchurched young people in our community. We believed for funding from the government and businesses to support faith-based community projects that would instill hope, value, and a sense of purpose in every young person we came in contact with. It was this dream that kept us going when we experienced initial setbacks and times of discouragement.

The dream that fueled me at Youth Alive was to see denominational barriers come down and see ministries unite to train and develop leaders, to fill stadiums with students praising and worshiping God, and to help young people find answers in Jesus Christ. It was this dream that kept us pressing on day in and day out, even when the challenges came.

The dream that fuels us at The A21 Campaign is that we can help stop human trafficking in our lifetime. It keeps us working day and night and energizes us when challenges and disappointments come.

I have a dream that our girls will love and serve Jesus all their lives, fulfilling every part of their God-given destiny and potential. That dream motivates the decisions I make as a wife and the choices I make as a parent.

There is a real difference between a goal and a dream. With natural planning and ability, we can make a goal a reality. A dream, on the other hand, needs God's supernatural power to bring it to fulfillment.

Dreams take faith. Don't just set small goals; dream big, audacious dreams.

MOMENT OF REFLECTION

Do you have dreams for the different areas of your life or merely manageable goals?

October 19

Our Defining Moment

Mordecai had a cousin named Hadassah, whom he had brought up because she had neither father nor mother. This young woman, who was also known as Esther, had a lovely figure and was beautiful. Mordecai had taken her as his own daughter when her father and mother died.

ESTHER 2:7

Esther was a Jew who became queen of Persia after finding favor in the eyes of the king. When the king later made a decree that all the Jews in the land were to be destroyed, Esther was their only hope. She had a choice to make: reveal her true identity to the king to save her people or keep it hidden and save herself. Esther chose to put God first.

The book of Esther reveals how God gives each of us a defining moment. Every day we have the opportunity to make an eternal difference in the lives of others. It rarely looks glamorous or comes with music and fanfare. The things we do may not seem significant, or to be making a difference, but they may very well be our "time such as this."

That moment may come while we're taking someone to an appointment, counseling someone on our day off, sacrificing yet another social invitation because someone has an immediate need. If our focus is on what we could be doing instead of where we are right now, we run the risk of missing our God-given opportunity.

We must never despise what we are doing right now because we do not know the eternal consequences of the seed we sow today. That young man we pick up for church each week or the woman we seem to spend hours talking to about her challenges at home may be the next great evangelist, world leader, or business person that God is touching through our lives.

MOMENT OF REFLECTION

Who has God put in your life to minister today?

October 20

What Are You Waiting On?

Those who wait on the LORD shall renew their strength; they shall mount up with wings like eagles, they shall run and not be weary, they shall walk and not faint.

ISAIAH 40:31 NKJV

No doubt you awoke this morning, as I did, mentally rehearsing the endless list of things you have to accomplish today. It can be overwhelming and exhausting just thinking about all our responsibilities, commitments, and obligations.

But then I remembered this verse from Isaiah.

In God, we already have all the strength we need to do whatever we are meant to accomplish today. Our only requirement is to wait, trust, and rely on him and his strength. If we are willing today to be utterly dependent on God, then he will supernaturally enable us to do all he has called us to do, and we will not be weary at the end.

This puts a smile on my face. As I embark on a day of being a wife, mother, team leader, writer, visionary, and "whatever it takes" person, my only real goal is to wait on God. He is the renewer of my strength and the enabler of my responsibilities.

I am going to run forward; only to WAIT on God.

MOMENT OF REFLECTION

Who are you waiting on today? Your spouse?
Your kids? Your boss? Your staff? Your business colleague?
Your town planner? Or your God?

October 21

Choose Friends Wisely

Whoever walks with the wise becomes wise, but the companion of fools will suffer harm.

PROVERBS 13:20 ESV

Someone once said, "Show me your friends, and I'll show you your future."

It's true, we will travel the same path as our friends — so we must choose wisely. Right relationships are the key not only to success but to actually staying on track with our God-given destiny. The relationships that we nurture either detract us from our calling or launch us toward his plan for our lives. When we get caught up with the wrong crowd of people, or have a negative and draining relationship in our lives, we can easily find ourselves in places we never imagined we could end up.

Even with the right relationships, we must always remember that no one person can be everything to us. We need people who will inspire us, challenge us, motivate us, and have fun with us, and people with whom we can share our hearts, prayer requests, struggles, and dreams. And of course, in our relationships we should both give and receive.

God has created us for relationship and friends are his gift to us. Let's ensure that the relationships we are building are taking us toward our destiny and not away from it.

MOMENT OF REFLECTION

Make a list of your close friends and the people that you "do life with." Are they helping or hindering your relationship with God?

October 22

Developing Your Gifts

You will say then, "Branches were broken off so that I could be grafted in."

ROMANS 11:19

God gives each and every one of us unique gifts, and we have a responsibility to develop and exercise them. If we exercise our gifts, they will grow strong. If we do not, they will most likely remain undeveloped and less effective than they otherwise could be. We should all commit to growing the gifts that God has given us so that we can produce optimum fruit-bearing lives here on earth.

I have found that the more I develop the gifts that God has given me, the more opportunities that God gives me to use those gifts. I am committed to ongoing learning and growth, so I actively seek out people who have done more and gone further than me. I am so blessed to have Joyce Meyer as my spiritual mother who has done so much as a woman of God in the kingdom of God. Every opportunity I have, I sit and glean from this woman who helps to sharpen my gifts. We are never too old to stop learning. Even if you do not have direct access to someone such as Joyce, you can still learn from his or her books and digital recordings. There is no shortage of material that can help us to grow.

I try never to compare my gift with anyone else's because I have been uniquely equipped to do what God has called me to do. It is so important that we keep our distinctiveness and don't try to become someone else. There is enough room in the kingdom for one of everybody, so why try to be a second-rate someone else when you can be a first-rate you?

We must always remember that we need to grow to where we need to go. I did not start by speaking to crowds in stadiums or writing books or running an international ministry. I started by helping to clean the youth auditorium, picking up kids for youth meetings in my car, and speaking to people one-on-one about Jesus.

As you faithfully use what you have right where you are, then God grows what you have to take you to where you need to go.

MOMENT OF REFLECTION

What can you do to further develop the gifts God has given you?

October 23

The Second Mile

If anyone forces you to go one mile, go with them two miles.

MATTHEW 5:41

Ownership creates a "whatever it takes" attitude and a "second mile" commitment. Great churches, ministries, families, marriages, friendships, and businesses are never built in the first mile. It's the second mile where the unexpected, above-and-beyond attitude is found.

I remember going to a store ten minutes before closing time only to be told by the clerk that she was finishing early for the day and I would have to come back the next day to make my purchase. I walked away thinking that it was obvious that woman did not own that business; if it had been her store, then she would have stayed open as long as it took me to buy the item I wanted. In fact, she would have been so thrilled to have a customer that she would have gone out of her way to accommodate my request.

Because the store was not hers, she had no desire to go the extra mile; she would simply perform the bare minimum requirements to keep her job. To live a life that is based on how little you can do is to lead a little life. How often do people ask, "How little can I do and still be paid? How little can I turn up and still be a member? How little can I contribute and still be included?" If you live by minimums, you will only accomplish a minimum amount of all that you were placed on the earth to accomplish.

An abundant life is a large, expansive, generous life. The life that God has called us to live is not one that says, "How little?" but "How much? How far? How big? How wide?"

God is able to do exceedingly and abundantly above all that we can ask or think. Our eyes have not seen, nor our ears heard, nor have our minds conceived what he has for us. Let's not think in minimums but act as sons and daughters of a limitless God.

Ordinary lives are lived in the first mile; extraordinary lives only happen when we are willing to go the second mile. Don't just do what is asked; choose to go above and beyond the minimum requirements so that you can have maximum impact.

MOMENT OF REFLECTION

What would it mean for you to take ownership and "go the second mile" in what God is calling you to do? How can you serve the bigger picture?

October 24

Empowering Others

He chose capable men from all Israel and made them leaders of the people, officials over thousands, hundreds, fifties and tens.

EXODUS 18:25

One of the best ways to build a culture of growth in the church is to ensure that we are constantly empowering people to fulfill their God-given purpose. We must never allow our own fear, insecurity, pride, or laziness to keep us holding on to things we should be empowering others to do.

Multiplication happens through empowerment. We need to give people permission to grow, learn, fail, all the while continuing to support and affirm them. We must be committed to releasing the gifts in others and achieving results through others.

It takes a lot more work and effort to pour our lives into other people so that God can do his work through them, but it is so worth it. Each one of us is responsible to raise up others in whatever sphere of life we are in. Multiplication and reproduction are woven into the fabric of our being as Christ followers. From the moment we were created, God told us to be fruitful and multiply. We are not here to do everything by ourselves but to raise up others as we go about the Father's business.

Let's never be people who try to keep others back so that we can keep moving forward. The kingdom of God is not built on the same principles as the world. In our world, everything is geared toward getting ahead, looking our best, getting all the credit and accolades; but in God's economy, the way up is down and the way forward is together and not alone.

As we keep growing, we give others permission to keep growing. The journey is so much better together, and the future of the church depends on it.

MOMENT OF REFLECTION

How can you empower someone else today to reach his or her God-given purpose? Is it difficult or natural for you to encourage others in this way?

October 25

The Body of Christ

But God has put the body together, giving greater honor to the parts that lacked it, so that there should be no division in the body, but that its parts should have equal concern for each other.

1 CORINTHIANS 12:24–25

Six months after snapping my right ACL and tearing my MCL and meniscus, I became more aware than ever that when it comes to the body, "If one part suffers, every part suffers with it; if one part is honored, every part rejoices with it" (1 Corinthians 12:26).

At the start of 2010, I did not even know I had an ACL (I always felt nauseous during anatomy classes), but I can testify that during that year no one piece of my body had more attention than my knee—and in particular the ligaments that you cannot see but that are responsible for all the movement. I have firsthand encountered the truth that "those parts of the body that seem to be weaker are indispensable" (1 Corinthians 12:22).

In the same way, every single Christian person is placed in the body by God for his purposes. God does not esteem or value any part more than any other part but has set each part in place so that the *whole* will function effectively.

In our celebrity-obsessed culture, it's easy to become lulled into thinking that if people are better known, more visible, or being used in a unique way by God at a particular time, it makes them better than any other part of the body. We need to take our God-assigned place in the body and not devalue it or aspire to a more prominent place. Prominence and significance are not the same thing. The liver is not prominent in the human body, but it is extremely significant.

We should not aspire to be the biggest and the best, but rather to be all that God has called us to be and to do all that he has called us to do.

MOMENT OF REFLECTION

If the church were a physical body, what part would you be? Do you hold that part to be just as important as others — but not more important?

October 26

Growing in Leadership

Do your best to present yourself to God as one approved, a worker who does not need to be ashamed and who correctly handles the word of truth.

2 TIMOTHY 2:15

As leaders, we must constantly be sharpening our skills—learning, reading, studying—so that we become more proficient in what we do. Things that are hard when we start leading will become easier in time.

When I first started driving, my dad made me learn to drive a manual transmission. I remember sweating as I tried to work out the exact moment that I should engage the clutch and change gears. (Let's just say that for months all I did was stall!) Now, many years later, I can not only drive a manual but do a few other things at the same time. In order to learn a new skill that would eventually give me so many more options in life, I had to be prepared to start at the beginning and make many mistakes doing something uncomfortable.

The degree to which we are prepared to place ourselves in situations where we are once again a novice is the degree to which we will learn new skills as we get older. So often we do not want to trade our proficiency or comfort at one level to learn something that will take us to a new level and open new doors of opportunity.

If we are to keep growing in our leadership capacity and avoid becoming stagnant, then we need to keep taking on things with a greater degree of difficulty. The more we increase our personal capacity, the more fruitful our lives will become. We all have more room to grow. That is what keeps us young in mind and heart. That is what keeps our spirit fresh and our passion for Jesus alive.

MOMENT OF REFLECTION

As you grow in leadership and understanding your calling, what are some things you can do to stretch your abilities?

October 27

God Without the Box

Jesus looked at them and said, "With man this is impossible, but with God all things are possible."

MATTHEW 19:26

I have discovered that whatever we believe about God determines whether he is big or small in our lives. The God of the universe is ultimately made big or small in the hearts of his people.

The truth is, God is who he is independent of our perspective. He is omniscient, omnipresent, and all-powerful regardless of whether we believe this or not. However, what he is ultimately able to do in and through our lives is absolutely determined by the limitations we place upon him.

When it came to understanding God, my own early religious tradition, education, culture, and experience had shrunk him to tiny proportions. My shrunken perspective didn't actually change anything about God, but it certainly limited his ability to work on the inside of me.

Because I viewed God in a certain way, I never believed him for big things, nor did I expect that he could or would do anything with my life to further his kingdom. During those years, my God was small, my life was small, my impact was small, and my expectations were small.

I had placed God in a box and never expected him to operate outside of the perimeters of that box. My life was compartmentalized, and I reduced God to the smallest compartment, to be opened once a week for a few hours. If I was going to fulfill the plan and purpose of God for my life, then my perspective of God's nature needed a radical shift.

MOMENT OF REFLECTION

How would you describe your perspective of God?

October 28

Climbing the Mountain

With your help I can advance against a troop; with my God I can scale a wall.

PSALM 18:29

After reading a biography of Sir Edmund Hillary, the first man to climb Mount Everest, I was so inspired. He had an extraordinary way of looking at the seemingly impossible task of climbing the mountain. After one failed attempt, he said to the mountain, "You cannot get any bigger, but I can." He also said, "It is not the mountain we conquer, but ourselves." He definitely understood the principle that in order to climb mountains and overcome external obstacles, we need to get bigger on the inside. We need to enlarge our capacity and become stronger.

Once we understand that God is big and that he needs to become bigger in us, then we are then left to work out how this can happen.

It is one thing to confront the facts with the truth, but quite another to become strong enough to do this. It is one thing to know that God is big, but quite another to allow him to be big in us. In our world, we have a lot of mountains to climb and giants to defeat, but we can only do so when we rely on the big God who lives within each one of us.

I have found that when I am trying to make God bigger than a giant in my life, God ensures that I keep coming up against that giant. We must be willing to stop running from our giants and run toward them if we are finally going to overpower them. It may take several attempts, but as long as we do not give up, we will eventually emerge victorious. It is not easy, or painless, and we must be committed to the process, but when that sweet day of victory comes, it is worth all the effort.

Go and face your giant again today—and if necessary, again and again—until it no longer has power over you.

MOMENT OF REFLECTION

What mountains are you called to climb?
How can God become bigger in you
to allow you to conquer those mountains?

October 29

Whatever It Takes

For everyone born of God overcomes the world. This is the victory that has overcome the world, even our faith.

1 JOHN 5:4

When my girls were little, their favorite ride at Disneyland was "It's a Small World." As much as I loved going on this ride with them, I knew that the theme song "It's a Small World" would be stuck in my head for hours afterward.

Many people like to think it *is* a small world—and they do everything they can to keep their world small, safe, convenient, and protected. This may be a great ride at Disneyland, but it is not the ride God wants us to take through life. It is not a small world we live in but a big one. It is not a small God we serve but a big one. He does not want us to have a small sphere of impact but a big one.

Instead of trying to shrink our lives, we should be asking God to enlarge *us* so that we are able to reach and influence more people with the gospel. We were created by God to have lives that multiply and expand. We were not created to get smaller but to get bigger and have a greater impact.

We live in a big world with billions of people who still need Jesus. We are called out and then sent out into this world to bring them the light, love, hope, grace, and mercy of Jesus.

Let's show our world how great our God truly is.

Let's stop trying to live small lives and start living the big life Jesus came to give us.

MOMENT OF REFLECTION

Enlarging your circle of influence starts with prayer.
Start right now by praying that God
will give you the desire to reach more people.

October 30

Wake Up!

And do this, understanding the present time: The hour has already come for you to wake up from your slumber, because our salvation is nearer now than when we first believed. The night is nearly over; the day is almost here. So let us put aside the deeds of darkness and put on the armor of light.

ROMANS 13:11–12

As we dare to wake up to the world around us, we must make God and his purposes in our lives bigger than the temptation to stay warm in the comfort of our Christian bubble. We are not to fall asleep between the first and second coming of Christ; we are called to action. In the book of Romans, Paul instructs us on how we are to live as followers of Christ. Listen to today's Scripture from *The Message* paraphrase:

> But make sure that you don't get so absorbed and exhausted in taking care of all your day-by-day obligations that you lose track of the time and doze off, oblivious to God. The night is about over, dawn is about to break. Be up and awake to what God is doing! God is putting the finishing touches on the salvation work he began when we first believed. We can't afford to waste a minute, must not squander these precious daylight hours in frivolity and indulgence, in sleeping around and dissipation, in bickering and grabbing everything in sight. Get out of bed and get dressed! Don't loiter and linger, waiting until the very last minute. Dress yourselves in Christ, and be up and about!

Ultimately, choosing to awaken means that we have to turn the lights on so that we can dispel the world's darkness. We must be alert, responsible, and engaged in the world in the unique and creative way that God has called us to. So many of us are sleepwalking through our days, getting through our to-do lists, and not even realizing there is a bigger purpose God is outworking around us. Waking up does not mean that we all need to make a geographical shift, but to wake up in our own communities, workplaces, schools, and lives. Instead of focusing only on *our* small world, *our* needs, *our* families, and *our* friends, we need to see what God sees, feel what God feels, and hear what God hears in the cries of people everywhere.

MOMENT OF REFLECTION

Do you need to wake up to the needs around you?

October 31

Every One Matters

For I, the LORD, love justice; I hate robbery and wrongdoing.

ISAIAH 61:8

It is easy to look at an issue like human trafficking and become overwhelmed by the magnitude of the problem. After all, the reality of the situation is of epic proportions. There are an estimated twenty-seven million people who are enslaved on the earth today. This is a huge, extraordinary, and almost incomprehensible number. Could we really make a difference? Would anything we do actually matter?

Numbers have a way of numbing us. They are dehumanizing and desensitizing. It is easy to ignore suffering when it does not have a name or a face, but in my situation I could no longer walk by in ignorance. I had seen the posters; I had heard the stories; and it wasn't long before I met the victims. These numbers were no longer nameless faces; they were real people who were caught in a living nightmare. I could not ignore their suffering. They began to fill my mind, my thoughts, and were the topic of my conversations.

In my dreams I heard their screams and cries, and one night I even woke up, dripping with sweat, and yelling, "We are coming to get you!" This was not about twenty-seven million, but it was about every single one of those girls who have been trafficked. Every one of those twenty-seven million victims has a name and a face. Behind every number is a person. It is just as someone once said, "A million is just a statistic until you meet the one."

I have met the one, and another one and still another one.

There are so many more ones out there waiting for you and me.

MOMENT OF REFLECTION

When have you been so moved by an individual human story that you felt called to tackle a very large injustice?

November

SEEKING THE LOST

November 1

Search and Rescue

I will search for the lost and bring back the strays. I will bind up the injured and strengthen the weak.

EZEKIEL 34:16

It is so natural, after being rescued, to simply go back to your own life, to business-as-usual. After a harrowing experience, you yearn for normalcy. You want to—and sometimes do—forget that hopeless, horrifying moment of being forgotten in darkness. Going back there to warn others is hard work—and trying to rescue others in those perilous places sounds risky. It's true; many of us fear the lost, and because of that, we're reluctant to go out into the world to seek them.

Why would we fear the lost? Maybe because, often, they're so needy and desperate. We're afraid that they will attach themselves to us, leechlike, and beg for one thing after another: our time, our money, our emotional support, a place in our homes ("Just until I get back on my feet"), a ride to work, and on and on.

Or we might fear them because they are so "other" than us—different lifestyles and different life choices. They may have a different language and clothing styles, different food and music preferences, or a different sense of humor. Will they accept us? Will they laugh at us behind our backs? Will they despise us even as we sacrifice for them? Are they, perhaps, even a danger to us? Might they be willing to take by force those things we don't offer freely? Will we feel uncomfortable, uneasy, in their midst?

For the desperate, the hungry, the oppressed, for those in pain, no rescue can come soon enough. And when the lost call to us for rescue, God doesn't command us to be supermen. He commands us to be willing. He'll do the rest.

MOMENT OF REFLECTION

How do you feel about reaching out to the lost?
In what ways are you reaching out to the lost?

November 2

The Lost Coin

Suppose a woman has ten silver coins and loses one. Doesn't she light a lamp, sweep the house and search carefully until she finds it?

LUKE 15:8

In the story of the lost coin, the coin didn't lose itself. A woman who had ten silver coins lost one. Some people are lost not because of something they willfully did, but because of a place they fell into or circumstances beyond their control. They are lost because of the words of an insensitive teacher, the neglect of an absent parent, the malice of an abuser. Maybe they've been abducted by a trafficker who sees them not as persons but as commodities to be bought and sold to the highest bidder. Maybe a corrupt ruler has mismanaged all of his country's resources, leaving the innocent poor with no food, water, health care, education, or basic human services. In any case, the lost are people who have lost their purpose, their potential, perhaps even their destiny.

This might be a single mom whose income pays only some of the bills and is maxing out her credit cards to cover the rest of her family's necessities. Or this might be the couple working so hard at their jobs and managing their home that they're drifting apart, and the intimacy of their marriage is being lost. Or this could be the CEO who has worked his way to the top of the corporate ladder—but is experiencing dissatisfaction and malaise.

On the other hand, the *one* may be someone who has lived a life of crime or willfully hurt another. We should remember that Jesus stood up for a woman caught in adultery; a greedy, dishonest tax collector; and the thief hanging on the cross next to him. He didn't distinguish between those lost because of circumstances beyond their control and those who willfully and willingly put themselves there.

God's heart beats for every lost person every single second of every single day. That's what he wants us to remember. We too were once lost, but now we are found. And because we've been found, he has called us to be part of his search-and-rescue team.

MOMENT OF REFLECTION

Who are the lost in your neighborhood?
In your own family?
What can you do to help?

November 3

Obeying Matilda

In him we were also chosen, having been predestined according to the plan of him who works out everything in conformity with the purpose of his will.

EPHESIANS 1:11

Nick and I have a Global Positioning System (GPS) in our car, and Nick loves it. He gets in the car, types in our destination, and immediately the familiar, soothing voice tells us she is coming up with the most direct route for our trip. Nick waits until she is done and then follows her instructions obediently. She has become such a constant companion during our driving outings that we have even given her a name: Matilda. Whenever we find ourselves lost, Matilda can always show us how to get where we want to go.

Nick has a special affection for Matilda. He not only loves that he never has to stop and ask for directions, but I think he's also happy that he doesn't have to listen to me telling him my opinions on the best route (which are invariably correct, of course). I, on the other hand, often get annoyed with Matilda. She can be such a know-it-all sometimes, and there are days (although never when Nick is in the car) when I can detect a bit of condescension in her happy, velvety voice. Sometimes just to show her who's boss, I disobey her vocal navigations and pass up the turn she is insisting I make. I think it's funny to hear her start to flip out and then go silent. But after a few seconds, the ever-faithful Matilda gets over her meltdown and says, "Rerouting. Please stand by. Rerouting."

When I hear Matilda repeat the "rerouting" mantra, it reminds me of the church's core mission. In a sense, we are God's spiritual

GPS, sprinkled throughout the planet. He has placed us in our environments to help people who are lost reroute their lives. Jesus came to seek and save that which was lost, and we as his body are to continue this mission.

Just like Matilda — only hopefully in a much less annoying voice — we get to influence the people around us who have not yet chosen to believe in Jesus. By our example and through the relationships we build, we can communicate the deep love God has for them and gently steer them closer to his destination for their lives.

MOMENT OF REFLECTION

What is your mission in influencing the people around you for Jesus?

November 4

Lighting Up the World

Let your light shine before others, that they may see your good deeds and glorify your Father in heaven.

MATTHEW 5:16

Our daughter Catherine is constantly taking our emergency flashlights from the drawer and carrying them around with her. When she first discovered them, she would walk around all day with a flashlight by her side, shining it everywhere. I tried to explain to her that flashlights are really not of great use during the day. After all, how much can you illuminate a room that is already well lit? But you know how kids are — most of their fun is had in discovering new things.

I remember the first time Catie "got" how a flashlight is really supposed to be used. As Nick and I were putting her to bed one night, we turned off all the lights so that it was pitch black in her room. The look on her face was priceless when Nick turned on the flashlight and she realized how brightly it beamed in the dark. We thought this demonstration would alleviate Catherine's need to tote around the light throughout the day. However, it had the opposite effect! We had unwittingly made it a challenge for her to find the darkest places she could to light a path for all her toys.

For the next two weeks, my afternoons were spent in the dark as Catherine took my hand and guided me through the maze of furniture. Just the thought of me hurting myself in the dark deeply concerned her, as was evidenced by her shining the flashlight meticulously in every possible corner. She was so proud that her little light allowed her to bring me to a place of safety.

This is a perfect illustration of how we as Christians have the privilege to walk in his light and experience the life that is illuminated by his Word. We then have the privilege of sharing that light with the whole world.

MOMENT OF REFLECTION

In what ways are you letting your light shine before those in your immediate world—your home, community, and workplace?

November 5

Never the Same

Religion that God our Father accepts as pure and faultless is this: to look after orphans and widows in their distress and to keep oneself from being polluted by the world.

JAMES 1:27

Some years ago, an incredibly powerful visit to Auschwitz left me with an unshakeable conviction that I could not continue to sit on the sidelines. I wondered if I would have been able to persevere even unto death, as the great German Lutheran Dietrich Bonhoeffer had. I did not know. Would I have had the courage to hide Jews in my home as so many had, knowing well the incalculable dangers? Would I have been able to devise a scheme to save as many as possible, as the German businessman Oskar Schindler had done?

All I knew was that I could no longer turn my back on human suffering, on injustice, on those who cried out in pain and terror. I had to stand up and be counted. I looked to heaven and whispered a prayer, a vow: "God, help me not to close my eyes to other people's horror or ignore injustice. Help me fight the injustice you hate. Help me value people and speak up for those who have been silenced. God, you have loved, chosen, and healed me, and I want to help others be set free. If anything—anything!—like this happens in my lifetime, help me not to sit back and pretend it does not concern me."

And then I sensed God saying something directly to me: "Christine, right now, all over the world, in too many lives, something like this is happening. I am going to awaken you to things you did not know were taking place."

MOMENT OF REFLECTION

How has your heart been changed by human suffering?
In what ways can you speak up for those who have no voice?

November 6

I See You

Arise, shine, for your light has come, and the glory of the LORD rises upon you.

ISAIAH 60:1

Nick and I sat talking to fourteen young women brutalized by sex traffickers—evil men of evil intent. One of the women, Sonia, had asked a piercing question: "Why didn't you come sooner?" Realizing that excuses were trifling, I had simply asked for their forgiveness. Nothing else mattered to me at that moment but these girls, their despair—and what healing God could bring to them.

"I want you to know," I said with new conviction, "that I have now heard your cries. I have seen you. I see you now." I turned to Mary. "I *see* you, Mary. And when I see you, I see Anna." I turned to Sonia. "I see you, Sonia." I looked intently at each girl seated at the table. "I see each of you. I hear you. I know you by name. I have come for each of you."

I wanted to see these girls as Jesus saw them—not as a sea of needs, but as individuals he had called by name, chosen one by one, and loved. I heard his words before I spoke my own: "Tell them I have their names written in my book. That I came to give the good news to the poor. To heal the brokenhearted. To set the captives free. Tell them these promises are for here. Now. As well as for eternity."

"You will no longer be hidden," I told Sonia. "From now on, wherever I go, I will tell people you exist." I focused on each girl, one at a time. "I will ask them the very same question you've asked me. I will not sit back waiting, hoping, wishing, for someone else to do something. I promise you: I will *be* the someone. Now that I have found you, I will find other girls like you. I will do everything I can to stop this."

MOMENT OF REFLECTION

Will you speak up? Will you pray?
Now that you know, what will you do?

November 7

His Hands and Feet

If anyone obeys his word, love for God is truly made complete in them. This is how we know we are in him: Whoever claims to live in him must live as Jesus did.

1 JOHN 2:5–6

One Friday afternoon in the checkout line at the grocery store, I was getting frustrated that the clerk at the register, a young girl, was taking so long. I grumbled to myself, "Can't you hurry?"

God heard my unvoiced question and nudged me. "Christine," I heard him say, "that girl is scheduled to have an abortion on Monday."

I was puzzled. "God, what can I possibly do? She doesn't know me! She'll think I'm crazy if I say anything to her about it!"

But God pushed harder, this time more like a shove: "If you are my hands and feet on the earth, then do the work that I would do. Do all you can to let people know that I've not abandoned them. I will do the rest."

I looked again at the girl, scanning the items of the customer ahead of me. Suddenly I saw a girl perhaps scared inside, preoccupied with a million questions, hurting, frustrated. I prayed, waiting for God to give me the right words. Suddenly what I'd thought was an everyday shopping stop took on much greater significance.

When I got to the front of the line, I smiled at the girl as she scanned my items. I said quietly, "Excuse me. I know you might think I am crazy, but I just wanted you to know that the thing you have scheduled to do on Monday isn't the only option. There is another way. You don't have to do it."

The girl looked up at me. She began to cry.

"It's going to be okay," I told her. "Would you like to talk about it when you get off work?"

She wiped her tears. "Yes," she said. "Yes."

I asked her name.

"Katia," she said. We agreed on a place to meet, and I walked out of the store knowing that God had just wakened me to something great.

Later, after chatting with Katia, I realized God had prompted me to help save a life. He had wakened me to be his hands and feet because there are people everywhere who are hurting and dying. I never saw Katia again, but she did allow me to pray for her and give her a list of alternatives to abortion, with contact information. And I got the impression that she had definitely concluded that God was real—how else could someone speak openly to what she had been hiding? On that afternoon, Katia felt *chosen*—which totally changed the decision she was about to make.

MOMENT OF REFLECTION

Are you willing for God to use you to bring hope to others?
Are you awake to those around you?

November 8

Being Involved

At once Jesus realized that power had gone out from him. He turned around in the crowd and asked, "Who touched my clothes?"

MARK 5:30

If we are living an authentic Christian life from the inside out, we can never be ashamed of the gospel. We are living testimonies of its transforming power in our own lives, and we are passionately committed to seeing it work in the lives of others. When we truly love our neighbors as we love ourselves, we cannot help but proclaim this life-saving Word to them.

Yet in order to be able to share the gospel with our neighbors, we must be willing to stop and take notice of what is going on in their lives. Jesus always stopped and noticed what was going on around him. He brought restoration to the physically sick, emotionally damaged, and spiritually destitute. Although he was on a mission to save all humanity, he was never too busy to notice the crippled man by the pool, the woman at the well, or the woman with the hemorrhage. He was always on the way to somewhere else, but he was ever prepared to be interrupted and to get involved in the lives of individual people whose paths he crossed.

In our fast-paced modern world, we often feel that we can barely keep up with our own lives let alone take on the interruption and inconvenience of someone else's. But if we are to truly *be* Christians and not just *act* like ones, we must be prepared to love our neighbors as we love ourselves and express this through our tangible involvement in their lives.

In a world longing for authentic relationship, we need to get up close and personal with those who are hurting and lost. The church must be seen, felt, and heard in the trenches of human experience. This could include shopping for a friend or neighbor who is incapacitated, visiting the sick, taking time to listen to a coworker's personal struggles, helping someone in need, or visiting the aged in a nursing home. Yet each one of these "ordinary" good works contains within it the seed for a supernatural encounter.

MOMENT OF REFLECTION

What would you see as the difference between noticing the lives of others and intruding in the lives of others?

November 9

Carry the Light

I have come into the world as a light, so that no one who believes in me should stay in darkness.

JOHN 12:46

Light and darkness cannot coexist; whenever light encounters darkness, darkness is dispelled. In a world full of pain, confusion, and hopelessness, people are looking for healing, direction, and some semblance of hope for their future. The shining light of Christ is intended to not only guide our own path but to help those around us find a way through their darkness and point them toward the life God has waiting for them.

Light is always stronger than the darkness. We need not fear or condemn a dark world; rather we must go into that world and radiate hope, grace, mercy, love, justice, and truth. As long as the light is absent, the world will always be dark.

The light of Christ is attractive, magnetic, and transformational. But how brightly are we shining that light? Are we a flickering candle, a seventy-five-watt bulb, or a stadium spotlight? If our spiritual core is weak, broken, or fragmented, then our light is dimmed.

It will take each and every one of us to personally rise up and shine our fullest light into the darkness around us. Are you doing your part?

MOMENT OF REFLECTION

How strong is Christ's light shining through your life?

November 10

Because I Was Rescued

It is for freedom that Christ has set us free. Stand firm, then, and do not let yourselves be burdened again by a yoke of slavery.

GALATIANS 5:1

As I reflect on all that the cross and resurrection represent in my life, I am reminded of the "why" behind our commitment to seeing people rescued and their lives restored.

"It is for freedom that Christ has set us free." When I look at my own life, and the situations God has lifted me out of and rescued me from, I am filled with such gratitude and awe. I have been set free from my past, and by his grace I am able to live in the fullness of his promises.

But I am also aware of the weight and responsibility that I, being rescued, now have to live my life as a rescuer. Christ did not die on the cross for us to live safe, comfortable, self-centered lives. He died so that we would know what it is to walk in his freedom, and then to extend that freedom to those around us.

We have the opportunity to share the hope and freedom found in Christ through The A21 Campaign. Not only does this movement allow every one of us to share the "why" behind our stand against human trafficking, but it is also an opportunity to take action. Human slavery is an abomination because God created every human being to be free. No one has the right to buy or sell another person created in the image of God.

This is why I, who have been rescued, am committed to the fight to see young women set free from the clutches of sex slavery:

BECAUSE ... we serve a God of justice.
BECAUSE ... he has set the captives free.
BECAUSE ... compassion is more than a feeling, it is action.
BECAUSE ... she was worth him dying for.
BECAUSE ... ONE is too many.
BECAUSE ... I can choose what I want to do today, but she can't.
BECAUSE ... it was for freedom that Christ has set us free!

BECAUSE ... we need to protect our daughters and sisters near and far.

BECAUSE ... BECAUSE. That's enough.

Allow God to speak to you today about any areas in your life where you are not yet free. Surrender those things to him, and allow his love and grace to transform you from the inside out. Decide today to live your life to reach those who are broken, enslaved, and hurting with the message of restoration, hope, and life through Jesus Christ.

MOMENT OF REFLECTION

Why don't you go online to TheA21Campaign.org and see which one of the twenty-one things you could do today to help set a captive free?

November 11

Mrs. Jones

As a prisoner for the Lord, then, I urge you to live a life worthy of the calling you have received.

EPHESIANS 4:1

More than any words, programs, or doctrine, it's our very lives that speak the loudest. Consider the people in your life who you respect and admire most. Does your respect and admiration for them come from their words alone or from the actions they put behind them?

I remember my high school teacher, Mrs. Jones, and the impact she had on my life growing up. She was always available to listen, encourage, and go out of her way to assist us. Her positive attitude and consideration for others taught me that my actions really do matter. Mrs. Jones wasn't an amazing orator, evangelist, or pastor. She was simply a woman determined to impact as many lives as she possibly could by her encouragement, openness, and love. The most valuable lesson I learned from her was this: A person's everyday life speaks louder than one thousand sermons. The example of Mrs. Jones's life spoke volumes to every one of her students.

Just think of the Christian impact we could have if every single one of us determined to allow the example of our lives to do more "witnessing" than our mouths. Just by helping out another mom at our child's preschool, by reaching out to that neighbor who seems like an outcast, by letting someone know we are praying for him or her, or by giving a sincere compliment to an acquaintance, we can show the goodness and devotion of God. I have found that our good works, kind thoughts, and uplifting words often open the door for us to be able to share the good news.

MOMENT OF REFLECTION

What are some practical ways you can be an example for others to follow?

November 12

Prisoners of Hope

Return to your fortress, you prisoners of hope; even now I announce that I will restore twice as much to you.

ZECHARIAH 9:12

As I've mentioned, I am involved in helping to rescue, restore, and rebuild the lives of young women who have been trapped in the horror of human trafficking. We have offices all over the world and have dealt with some deeply distressing and horrific cases over the years. If our team was not full of an eternal hope, then we could easily get discouraged and give up. The problem seems too overwhelming; the disappointments are many; the statistics are stacked against us. Yet we have determined that we will remain prisoners of hope in the midst of what could be overwhelming hopelessness and focus on each *one* life that is rescued. We will not be defeated by what is *not* happening but rejoice in what *is*.

I remind our teams regularly that we must faithfully do certain things if we are to stay hopeful:

1. Stay focused on Jesus. (Hebrews 12:2)
2. Draw near to Jesus. (Hebrews 10:22)

3. Hold fast the confession of our hope. (Hebrews 10:23)
4. Stay confident in Christ. (Hebrews 10:35)
5. Pray. (James 5:16)
6. Listen to the right voices. (Romans 10:17)
7. Remember God's faithfulness thus far. (Joshua 4:7)
8. Remain steadfast. (1 Corinthians 15:58)
9. Remain generous. (Proverbs 11:24–25)
10. Be thankful. (1 Thessalonians 5:18)

If we are feeling hopeless instead of hopeful, it is possible that we have neglected to do one of these ten things. In order to be filled with hope again, it may be time to make a slight adjustment and get back in prison. There is only one type of prisoner that I want to be—and that is a prisoner of hope.

MOMENT OF REFLECTION

Meditate on the list above and assess where you are on the scale of hopeful to hopeless.

November 13

What Will Your Legacy Be?

But if serving the LORD seems undesirable to you, then choose for yourselves this day whom you will serve, whether the gods your ancestors served beyond the Euphrates, or the gods of the Amorites, in whose land you are living. But as for me and my household, we will serve the LORD.

JOSHUA 24:15

A legacy is that which a person leaves behind to be remembered by. It is more than just the memory of a person's profession, successes, or failures; it is the memory of the themes that governed that person's life.

When I think of the word *legacy*, I envision a mailroom filled with packages all addressed to different people. Each one of these packages contains the sum of someone's life. Some packages are filled with faith, forgiveness, hope, love, compassion, and generosity. Others contain such things as anger, greed, racism, bitterness, and rejection. Then there are those packages that contain a little of both. Regardless, every single package has a destination, and more importantly a life that will soon open it and be affected by whatever is inside.

The reality is that every single one of us will leave behind some sort of legacy when we are gone, whether it's at the end of a season or our life as a whole. We can consciously choose to leave a specific kind of legacy or we can let it happen by default. Quality legacies are the result of determined doing.

I believe the quality of the legacy we leave for the next generation is directly determined by how big we really believe God is. If we choose to live a life that extends beyond just ourselves and beyond today, then we are showing a generation there is Someone big and grand who is worth living and giving our lives for. They are watching and learning from us. This is why it is so crucial that we do not grow weary in doing good, stop running our race, or drop the baton.

Our lives are not only about us but also about those who are coming after us. What type of legacy do you want to leave?

MOMENT OF REFLECTION

If you were to die today,
what would your legacy be?

November 14

Dispelling the Darkness

Truly I tell you, whatever you did for one of the least of these brothers and sisters of mine, you did for me.

MATTHEW 25:40

We have to do whatever it takes to turn on the lights and dispel the darkness that plagues the world we live in. Time is ticking away and there is no more grace to press the snooze button again. We must awaken from our slumber. We cannot sleep through one in five human beings suffering, often with wounds created by our lack of attention and indifference. These are people who, like us, have been created in the image of God and are not somehow lesser or secondary.

We, the church, have a responsibility to bring the light, life, hope, and help of Jesus to all people. In the same way Jesus received us, so must we receive them. Genuine love and compassion is the only thing that can ultimately dispel the darkness that surrounds them.

As I reflect on today's Scripture, I am sobered by the thought that Jesus said whatever we do for "the least of these," we actually have done for him. This shows me that when we reach out to the poor, the marginalized, the prisoners, and the broken, we are not being like Jesus to them: *they are like Jesus to us.* That is a very powerful revelation. If we understood the implications of this, we would far more readily respond to the needs of others around us. We have the opportunity to touch Jesus in those we have the privilege to serve. Don't miss such a sacred moment.

MOMENT OF REFLECTION

How can you start reaching out to the poor, broken, and marginalized in your community?

November 15

Rescue Comes

For the Son of Man came to seek and to save the lost.

LUKE 19:10

One of my companions, Kylie, jolted me. "Do you hear that?" she whispered, breathless.

"What?" Paul asked.

I listened.

All I heard was Kylie rustling, trying to stand. "She's delirious," I thought.

Then I felt a slight vibration, a tremor in the trees, on the ground, followed by the sound of a steady, beating whir. I rubbed my ears.

The sound didn't go away. In fact, it was getting louder. I felt a force of air and opened one eye.

Kylie, Sally, Mick, Paul, and I had been lost in the Australian Daintree Rainforest for more than twenty-four hours and we had all but given up hope of rescue.

But now, Kylie and Paul were standing, waving madly at the sky, shouting, "Here! We're here!" Their shouts and an even stronger rush of air made me sit up and look around to see—a helicopter. Mick had gone for help and we wondered if we would ever see him again. But there he was leaning out from the side of the rescue chopper as it hovered just above us.

I jumped up and ran to the cliff's edge. I will never forget standing there on that precipice, yelling, "We're saved! We're saved! We're saved!" Overjoyed and relieved and incredulously happy, I wanted to hop up and down. Instead, I froze.

It wasn't just the sharp drop over the cliff's edge or my sore feet and aching limbs that stopped me. It was the words. As clearly as I have ever heard the voice of God, I heard him that day: "Yes, Christine, you are saved. Remember what it is to be saved. Remember what it was to be lost. Remember the darkness and the difference between feeling carefree one morning and by evening sad and scared and sorry for being careless. Remember that I am here. Remember that I want to save every soul. And remember what it is to be unable on your own ability to get out of the dark."

This was a defining moment for me. God allowed me and some friends to be lost overnight and then rescued by a helicopter so that I could once again feel the reality of what it was to be lost and then found. It is crucial that we regularly remind ourselves that the same God who rescued us then sent us into the world to help find and rescue others. We are God's search-and-rescue team.

MOMENT OF REFLECTION

Can you remember what it was like
to be lost and then found?

November 16

Seek and Save

Suppose one of you has a hundred sheep and loses one of them. Doesn't he leave the ninety-nine in the open country and go after the lost sheep until he finds it?

LUKE 15:4

In Luke 15, Jesus reveals to us the principle that when we have lost something of great value, we'll stop at nothing to find it. When the shepherd loses one sheep, Jesus tells us, he will leave all the others who are safe in the fold to search for the one that is lost. This man lives from the inside out—he leaves the ninety-nine sheep on the inside because he realizes the one that is outside the safety of the herd is in harm's way.

He also knows that sheep do not get lost on purpose. The one lost sheep may have simply found a ridge with some super-tasty grass. Similarly, people do not get lost on purpose. Often they simply get caught up in the turmoil of day-to-day life—just trying to survive, pay the bills, raise their kids. We need to be like the shepherd, willing to do whatever it takes to find those lost sheep.

When we seek out that which is lost, we are loving our neighbors as we love ourselves and valuing people as God values them. We will be so occupied and fulfilled with doing what the church was placed on this earth to do—taking what is inside the church out into a broken world—that our doors will never close.

Instead of judging the lost, blogging about the lost, talking about the lost, blaming the lost, avoiding the lost, or ignoring the lost, Jesus shows us that it is our job to do whatever it takes to *find* the lost. We have a world so preoccupied with trying to survive, they do not even know that without Christ they are dead. They think surviving is somehow living, but abundant life can only be found in and through a relationship with Jesus Christ.

Jesus did not come to make bad people good; he came to make dead people alive. Let's go out and find the lost sheep and show them that because Jesus is alive, they too can live.

MOMENT OF REFLECTION

Do you remember what it was like to be so preoccupied with just trying to survive that you were not even looking for what you never knew existed — abundant life?

November 17

Awakened to Love

Multitudes who sleep in the dust of the earth will awake: some to everlasting life, others to shame and everlasting contempt. Those who are wise will shine like the brightness of the heavens, and those who lead many to righteousness, like the stars for ever and ever.

DANIEL 12:2 – 3

When you decide enough is enough — that the darkness of this world must be lit with the hope of Christ and his transforming love, and that you are a conduit of that love — you will not rest.

Once God opened my eyes to the horrors in this world, my restlessness grew. The horrors were not in another time or place, but next door, along my streets, in my community, and wherever I traveled.

And so many of them could so easily have been mine. My life might not have turned out as it has. I too had once been trapped. I too had once been unloved, forgotten, and broken. What if I'd remained in that dark place? What if, as number 2508 of 1966, I'd been born in Moldova or Bulgaria or Romania and left in an orphanage instead of a hospital in Sydney, Australia? What if I'd never been adopted by loving, kind, generous parents? What if those who took me home from the hospital were traffickers? What if my abuse had never stopped, if I could not have escaped it?

Every day has been a deeper awakening to this truth. God has shaken me alert to the suffering in this world, the imprisonment of people who languish. Sometimes the bars are visible. More often, they're not. What I know for sure is that for all its goodness, all its beauty, this world is too dark for us to be content to slumber. Every dawn is a reminder that we have a new day, another chance to make a difference. Every sunset is a reminder that there is one less day left for me to make a difference.

MOMENT OF REFLECTION

Have you been awakened to love the lost?
How will that manifest itself in your life?

November 18

Living Like We Truly Believe

For the word of the LORD is right and true; he is faithful in all he does.

PSALM 33:4

John Stuart Mill said, "Christians seem to have the amazing ability to say the most wonderful things without actually believing them . . ." I have not been able to get this thought out of my mind.

Just think of the amazing claims we make about the power of the cross of Jesus Christ, the power of the gospel to transform lives, communities, and nations. Imagine if we lived radical lives of faith that were in alignment with what we profess to believe.

Imagine the conversations we would have that we do not;
Imagine the acts of kindness we would do that we do not;
Imagine the inconveniences that we would endure that we do not;
Imagine the places we would go that we do not;
Imagine the money that we would give that we do not;
Imagine the serving that we would do that we do not;
Imagine the forgiveness we would extend that we do not;
Imagine the words of affirmation we would give that we do not;
Imagine the prayers that we would pray that we do not;
Imagine the offenses we would forgo that we do not;
Imagine the people that would be reached that are not;
Just for today . . . imagine.

Today why not choose no longer to imagine but rather to live every moment of every day, every conversation, interaction, and exchange like we really BELIEVE what we profess to believe? It would radically alter our lives and the world we are called to reach.

MOMENT OF REFLECTION

Time to be honest. Have you ever sung the words of a worship song, nodded approval to a sermon, or witnessed to someone about God's power, but the truth of those words have not yet become part of your own belief system?

November 19

Precisely the Right Place

Sow your seed in the morning, and at evening let your hands not be idle, for you do not know which will succeed, whether this or that, or whether both will do equally well.

ECCLESIASTES 11:6

Pastors Dimitri and Maria had been shepherding their small flock of believers in Thessaloniki, Greece for over twenty years. During that time they experienced numerous challenges and hardships, including the loss of their fourteen-year-old son, Peter, to cancer. They had many big dreams for their son, church, and nation, but everything looked hopeless.

You see, Greece is a very difficult mission field. It is a nation steeped in tradition and religion, and there is very little light shining in the midst of darkness. In the twenty years their church had been ministering in Greece, they had never been able to grow to a hundred members. In one way it seemed like the ground they were plowing was completely fallow and infertile, but in spite of this, they remained faithful and full of belief.

As it turns out, one day they would see that God had a much bigger purpose in store for them and their church. They were not only pastors, but lawyers, and for years could not work out why they had both a legal practice and were pastoring a church. They did not know that in the future God would require both of these facets of their lives to launch them into their destiny.

When we started The A21 Campaign in Greece we needed to assemble a legal team, and guess who we found to be in precisely the right place?

Literally overnight these pastors went from wandering on the backside of the desert to being on the front lines of the fight against human trafficking. If they had left their seemingly insignificant place, they would not have heard God calling them to the next place. He wanted to use them to help bring justice to a nation, and they are now a vital link in the chain of our campaign.

MOMENT OF REFLECTION

What past experiences have you had that seemed insignificant at the time but were later used by God for something important?

November 20

Welcome Home

While he was still a long way off, his father saw him and was filled with compassion for him; he ran to his son, threw his arms around him and kissed him.

LUKE 15:20

In the parable of the prodigal son, the younger of two sons asks for his share of his father's estate and soon after leaves for a distant country where he squanders his wealth in wild living. Finally, brought low, he returns home hoping his father will allow him to hire on as a servant. Instead, his father receives him back wholeheartedly. This does not sit well with the wayward son's older brother, who is angry and refuses to attend the "welcome home" celebration. In response, the father speaks to his older son about the younger: "We had to celebrate and be glad, because this brother of yours was dead and is alive again; he was lost and is found."

Because of his immaturity and selfishness, the prodigal son made a very bad miscalculation. He thought that a life outside of his father's house and without the father would be better than a life within the house with his father. He was proven to be tragically wrong, and he knew it. And so he headed home.

Despite the fact that the young man had brought great pain to his loved ones, his father did not condemn, reject, or ignore him. On the contrary, at the first sight of his son, he ran to embrace him! When a lost person comes home to be reconciled with Jesus, we the church must always have a "Welcome Home" sign ready, the doors wide open, and the table prepared with the finest feast. Let's love and never reject the prodigals.

MOMENT OF REFLECTION

In this story of how the lost becomes found, do you relate more to the wayward son or his older brother? Why?

November 21

Why? Why? Why?

We proclaim to you what we have seen and heard, so that you also may have fellowship with us. And our fellowship is with the Father and with his Son, Jesus Christ.

1 JOHN 1:3

Don't you hate it when you look in the mirror and you notice a huge piece of spinach between your teeth—and you ate that spinach at lunch *five hours ago*? You begin to mentally retrace your steps over the last few hours, and you think of all the people you know must have seen the garish thing and didn't say a word! The client with whom you were trying to close the deal, your boss, your coworker in the adjacent cubicle ... You suddenly realize that the guy at the espresso stand was not smiling at you because he thought you were cute; he was giggling about the head of spinach lodged between your teeth. "Why didn't anyone tell me about that?!" you wonder.

Carrying spinach around in your teeth isn't necessarily life-threatening (unless you are single), and the result of this lack of etiquette is usually nothing more than a few moments of embarrassment. But what if you were walking with a friend, not paying attention to where you were going, both laughing about the movie you just saw, and—*BAM!*—you walked straight into a pole! Your friend had delicately walked around it but had failed to point it out to you. As soon as you pick yourself up off the side of the road, first thing you would say is, "Why didn't you warn me about that?!"

Let's take it up a notch. You and a friend are at the playground with your children. One of your own children needs your attention, so you kindly ask your friend to watch your eldest child. As she is "watching" little Johnny, he wanders out into the street to pick up a penny. From across the park, you look up to see a truck flying down the street in the direction of your son. As you sprint to save him, I am sure one of your thoughts is, "Why didn't she do something about that?!"

There is a lost, broken, and hurting world all around us, and we have the answer in Jesus. If we, the church, don't speak up and do something about it, then who will? People's eternities are at stake.

MOMENT OF REFLECTION

Why is it important to preach the gospel?
What will happen if we don't?

November 22

Reaching the Lost

He said to them, "Go into all the world and preach the gospel to all creation."

MARK 16:15

If in fact 90 percent of all decisions for Christ are made before the age of twenty-five, then young people should be our primary target for evangelism in the world. Once we have trained up our own children in the Lord, we must teach them to reach out to the vast mission field ripe for harvest in our own backyards, our own communities.

It's our job as Christians to encourage our young people to build authentic and meaningful relationships with their unsaved friends at school, on sports teams, and at their jobs, with the intention of sharing the gospel. But reaching out doesn't always come naturally.

Our young people must be taught how to live a daily life of mission—and we do that by living that life before them. If we are simply telling young people to win their friends to Christ, we are not giving them what they need to be successful. But if we are regularly sharing with them that we have been witnessing or intentionally building friendships with unsaved people, they will then be able to understand the significant nature of evangelism.

Our reaction to a lost and broken humanity will be directly translated in the way our young people view the unsaved. If we make Christ's final command our first priority, our young people are likely to make it a priority in their lives as well.

I believe there is nothing that will keep a young person on fire for God like winning people to Christ. And by reaching out, they affirm their own importance to God. If we keep our young people fully engaged in the mission of God, then they will have much less time to become engaged in the activities of the world. I have found that most young people don't necessarily want to reject Jesus but are bored with religion and trying to "be good." If we inspire them to be about the Father's business, they are much less likely to get caught up in the wrong business.

Teaching our children to be soul winners is a responsibility—but more than that, it is a privilege.

MOMENT OF REFLECTION

In what ways are you modeling a daily life of mission before the young people in your life?

November 23

A Certain Danger

As you sent me into the world, I have sent them into the world. For them I sanctify myself, that they too may be truly sanctified.

JOHN 17:18–19

There is a certain danger that can increase when we have been involved in church life for a long time. Sometimes we get so involved with our Christian friends and Christian activities that we let go of our relationships with lost people and lose sight of the issues that affect them.

If we are going to reach the lost, we must consciously choose to stay connected to unchurched people. In the same way that you cannot impact a world that you are not in, you cannot influence people with whom you have no relationship. If we spend our time on earth avoiding the unchurched, then we are highly unlikely to see them in heaven. This is the only chance we will ever have to go into all the world.

If we get all caught up in church with no avenue for outreach, we are missing the point and will in fact implode. It is important that we are fully engaged in church life, but we need to remember that church is the place where we go to be trained and equipped to do what God has called us to do. It is where we gather so that we are strengthened for service when we scatter.

As Christians, we should always see the bigger picture—the one that includes those who do not know the Lord and need to hear about him from those who do. Our mission is to go out into the harvest and reach the world for Christ. This mission of God is far too important to leave to the missionaries alone. It requires all of us to be witnesses.

MOMENT OF REFLECTION

How many relationships do you have
with those who are not professing Christians?

November 24

A Divine Recalibration

Learn to do right; seek justice. Defend the oppressed. Take up the cause of the fatherless; plead the case of the widow.

ISAIAH 1:17

Christians in general are getting back to basics. We are sick of endless activity that is taking us nowhere and endless sermons that are not bringing change. We want our first love, first passion, and first priority back. We are simplifying, reordering, restructuring, repenting, and going back to our first works. The book of Isaiah refers to these sorts of endless and meaningless activities when it says:

> Quit your worship charades. I can't stand your trivial religious games: Monthly conferences, weekly Sabbaths, special meetings — meetings, meetings, meetings — I can't stand one more! Meetings for this, meetings for that. I hate them! You've worn me out! I'm sick of your religion, religion, religion, while you go right on sinning. When you put on your next prayer-performance, I'll be looking the other way. No matter how long or loud or often you pray, I'll not be listening. And do you know why? Because you've been tearing people to pieces, and your hands are bloody. Go home and wash up. Clean up your act. Sweep your lives clean of your evildoings so I don't have to look at them any longer. Say no to wrong. Learn to do good. Work for justice. Help the down-and-out. Stand up for the homeless. Go to bat for the defenseless. (Isaiah 1:13 – 17 MSG)

Those works that we are returning to are the works of the early church in the book of Acts: a church that was full of love, sold everything, helped anyone who had need, and shared the gospel. It was a church that "turned their world upside down."

People are no longer content to *play* church; they want to *be* the church. We want our lives to count for something, to be committed to a cause and not a religion. We want to see a big God who can bring transformation and change by using ordinary people to do extraordinary things. That's what I want and I believe that's what you want.

MOMENT OF REFLECTION

Are you yearning to see God do more in and through your life?

November 25

Wholeheartedly Following

Love the LORD your God with all your heart and with all your soul and with all your strength.

DEUTERONOMY 6:5

If you plow while looking over your shoulder, then your rows will become crooked and your fields will become difficult to harvest. Ploughmen are meant to fix their eyes on a point that lies near the end of the field, and steadily move toward it, not looking to the right or the left. In the same way we must fix our eyes on Jesus, the author and finisher of our faith, and let nothing stop us from wholeheartedly following him. It is about the priority of our love and commitment to him over any other love and affection.

It is crucial to regularly ask ourselves, "What is God asking me to do right now?" Each time we respond with "Yes, Lord, but first," we are really pulling the spiritual covers over our heads, pressing the snooze button, and going back to sleep. Consequently, this makes our big God very small in our own world, and his ability to work through us is limited.

But there is a world that is crying out for the church to arise, and in order for this to happen, we must all take our place in the body of Christ and be fully awake. It is through seeking God, trusting him, making him first in our lives, and walking in obedience that we are awakened and able to be a part of all he is doing on the earth.

Once we have decided to follow Jesus, we must make sure that there is no turning back. We are all in; and whatever happens to us, around us, or within us, we will continue to unflinchingly follow our Savior wherever he leads.

MOMENT OF REFLECTION

Is your hand still on the plow, or have you found yourself glancing backward recently?

November 26

To Do the Will of Him Who Sent Me

"My food," said Jesus, "is to do the will of him who sent me and to finish his work. Don't you have a saying, 'It's still four months until harvest'? I tell you, open your eyes and look at the fields! They are ripe for harvest."

JOHN 4:34–35

It is all an issue of our priorities. Many of the conflicts that we have, anxieties that we experience, and overwhelming feelings we encounter are because we have compartmentalized our lives; we fit Jesus in rather than putting him first. If we keep the divine order right, then we automatically have time and space for everything else we are called to steward and do in life.

We often experience guilt and frustration when we see the needs of the world around us because we do not know how we can fit anything else into our already very full lives. How can we help anyone else, hear their cries, or respond to their needs when we are so consumed with ourselves that there is no room for anything or anyone else?

We need to reorder, recalibrate, repent, and return to our first love. It is all an issue of what is first in our lives. When we make God our dominant priority, then our desire becomes to seek first his kingdom and his desires for the hurting world around us. When we shift our priorities and our focus, subsequently our actions shift as well. As we seek his kingdom first, he then adds whatever we need. He does not forget our needs, deny them, or ignore them. He provides for each and every one. The key to his provision is to put him first.

The amazing truth is that we never come second by putting God first. Let's be Jesus people who are sustained, nourished, filled, and fed by doing the will of the Father.

MOMENT OF REFLECTION

Do you find yourself trying to put everything in logical order before finally submitting to the will of God, or do you trust him to work it all out if you simply put him first?

November 27

Not Someday When

He has shown you, O mortal, what is good. And what does the LORD require of you? To act justly and to love mercy and to walk humbly with your God.

MICAH 6:8

When we were challenged to begin The A21 Campaign, I could think of so many reasons why it was not a convenient time to start rescuing the victims of human trafficking. We had geographical issues, a young family, financial concerns, and an already more-than-full life. I could have said, "Jesus, I will do this when my children grow up, when we are more established, or when my speaking engagements ease up." But he was asking us to begin then, not someday when.

As I was mentally listing all the reasons why I could not do this, I remembered a trip to Poland I had made earlier that year where I visited Auschwitz—the German concentration and extermination camp. As I walked around the dark, eerie, deserted buildings where over one million people died, I was inconsolable. Nothing had ever moved me so much as I thought about the terror, torture, pain, starvation, disease, executions, medical experiments, and gassings they had been forced to endure. I spent hours walking, thinking, crying, praying, and wondering what I would have done if I had been alive during the war. Would I have dared to be a voice for those who were oppressed? Would I have tried to stop this injustice? Or like so many others, would I have slept through this horror, pretending it was not happening?

I had made the commitment that if anything like this was to ever happen in my lifetime I would not be silent; I would do all that was in my power to stand up for justice. I would not sleep through a holocaust. I did not know that shortly afterward I would be confronted by the injustice of human trafficking. I now had the opportunity to play my part and do something to make a difference, and could not simply walk away because it was dangerous, difficult, and inconvenient. I had to make the choice to rearrange my life, recalibrate my priorities and schedule, and embark on a path I had never planned to walk down.

I am so grateful I said yes. There is no doubt that what we do involves great risk, much heartache, and discomfort, but the rewards are immeasurable. At least when you feel the pain, you know you are awake and alive. In order to do what we are called to do, we have had to miss family and friends' weddings, funerals, birthdays, and parties. We have had to sacrifice our time, energy, sleep, and so many other things in order to take hold of all that God has called us to.

Even though the journey has been challenging, it has been completely worth it because we have seen so many miracles, and lives rescued and restored. We know we are doing what we are called to do. If I could go back, there's not much that I would change, except this: I would have gone even sooner.

MOMENT OF REFLECTION

What is Jesus asking you to do right now?
Who are the lost people he's called you to save?

November 28

God So Loved the World

For God so loved the world that he gave his one and only Son, that whoever believes in him shall not perish but have eternal life.

JOHN 3:16

The world is too dark for the church to remain sleeping. The sobering truth is that it's our *responsibility* as Christians to be light bearers in this world. When we walk in the light, then others are brought to the light. As long as we, the church, remain asleep, we will never be able to take the light that is in us and penetrate the dark world around us. As a result, so many people will continue to wander in darkness. We of all people ought not to be sleeping through the alarm clock. Time is literally ticking away and we have a mission to fulfill.

Each time we are sidetracked, distracted, apathetic, or indifferent, we are pressing the snooze button and allowing the world to linger in darkness longer. Every single day brings opportunities and opens doors for us to walk in the light with holy living, acts of kindness, words of life—extending love, grace, mercy, truth, and justice. It is only when we are awake that we can see well enough to help others awaken from their deathly slumber.

If we, the church, keep pressing the snooze button, we will sleep through the very reason we were sent into the world. If I sound urgent, it is because I am. We literally do not have the luxury to keep pressing a button that does not exist on the eternal time clock. Time is running out. This is our moment to do what we have been commissioned to do, so let's all go into of our various parts of the world and do what Jesus told us to do.

Remember ... God so loved *the world.*

MOMENT OF REFLECTION

What can you do to build relationships with people who do not know Jesus?

November 29

The Sleepwalking Church

You are all children of the light and children of the day. We do not belong to the night or to the darkness. So then, let us not be like others, who are asleep, but let us be awake and sober.

1 THESSALONIANS 5:5–6

I have often been woken up in the night only to see Catherine sleepwalking or hear her sleeptalking. In fact, I have had many lengthy conversations with her in the middle of the night of which she had no recollection of in the morning. I have heard her ramble in her sleep, making absolutely no sense. I have stopped her from walking out the front door or trying to go back to bed in the refrigerator.

Most of these incidents have been harmless and often very funny, but through them I have noticed that when someone sleeptalks they say a lot, but really say nothing; they walk a lot, but really go nowhere. Most of the time they simply end up back in their bed asleep.

For a long time, we the church have heard a lot of talking and have done a lot of activity, but we have not necessarily been saying anything or going anywhere. We end up back in the comfort of our Christian subculture, pull up our spiritual blankets, and go back to sleep until the next week. We like our warm, comfortable sermons, conferences, activities, and lifestyles, but we are going nowhere and saying nothing.

It is time to wake up, start saying things that make sense, and start walking into the darkness with the light of Christ. It is time to be up and about.

God is waiting for his church to get out of bed and to start being involved in what he is already doing in the world. Humanity is waiting, and justice and compassion are the languages they understand.

Let's roll up our sleeves and jump into the trenches of life, helping to pull people out of darkness into light.

MOMENT OF REFLECTION

In what ways are you sleepwalking or standing on the sidelines? How can you help others?

November 30

With God All Things Are Possible

Do you not know? Have you not heard? The LORD is the everlasting God, the Creator of the ends of the earth. He will not grow tired or weary.

ISAIAH 40:28

In my own life, I have been rescued from a seemingly hopeless situation of abuse and pain. I believe that because Jesus stepped into my life and brought healing to me, I now have a responsibility to see that others who are suffering in the world are rescued. I have not been set free to merely indulge in my own life but to use my life to set at liberty those who are oppressed.

We began The A21 Campaign for the one, and have since seen the one rescued and restored, and then that one reaching out to the next one, who was also enslaved. I believe that we will only continue to see more girls rescued; and that their lives will be a testimony to the truth that God is a redeemer, restorer, and rebuilder of destinies, hopes, and dreams. It is my prayer that these girls will not only fulfill all that God has for their futures, but that they will actually reach out to others who are enslaved and help them to find freedom and hope in Christ as well.

If every one of us who has been rescued took on the responsibility of reaching out to one other still waiting to be rescued, then we could potentially fulfill the Great Commission in less than a week. Jesus did not give us an impossible mission to fulfill; it is entirely possible if each one took responsibility for one.

MOMENT OF REFLECTION

Who is one person that you are actively believing God to see saved?

December

HEALING THE WORLD

December 1

His Witnesses

In your hearts revere Christ as Lord. Always be prepared to give an answer to everyone who asks you to give the reason for the hope that you have.

1 PETER 3:15

We often pray that God would use us to help change the world, yet we simultaneously underestimate the opportunities that await us in our everyday lives. All of us are in this world (after all, we don't live on Mars), and that means that we have the potential to transform our world one life at a time simply by choosing to *be* Christians in the course of our everyday routine.

When my husband, Nick, was working in the banking industry, his corporate life was very busy, and he spent much of his time extremely frustrated because he wanted to be "doing more for God." Then one day an encounter with a colleague made Nick realize that his workplace *was* his mission field.

One of Nick's coworkers, John, a former professional athlete, was now one of the most successful salesmen in the firm. However, he had recently broken up with his longtime girlfriend, and his personal life was in shambles. One day, he approached Nick and said, "How do you do it?" At first, Nick wasn't sure what John meant because, although Nick was also doing well, he was still one of the newer reps. "What do you mean?" Nick asked. "Your life. I mean, you've been here six months, and I've never heard you say one negative thing about anyone. When you talk about your wife, it's clear that you actually love and respect her, and I've never seen you so much as glance at another woman! At our office parties, you never get drunk or out of control. I've never heard you stretch the truth when dealing with a client's finances, and your commissions are still high! How is that? Everyone here loves you and considers you trustworthy; you're always happy; and you've become the go-to guy for anyone here who needs advice. What makes you so different?"

ust how much of an impact he *was* mak-
ian in his workplace.

MOMENT OF REFLECTION

Do you see your workplace as your mission field?
How does that work in your particular life?

December 2

Pure Religion

And if anyone gives even a cup of cold water to one of these little ones who is my disciple, truly I tell you, that person will certainly not lose their reward.

MATTHEW 10:42

Not long ago, we decided to take Catherine on a trip to South Africa with us. We thought that it would be good for her to see how 70 percent of the world's children live and to learn to appreciate just how truly blessed we are as a family.

As we were driving through one of the townships, I could see Catherine's confusion as she saw the children living on the side of the road. She was glued to the window of the car, studying every person we passed. "Mummy, why are those girls sleeping on the ground? And how come that boy's shirt is so dirty and ripped?"

Before I could answer her, she then said, "That girl over there looks very sad. Can we stop and give her one of my dollies to play with?" When she later found out that these children didn't go to school, she said, "I have an idea! Let's just buy them all school uniforms so that they can go to class!"

As I listened to Catherine's questions, I was reminded of the purity, innocence, and simplicity with which children process situations. The solution was so simple to Catherine that day—and you know what? In many ways, it *can* be this simple. Imagine what the world would look like if we all considered it our personal responsibility to make a difference in our corner of it.

Nick and I are committed to ensuring that our daughters do not grow up oblivious to the needs of the people in their world, even beyond their immediate sphere of influence. We want them to know that they are blessed by God to be a blessing to others.

Instead of being daunted by the immense need on the planet, we are determined to be part of the solution by helping to change the world, one life at a time. We cannot do everything to alleviate all the pain and injustice on the earth, but we must each do something.

MOMENT OF REFLECTION

What can you do to make yourself more aware of the needs of the people who live on the other side of the world? What about those who live nearby?

December 3

Good Works

What good is it, my brothers and sisters, if someone claims to have faith but has no deeds? Can such faith save them?

JAMES 2:14

It is easy to become overwhelmed with all the needs in the world—and to think that our small contribution will not make any real difference. The thing that we must understand is that we are only responsible for the good works that God has called *us* to do. We cannot do everything, but we can each do one thing. We do not need to assume responsibility for anybody else's good works but simply do what we are supposed to do.

If we all did this, I believe we would fulfill Christ's mission on the earth. We must begin to value our seemingly mundane lives and routines, understanding that each day God has opportunities waiting for us to meet the needs of others.

No matter where we live, we are all surrounded by people who need to know the practical love of God. We cannot just sit back and pray and hope that *somebody else* does something. James teaches us that faith without works is dead. If we are to perpetuate a Christianity that truly changes our world, our faith must be accompanied by good works.

Don't forget that we are often the answer to our own prayers. We are waiting for God to do what he has already equipped and empowered us to do. We just might be the someone that somebody is waiting for.

MOMENT OF REFLECTION

What motivates you to reach out to someone in need?
Which do you think is easier to reach out to —
someone you know or a stranger?

December 4

Being a Witness

Then Pilate said, "So, are you a king or not?" Jesus answered, "You tell me. Because I am King, I was born and entered the world so that I could witness to the truth. Everyone who cares for truth, who has any feeling for the truth, recognizes my voice."

JOHN 18:37 MSG

Being a witness is not a program; it's a lifestyle. God has given us the power to be a witness in our seemingly insignificant day-to-day lives. At the kids' school, at moms group, at the grocery store, at the gas station, at the sports club, at the office, there are endless opportunities to bear witness to his truth. We show our "neighbor" what authentic Christianity looks like in a practical way when we live lives that are flourishing and that demonstrate the claims of Christ actually work where the rubber hits the road.

When Jesus was speaking to Pilate, he said that he came to earth to *bear witness* to the truth, and his words have profound implications for each and every one of us. Jesus did not come only to proclaim the truth (which is imperative) but also to ensure that every aspect of his life was bearing witness to that truth.

Similarly, our lives ought to be bearing witness to the truth of God's Word: in our relationships, our lifestyles, our habits, our spending priorities, the moral choices we make, our values and dreams. If we fail to live according to the Word we preach, then we will have little or no impact on the world around us.

Our friends do not want to be exposed to a series of religious rules or rituals; they want to see that this faith-life works. Then they will believe that it is true.

MOMENT OF REFLECTION

What truth about God have you learned through experience? How does that truth influence your thoughts and behaviors?

December 5

Seizing Opportunities

As we have opportunity, let us do good to all people, especially to those who belong to the family of believers.

GALATIANS 6:10

I recently had what I'd like to call my very own Good Samaritan opportunity. As I sat in my living room, which faces onto the street, I noticed one of my neighbors packing up his truck. I didn't give it much thought, as there were a lot of garage sales at that time of the year and I assumed he was going to drop off the things somewhere. However, the next day, as I was talking to this man's wife, Nicole, she broke down and revealed that her husband had left her and their two children for another woman.

At that moment, as I stood in my driveway and watched my neighbor weep, I had a choice to make. Would I simply hug her, tell her I was sorry, and pray for her? Or would I choose to get involved in her pain? In all honesty, the former would have been simpler, but I chose to get involved and invited Nicole and her kids to my home for dinner.

During the next few weeks, we spent a lot of time talking and crying. I was able to shine the light of Christ in the midst of very dark circumstances, and what could have been simply another statistic turned into a great testimony. Over time a platform was built upon which I could proclaim the gospel to her. If I had tried to do this without the corresponding good works, I do not think she would have listened. I am thrilled to say that in time Nicole became a follower of Christ. She and her children are now firmly planted in a local church and are building their lives on the foundation of God's Word. Such is the transforming power of the gospel.

MOMENT OF REFLECTION

As you work to make a difference in the world,
do you know someone who could use some encouragement?
How would you go about showing that person the love of God?

December 6

Don't Forget to Remember

Be careful that you do not forget the LORD, who brought you out of Egypt, out of the land of slavery.

DEUTERONOMY 6:12

Have you ever forgotten anything? It seems like the older I get, the more often I forget things unless I intentionally choose to remember them. From birthdays, to meetings, to dinners, I have to write things down or input them into my calendar so I remember my appointments.

As Christians, it is so important that we actively choose to remember the promises of God in his Word or we will forget them.

When we *remember* what God has said, then we have courage to step out and act in faith. When we *forget* what God has said, then we tend to react to our circumstances in fear. Faith activates us; fear cripples and immobilizes us. Each day we must not forget to remember to walk in faith not fear, belief not defeat.

Today I want to remind you to never forget to remember that greater is he that is in you than he that is in the world. God gives us beauty for ashes; God will never leave you nor forsake you; and nothing can separate you from the love of God in Christ Jesus.

Why? Because you have been created for good works in Christ

Jesus; because you can be still and know he is God; because his grace is sufficient for you and his mercies are new every morning. He who promised is faithful, and there are no expiration dates on God's promises.

MOMENT OF REFLECTION

You were born for this day.
Don't forget to remember that
God is on your side!

December 7

Staying Battle Ready

For our struggle is not against flesh and blood, but against the rulers, against the authorities, against the powers of this dark world and against the spiritual forces of evil in the heavenly realms.

EPHESIANS 6:12

I was recently experiencing a bit of sleeplessness on yet another flight across the Atlantic Ocean. So I began to flip through the movie channels and was instantly drawn to a very moving scene in what looked to be a powerful movie about World War II. In this particular scene, an entire battalion was retreating, under siege from the opposing army.

These men strategically set up another camp, hidden from the enemy, and took the needed time to regroup and recuperate. After a few days, the commander began to rally the troops to reenter the fight. He delivered a very passionate and motivating speech, but no one moved. This scene seemed to last forever as all the soldiers (save two) sat in awkward silence, refusing to engage in another battle. They had lost their will to fight.

As a group, these troops wanted to stay in this defensive posture until the war was over. Their courage and vision had vanished, and they no longer wanted to risk their lives. Even when they received orders from the commanding headquarters to resume their battle positions, they refused. Some of the army's best men were in this unit, but they had exchanged a mind-set of attack and advance for one of survival and retreat. The commander had big plans for these capable men, but finally, he had to face the fact that these soldiers were now defeated. He said that the men were now peripheral to the mission and no longer central. The result was devastating.

When I saw this, I thought to myself, "Has the church come to this? Have we retreated from the world and simply set up a defense fortress while we await the rapture?"

We must ensure that we remain actively engaged in the spiritual battle to which we have been enlisted.

MOMENT OF REFLECTION

Do you consider your faith
something worth fighting for?
Why or why not?

December 8

Mrs. Jones Is Back

Do not withhold good from those to whom it is due, when it is in your power to act.

PROVERBS 3:27

"Excuse me, are you Christine Caryofyllis?" I was sitting in the hair salon and was very surprised to hear my maiden name. When I spun around in my chair, I was delighted to see Mrs. Jones, one of my teachers from high school! She sat down in the empty chair next to me, and we immediately began sharing what had been happening in our lives over the last quarter century.

It was just as easy to talk to her that day as it was when I was a student, and I was very glad to have the opportunity to express to her my appreciation for all she had done for me during those years at school.

She had been an excellent teacher, full of life and joy; I cannot remember her ever being in a bad mood. She truly believed in all us girls, and she always was available to listen, encourage, and go out of her way to assist us. I have to admit that I cannot remember anything she taught me in class, but what she taught me about attitude and consideration for other people was invaluable.

Mrs. Jones wasn't a famous evangelist. She was simply a woman determined to impact lives with the love of God. Just think of the impact we could have if every single Christian was determined to allow the example of our lives to do more "witnessing" than our mouths.

MOMENT OF REFLECTION

Twenty-five years from now, what do you think people will say about the impact you had on their lives? How will you make a difference?

December 9

Reason for the Season

For to us a child is born, to us a son is given, and the government will be on his shoulders. And he will be called Wonderful Counselor, Mighty God, Everlasting Father, Prince of Peace.

ISAIAH 9:6

Watching Sophia's school Christmas production, I was reminded of the power of a simple and passionate faith in Jesus.

I found myself captivated by the children in the production. Hundreds of beautiful faces were full of genuine joy, peace, and love. I decided, then and there, that I was not going to lose the joy of the "reason for the season" in the midst of the craziness that comes in the pre-Christmas lead-up.

When the kids sang "Happy Birthday, Jesus" and "Christmas Isn't Christmas," I shed a tear as I frantically snapped photos along with all the other proud parents. I wondered, "Is it really any more complex than their simple and true love?"

I think not.

Over the next few weeks, remember:

- Pause often.
- Breathe regularly.

- Exercise when you can.
- Rest as much as you can.
- Sing tons of Christmas carols.
- Eat loads of food.
- Laugh a lot.
- Don't spend more than you can afford.
- Give people the gift of TIME.
- Let people have the parking spot at the mall.
- Let the other shopper take the last toy.
- Offer that special friend or relative another chocolate.
- Send a kind note to someone.
- Help someone else.
- Look up and smile often.

Remember, Jesus is the reason for this season.

MOMENT OF REFLECTION

Have you found yourself getting so caught up in the stress of all that has to be done by Christmas that you have forgotten to remember the Christ of Christmas?

December 10

Wake Up!

"Wake up, sleeper, rise from the dead, and Christ will shine on you." Be very careful, then, how you live—not as unwise but as wise, making the most of every opportunity, because the days are evil.

EPHESIANS 5:14–16

Yes, great suffering is to be found in every part of the world. But we don't have to leave our own country, state, or neighborhood to find people who are facing oppression in many different forms. They are all around us—people trapped by fear, stuck in horrible places, stripped of identity and belonging, disconnected, disenfranchised.

We all know single moms and single dads who are trying to make a family on their own—playing roles of nurturer, provider, disciplinarian, taxi driver, home manager, play-buddy, and spiritual leader

—until they are exhausted, worked to death in spirit, used up and emotionally wrung out. Many people are alone, having everything they need to live except companionship—isolated, tormented, restless, anxious, hopeless, fearful. Others wonder how they are going to pay their mortgage or put their kids through school. They wonder if anyone cares if they live or die. Runaway kids are looking for love and a next meal and a safe place to sleep, ever afraid and ever in pain, hopeless. Addicts held hostage by a drug or a bottle, in a humiliating search for the means to get those things, experience emptiness and shame between fixes, subject to horrible twists and turns in body and mind inflicted by their drugs.

I had been asleep. Now God had awakened me so that I could rise ready to do what he was calling me to do. When we are asleep, injustice and pain can run rampant across the earth, but we may not even see or know of the nightmare someone else is living. Once we've been awakened, we can see the evil and respond. We are up, alert, ready to take the first or next step, ready to make a difference.

Of course, I can't do everything, but I can do the part God has assigned to me. That's all he asks of us—to be willing to do our part.

MOMENT OF REFLECTION

What is God speaking to your heart right now?
How will you respond?

December 11

Rising Ready

Be devoted to one another in love. Honor one another above yourselves. Never be lacking in zeal, but keep your spiritual fervor, serving the Lord. Be joyful in hope, patient in affliction, faithful in prayer.

ROMANS 12:10–12

Every day, situations in our normal routines require us to be the light of Christ in darkness. Waking up spiritually is not just about participating in life-changing efforts of worldwide importance, such as stopping genocide. It is walking through our lives wide awake, rising ready right where we are, with what we have. It is seeing people where they are and meeting their needs, being the hands and feet of Jesus to them.

It means seeing others instead of always looking out for ourselves. For some of us, that means being a better spouse and parent, a kinder neighbor, a more engaged church member.

It may mean offering grace to the server at the restaurant who forgets to turn in our order, causing us to wait an extra fifteen minutes to get our food. It may mean forgoing our two-lattes-a-week routine in order to sponsor a child through our church's missions program.

Rising ready may mean giving a friend who just lost a job a Starbucks card or buying her lunch, offering to do some shopping for a neighbor trapped at home with a screaming newborn, taking the time to listen to a heartbroken friend whose husband was just diagnosed with cancer. It may mean going through your closet and giving clothes to the local women's shelter.

When you're fully awakened, when you're rising ready, you will find that you've been missing out on seeing some great wonders.

MOMENT OF REFLECTION

Are you fully awakened to the needs of others?
What are the top three needs you see right now?

December 12

Lighting the Dark Places

See, darkness covers the earth and thick darkness is over the peoples, but the LORD rises upon you and his glory appears over you.

ISAIAH 60:2

God's glory is upon us. It can break through the darkest night. It is in us ready to burst out and overwhelm the darkness. That is what light does; it makes the darkness disappear. That is why God brings us each new morning. But although the light and the power are God's, he wants us to partner with him in bringing light into the dark places where oppressors try their best to shut people away.

We can get worn down and wearied by the needs of this world. We need sleep, rest, restoration, recuperation. That's why God gives us the end of a day; he doesn't begrudge us our rest. He doesn't want us to come to the end of ourselves and be defeated and enslaved in a spiritual Auschwitz, tormented, thinking it is *the work we do* that sets us free. No, he doesn't want us to burn the candle at both ends so that we end up lethargic, fatigued, burned up, and burned out. To do that is to walk into the lie that was wrought in iron over the arched entrance of Auschwitz—to be held captive by the idea that work sets us free. Working ourselves into a frenzy is not freedom. It is enslavement.

But we are not slaves; we are free. And we have been freed for a purpose: to share what we've been given, partnering with God to fulfill his purposes on the earth. Some days, that may mean nothing more than doing a dozen little things throughout our waking hours: providing a listening ear, a casserole, and a shoulder to cry on to the neighbor whose husband has just walked out on her; acknowledging the pain in the eyes of the girl at the checkout register; or opening our home to a family who has just lost theirs until they can get back on their feet.

Let's not miss any opportunity to do good ... because a small thing for you and I can make a huge difference to someone else. Little things have always made a big difference.

MOMENT OF REFLECTION

What do you think is the difference between working for God and working with God?

December 13

Crossing the Street

Let us not love with words or speech but with actions and in truth.

1 JOHN 3:18

In the dark hours of the morning, I came awake suddenly, shaken. It took me a minute to think where I was—the hotel room. Yes.

Thessaloniki. My own tossing about had roused me. I fluffed my pillow and turned over to try once again to fall asleep. But there would be no more sleep tonight. I sat up and threw back the covers.

Jesus' story of the Good Samaritan was on my mind, because I was going to preach on it in a few hours. I knew the passage by heart. A Jewish man was traveling from Jerusalem to Jericho when he was beaten and robbed by thieves. A priest and then a Levite passed by as he lay wounded along the side of the road. Then a Samaritan man came along. Though the Jews and the Samaritans were not friendly, he helped the man, bandaged his wounds, and carried him on a donkey to an inn where he could rest and heal. He paid for the man's care and then promised to return to check on him.

I thought of the many people like this man. Hurt and wounded in different ways, lying on the side of so many different roads—left behind by abuse, addictions, imprisonment, loss, famine, disease, violence, tyranny, and oppression. People broken by injustice and stripped of their belongings, dignity, identity, and self-worth.

Before, I had always thought of myself as the Good Samaritan. After all, I was an itinerant evangelist who spent most of the year on the road, literally making it my business to go to *them*—the broken and those dying in ditches—perhaps in ditches of their own making, perhaps thrown there by the cruelty of others. Now I was reading between the lines of Jesus' story.

Nowhere does it say that the priest or the Levite were bad people. But they were so consumed with keeping their schedules that they ended up walking past someone they should have helped. Then the Lord said to me, "Christine, the only difference between the Samaritan and the religious people was that the Samaritan actually crossed the street. Compassion is only emotion—until you cross the street. Compassion means action."

MOMENT OF REFLECTION

How would you define the word "compassion"?

December 14

Sowing and Reaping

Whoever sows sparingly will also reap sparingly, and whoever sows generously will also reap generously.

2 CORINTHIANS 9:6

If our world is only about "me" and "my needs," we are building a very small world for ourselves. Worse still, we won't be sustained and refreshed by God in the same way that we would if we lived beyond ourselves and learned to "water" the lives of others. If ever I find that I'm a bit frustrated because I'm believing God for something that hasn't happened yet, I find the best thing I can do is seek to meet someone else's need. Whenever I do, the results are amazing! As I take my eyes off myself and my needs and begin helping others, I see God taking care of me, and often those deep desires of my heart quickly come to pass.

Even when I was working through the emotional issues of my past and dealing with rejection, unforgiveness, abuse, and pain, I found that if I extended my hand to help someone else, my own healing process was accelerated and became much more bearable.

In our ministry, whenever Nick and I have a need, we begin to sow into someone else's need and invariably find that God meets ours. We were recently able to buy some new office premises that we needed because our team had expanded. I believe God blessed us with the funds to do that because we have sought to sow into the needs of others. Whenever we visited other churches around the world, we would always sow something into their building fund.

It is a spiritual principle that when we live a generous life, we're going to be watered by God. As we continue to live generously, our lives, impact, and influence will continue to expand. It is our giving that opens doors, not our receiving. Jesus did say that it was better to give than to receive, so let's not miss any opportunity to sow seed and to be generous.

MOMENT OF REFLECTION

Can you think of someone whose need you might be able to meet? What can you do to help?

December 15

Open to Interpretation

The LORD is righteous in all His ways, gracious in all His works. The LORD is near to all who call upon Him, to all who call upon Him in truth. He will fulfill the desire of those who fear Him; He also will hear their cry and save them.

PSALM 145:17–19 NKJV

As we reach out to people in our communities and strive to touch others with the message of Christ's love for them, we must remind ourselves of the mind-set prevalent in today's society. We aren't dealing with the same world we once knew. In earlier times, religion and the church were the backbone of society, providing a blueprint for our moral and spiritual lives.

Today, "God" is open to interpretation and beliefs about him are negotiable and relative to the individual. That is, "What is true for you may not be true for me." Many people do believe in a higher power but struggle to decide which one! Our young people no longer want to accept someone else's faith; they want to understand for themselves what they believe and why.

Browsing popular media, it is clear that interest in spirituality as opposed to religion is increasing. Marketing companies are catering to our culture's interest in the mystical and unexplainable through a diet of television programs and literature about witches, wizards, astrology, and the supernatural. This makes people vulnerable to deception, but it also makes them open to a genuine encounter with God.

We as Christians must lead those who do not yet know God to a genuine experience of and connection with him. When people encounter God as opposed to just hearing about him, they cannot help but believe he is real and worth investigating. We must ensure that our homes and churches are places where people meet with a supernatural God who saves, heals, delivers, and restores lives. If Jesus is real in us, he will become real to others.

MOMENT OF REFLECTION

As you aim to make a difference, how will you communicate God's truth in a relativistic world?

December 16

Servanthood

There are different kinds of service, but the same Lord.

1 CORINTHIANS 12:5

It would be a mistake to think that what God has called us to do will always be glamorous and fun. I can tell you, that's just not the case. Back when I was involved in youth work, I spent every Friday night volunteering at my local youth center. On one particular night, I was standing outside with some other members of the team when a young man came stumbling toward us. Clearly, he was very drunk and about to be sick. Right there in front of us, the young man vomited and then fell face first into it.

I was feeling pretty faint myself at that point, but I motioned for one of the girls to go get something to clean up the mess. She brought me two rolls of toilet paper, and I went to work. As I did so, I sensed the Lord say: "Christine, this is what you are going to spend your life doing—wiping up the vomit off a lost and broken generation." It was while wiping up the vomit, that I made a conscious decision to spend my life helping others find answers in Christ.

I was reminded of this incident eight years later when I was approached by the Australian *Rolling Stone* magazine wanting to feature one of our Youth Alive rallies in their next edition.

When the magazine featuring the article came out, I could not believe my eyes. It was a centerfold, four-page, color spread, featuring thousands of young people praising and worshiping God. I was overwhelmed as I read the comments: "Caine comes across as that young, groovy teacher at school who you had a bit of a crush on. She's savvy to what you got up to on the weekend. When you passed out drunk at a school dance she woke you up and *wiped up the vomit.*"

I gasped as I read that line. I believe that as sure as the Holy Spirit penned the Bible through the hands of human writers, he took the hand of the magazine writer that day, and especially had that line included to remind me of my mandate.

Serving the purposes of God in our generation is why we are here.

MOMENT OF REFLECTION

Do you live your life as a servant of Jesus Christ?

December 17

Combating Evil

For if you remain silent at this time, relief and deliverance for the Jews will arise from another place, but you and your father's family will perish. And who knows but that you have come to your royal position for such a time as this?

ESTHER 4:14

Some days we partner with God in many small ways—a kindness here, an encouraging word there, a caring gesture for someone else. And some days, it means bigger, more dangerous tasks.

In the book of Esther, King Xerxes is persuaded by an adviser to issue an edict condemning all the nation's Jews to death. Esther, a Jew, but chosen by King Xerxes as his queen, seems uniquely positioned to persuade the king to withdraw the edict—and, in fact, is urged to do so by her uncle Mordecai, who says that God has placed her in her royal position just for this purpose. Her decision to obey Mordecai could have cost her life; saying yes was literally a matter of life and death for Esther.

Even though you and I may not be in a human king's palace, we are serving a King and living in his kingdom. The lives of those on planet Earth in our generation are at stake, and every single day our decision to obey or ignore God can be the difference between life and death for those on the other side of our obedience.

If we approach Bible stories as though they are fairy tales, then we can easily disconnect ourselves from the people in the Bible as if they are somehow other than us. But if we believe that the Bible is true and its characters are people just like you and me, then we approach it very differently.

We realize that the same issues are at stake—that we need to overcome the same fears, doubts, and challenges that they did. And in the same way that we celebrate Esther for her obedience, others will celebrate our obedience because they had an opportunity to be introduced to Jesus and rescued from death.

Don't ever underestimate what your obedience can accomplish, what is at stake for people. Eternity. The fact that you and I are alive in this moment means that this is our "time such as this." There is no point waiting until we are dead to do what God has called us to do; it will be too late then. Now is the only moment we have. Here is the only place that we have.

MOMENT OF REFLECTION

How are you using your light to combat the darkness in your world?

December 18

The Gospel

I am the way and the truth and the life. No one comes to the Father except through me.

JOHN 14:6

The essence of the gospel message is totally opposite to today's thinking; it is based on *absolute truth*. Jesus said that *he* is the way, the truth, and the life. He did not give a range of options for getting to God but presented himself as the only means of salvation. So many believe that there are many ways to God, but I am glad that Jesus made it simple for everyone to understand: there is only one way, and that is through him.

The challenge for us as Christians is to present this absolute truth to those who are raised in a pluralistic secular society that espouses tolerance and relativism. In fact, our culture confuses tolerance with endorsement and considers it a negative thing to stand for something absolutely. The only thing we want to say absolutely is that there are no absolutes. Yet, I have discovered that if we don't stand for something, then we will fall for anything; and that is evident in our world today.

Proclaiming an absolute message in a relative world can be both a challenge and an opportunity. Contrary to popular opinion, people across the globe are searching for truth, meaning, significance, security, and unconditional love. As Christians, we know the source of all truth and love, and can offer seekers a life of eternal significance through Jesus Christ. If people can see that what we proclaim is really working in our lives, then they are very open to hearing about the One who makes it possible. *If we live what we believe, then others will believe what we live.*

We have been called to reach the world with the gospel of Jesus Christ. To do that, we must be certain of what we believe and ready to present the unvarnished truth to those we touch each day.

MOMENT OF REFLECTION

How are you able to present absolute truth in a relative world in a way that is filled with love and compassion?

December 19

Working Together

Just as a body, though one, has many parts, but all its many parts form one body, so it is with Christ. For we were all baptized by one Spirit so as to form one body—whether Jews or Gentiles, slave or free—and we were all given the one Spirit to drink.

1 CORINTHIANS 12:12–13

The body of Christ on earth today is the visible representation of an invisible God. The God that people see, feel, touch, and hear is the one his church depicts. God wants to be made big in the world through his church.

When the church is unified, functioning together like a healthy body, then we will depict a big God who is able to do big things on the earth. We will work together without comparison or competition, complementing and assisting one another. Conversely, if the church is a disjointed, divided body, then we will depict a small God to our world.

A healthy, dynamic, vibrant church can be a huge force of good, shining a bright light in the midst of darkness and adding much flavor to what is otherwise bland and tasteless. No other organization on earth is like it. As we continue to tear down walls and build bridges between denominations and different sectors of the church, we will even more readily show the height, breadth, width, and depth of God's magnificent love.

Let's keep loving the church of Jesus Christ by working together for his sake. She is glorious and rapidly growing over all the earth.

MOMENT OF REFLECTION

Do you see the potential impact of a unified church more now than at the start of the year?

December 20

No Consequences

All your words are true; all your righteous laws are eternal.

PSALM 119:160

In our society, the distinction between right and wrong has been grossly diluted. Celebrities have replaced God as a moral compass. Television, the big screen, and radio deliver the "sermons" that frame our worldview. Social, political, and educational policies have bowed to political correctness, encouraging us not only to accept ungodly practices but at times to celebrate them. As a result, our society lacks a true source of strength with which to live, goodness by which to live, and freedom in which to live.

I was powerfully reminded of this reality after speaking at a conference in Victoria, Australia. I had just finished when I turned to see a very nervous young woman standing behind me. My heart melted as I saw the deep pain in her eyes. We started to talk about life.

I quickly established that Rachel was not a Christian and that her mother forced her to come to the conference. She had lived a wild life for someone so young, and the scars of rejection, bitterness, hurt, and loneliness were already evident.

After about an hour, Rachel stated, "I had an abortion two weeks ago, and my boyfriend has left me." As we talked for a while longer, I realized her main concern was not the fact she had aborted a child, but rather, that she no longer had a boyfriend. I asked her, "Rachel, do you think you did anything wrong when you had the abortion?" She looked at me like I was crazy. "Of course not! What else could I have done? After all, I really want to travel."

I am not suggesting that all young people hold Rachel's view about abortion. Her story does, however, provide us with insight. Many in our society have little or no point of reference for distinguishing between right and wrong.

Some of you may be thinking, "Can we really make a difference?" I believe the answer is yes, but that difference will never be made by judging others or condemning a broken world; it will be made by loving the lost and living out God's truth in our own lives.

Let's ensure people can see the difference Jesus makes in our lives.

MOMENT OF REFLECTION

To make a difference in the world,
how will you communicate
God's ideas of right and wrong?

December 21

Joy to the World

But the angel said to them, "Do not be afraid. I bring you good news that will cause great joy for all the people."

LUKE 2:10

I love Christmas. I love the anticipation on my girls' faces and in their hearts. I love the mess (did I say that?), the extended family time, and the planning that goes into gift giving (my primary love language). I love the food (of course). I love all my crazy, affectionate family getting together. I love that there is no scheduled time, except girls rising at 4:00 a.m. to unwrap presents. I love looking at all the lights and displays.

And I *love* that for a period of time, in the midst of hyper-consumerism and secularism—when a man in a red suit is being transported by reindeer through a world full of pain, heartache, challenge, and adversity—that we get to exalt the name of JESUS.

One of my favorite Scriptures in the entire Bible is Luke 2:10, where the angel of the Lord declares Jesus' birth to the shepherds.

From that, we know our message is GOOD NEWS.

Our message brings GREAT JOY.

Our message is for ALL PEOPLE.

Let's determine to keep a great spirit at Christmas. Let's make sure that we don't get cynical or judgmental, but that we actually look like people with good news to tell. We want to spread that news with great joy and not exclude anyone from hearing it.

Let's ensure that our hearts and homes are full of love, joy, peace, kindness, generosity, laughter, warmth, and celebration at this time. Perhaps you have family members or friends who need to be forgiven, embraced, included, and loved ... why not determine to make this the year *you* cross that threshold and make a move toward forgiveness and reconciliation?

MOMENT OF REFLECTION

Who in your circle of family and friends needs to hear the good news of great joy? How will you bring them this message?

December 22

Favor Is for Purpose

But the angel said to her, "Do not be afraid, Mary; you have found favor with God. You will conceive and give birth to a son, and you are to call him Jesus."

LUKE 1:30–31

Can you even imagine what it would be like to have an angel drop by while you are putting on your mascara and declare that you have found favor with God? I would probably pass out if I had this kind of unexpected visitation, but apparently Mary did not flinch at the sight of Gabriel. This makes me wonder whether she was accustomed to angelic visitations. Had they met before? I'm not sure, but I do know this: it was a different greeting than anything she had heard before, especially when he went on to tell her that she—an unwed, betrothed, ordinary teenage girl—was the woman chosen to give birth to the long anticipated Son of God.

Mary's divine assignment was given in obscurity and privacy. There was no celebration or huge public announcement. There were no witnesses, TV interruptions, or social media messages. Mary had simply been chosen for a purpose and God had promised that he would be with her so that she could fulfill it.

I wonder if she knew what was coming and that is why she was troubled.

This young woman was chosen to carry, birth, and raise Jesus Christ, the Son of God. I'm sure that this divine interruption was not on Mary's "to do" list that morning. I would also guess that she had not asked to be the mother of God during her prayer time that day. Perhaps all she had asked was that God would use her and God decided that he would turn her world upside down by answering her prayer.

The truth is that although this was the greatest honor for any woman in history, it was not an easy assignment. We all want to walk in the favor of God, but do we really want the responsibility, cost, and commitment that divine favor brings? Mary would have to tell her fiancé, family, and friends about her conversation with Gabriel, and she, unlike us, did not know how the details of the story would turn out. I'm sure when the angel left, Mary anxiously wondered whether Joseph would leave her, her family would ostracize her, or her friends ridicule her. How could anyone believe what had just happened? In fact, if she had not seen it with her own eyes and heard it with her own ears, she would struggle to believe it herself.

The decision to accept her divine assignment could have potentially cost her everything and everyone that she dearly loved. Yet, she still said yes to the will and purpose of God. She did not understand how it could happen, but she said yes.

If we want the favor of God, then we must be willing to accept the divine assignment that comes with it. Favor is for purpose, not for status.

MOMENT OF REFLECTION

Are you willing to pay the price to do the will of God no matter what it costs?

December 23

Choose Your Friends Wisely

At that time Mary got ready and hurried to a town in the hill country of Judea.

LUKE 1:39

As soon as Mary had accepted her divine assignment, she purposefully got ready and hurried to her friend and cousin Elizabeth's house. She did not procrastinate or take any detours, but went directly to someone who would confirm and affirm that she was carrying the Son of God. As soon as Elizabeth heard Mary's greeting, the baby in her own womb leaped and she announced that Mary's baby was blessed. Mary had not even told Elizabeth the news, but the Holy Spirit himself already confirmed it.

The wisest thing that Mary did once she had received God's promise was to go to a friend who would speak life, hope, faith, and blessing over the dream she was carrying. She placed herself in an entirely life-giving environment where there was no possibility of being exposed to negativity, doubt, unbelief, or naysayers. For three months Mary was cocooned in this environment that helped nurture the Promise that she carried.

When God gives us a promise, it normally comes to us in seed form, and what we do with that seed is crucial. It needs to be planted in nutritious soil and daily watered with faith. The people with whom we share our dreams are crucial to their birth. We must place ourselves in an environment that is full of faith, hope, and life, and separate ourselves from people who are full of negativity and unbelief so that the promise does not die.

Who we surround ourselves with in life is absolutely crucial. We need people who believe in us, will encourage us, and are committed to helping us run our race and finish our course. It is not easy to let go of people who do not want to come with us on the journey, but in order to fulfill our purpose, we must be more loyal to God and our destiny than we are to other people.

MOMENT OF REFLECTION

Are the people in your life committed to seeing you fulfill your purpose, or are they hindering you from walking out your destiny?

December 24

Your Song

And Mary said: "My soul glorifies the Lord and my spirit rejoices in God my Savior, for he has been mindful of the humble state of his servant. From now on all generations will call me blessed, for the Mighty One has done great things for me—holy is his name."

LUKE 1:46–49

I've always been deeply moved by Mary's faith. Not only did she accept her divine assignment, she did it willingly with thanksgiving and praise. After Elizabeth blessed her, Mary began to declare the goodness and faithfulness of God. She did not accept her purpose begrudgingly but with passion and humility. She considered that to obey the call of God was an honor and not a burden.

She gave all the glory to God, proclaimed his goodness and faithfulness, and even declared, "From now on all generations will call me blessed." It required great faith to make that statement in her condition. Remember, she was an unwed teenage girl and her reputation was at stake, but she chose to believe God despite the circumstances. She knew that he was worthy of her trust and so she entrusted her future to him.

Once Mary had decided to pay the price to fulfill her calling, she was all in. She wholeheartedly trusted that God was who he said he was and that he would do all he had said he would do. Instead of waiting for a physical sign that she was pregnant, Mary prophesied her future when the promise was still in seed form inside her womb. And guess what? On this Christmas Eve you and I are indeed calling Mary, the mother of Jesus, blessed.

There are so many lessons that we can learn from this amazing woman of God on this day before Christmas. She was relentlessly steadfast and kept her eyes unflinchingly fixed on the author of the Promise that she carried. She committed to enjoy and celebrate the journey and not merely endure this calling as a burdensome obligation. She surrounded herself with great faith-filled people and reminded herself of all the amazing things God had done for her people thus far. She knew that the same God who had been faithful to them would also be faithful to his Promise in her.

Let's determine to be people of faith who expect to hear from God through his Word, who will not hesitate to say yes to our divine assignments when he gives them to us, and who will surround ourselves with people who inspire us to see the dream come to pass. As we go forward, let's never forget to give him all the praise and honor that he is due and continually speak words of life that affirm the dream and the promise that we carry. Each word we speak either waters the seed or destroys it, so let's speak life.

MOMENT OF REFLECTION

Do the words that come out of your mouth bring life or death?

December 25

A Christmas Rescue

Before they call I will answer; while they are still speaking I will hear.

ISAIAH 65:24

With each step we took to form The A21 Campaign, our ministry to the victims of human trafficking, God was there to meet us. We prayed our way forward—for divine alignments, for favor, for resources, and for open doors—and God moved hearts and paperwork and houses, and delivered not only what was needed, but more.

When the Greek authorities who investigated human trafficking were hampered by cuts in the funding for their search-and-rescue missions, we prayed for them too.

"We have a safe house," we prayed, "so please, God, bring us the girls who need help."

"That's ridiculous," some people said. "The missing and lost don't come to you—you have to go find them—that's why we call it *rescue.*"

We prayed, in shifts, around the clock. "God, if you want us to rescue these girls, you'll have to make a way. If the police can't fund investigations, you'll have to convict the clients to help us. Work on their hearts."

One day a man walked into the police station with a girl who spoke only broken Greek. It turned out she had been a sex slave, and the man with her was a client. Except that after he'd gone to a brothel, paid for her services, and taken her to a designated room, he couldn't go through with what he had intended.

"Why?" he wondered. He had, after all, gone there for that purpose and paid for it.

"Why?" the girl wondered, confused but relieved.

He couldn't explain. Instead, he asked the girl if she had registration papers, the legal requirement for all registered sex workers. Breaking into tears, she told him her story in broken Greek. She had been trapped. She wasn't registered. She was a sex slave. The truth broke his heart. He snuck the girl out of the brothel and took her to the police, who brought her to our safe house.

The officer helping with the transition said that, in twenty years of police work, he had never seen such a thing. It was Christmastime—and we had our first client, the first woman rescued from trafficking through the ministry of A21.

I love the idea that on the day we remember that God sent his Son to earth so that he might rescue us, we had the opportunity to see someone rescued.

Because he came, we must go.

Because he rescued, we must rescue.

Because he loved, we must love.

MOMENT OF REFLECTION

Do you think God cared about the man in this story? Why or why not?

December 26

Sharing God's Love

Freely you have received; freely give.

MATTHEW 10:8

Whatever we receive from God is what he asks that we give to someone else. I saw the power of this the time my daughter Sophia and I were walking down a crowded street. I had a full day, but had promised to let her accompany me on it—a special treat for both of us. We'd been running hard and fast all that day to keep appointments and get things done.

Sophia, of course, would have been happy just to walk along and look at everything: the shop-window displays, the flowerpots and trees outside the buildings, the cars parked alongside the curb. But I was on a mission.

Suddenly I realized that Sophia's hand was no longer in mine. I grabbed at the air, reaching for her, but touched nothing. I whirled around to find her. Just steps behind, she had stopped to kneel at the curb next to a man who appeared to be homeless. She held out to him the dollar I'd given her that morning to buy a treat for herself. She had been holding tight to that dollar the entire day. It was a treasure, a rare gift for a special day with Mummy, and she'd been trying to decide exactly how to spend it on our day downtown. Now, without hesitation, she was handing it to a stranger.

"Jesus gave me this dollar to give to you," she said.

How easily she had handed over what was so precious to her. How powerful that mere dollar became.

The man she handed it to handed it back, tears streaming down his face. "Honey," he said, "you spend that on some candy for yourself."

He had been given something much more precious than her dollar. Sophia had given her heart—and so much more. She gave him hope. She reminded him that there was goodness in this world, and grace—even from a child. She had reminded him that God would provide—even from the least and most unlikely sources. God used her open hand to open a stranger's heart. And he used her willing spirit to show me that when we give what we have, the God of hope delivers all the rest.

Let's be people who not only freely give on Christmas day but every day.

MOMENT OF REFLECTION

What has God given to you?
How will you share his gift with others?

December 27

Small Things Make a Big Difference

A little yeast works through the whole batch of dough.

GALATIANS 5:9

Have you ever seen a big ship leave the dock as it prepares to sail the open seas? I recently watched a huge ship pulled out, turned around, and pushed out by a tiny tugboat as it left Sydney harbor for Tahiti. I was totally mesmerized by the power of a small tugboat; I could not believe such a small thing could literally turn around an entire ship.

I realized yet again that little things have great power. Small things in the hands of a big God can make a big difference.

We so often devalue things because they seem so small or insignificant, but never forget:

- A small attitude adjustment can make a big difference in a relationship.
- A small change in spending habits can make a big difference to your bottom line.

- A small shift in your thinking can make a big difference in your attitude.
- A small investment can yield a great return.
- A small change in diet can make a big difference in your health.
- A small change in your exercise routine can result in big fitness leaps.

We rarely move big distances in one jump. We normally make small, incremental changes that over the course of time make a big difference!

As we come to the close of another year and prepare to make some resolutions for the new year, why don't you consider identifying a number of small things that you are willing to work on instead of trying to tackle one big thing? One small course correction at this time of the year can set you up to soar as you start the new year.

MOMENT OF REFLECTION

List the little changes that you are going to make that will eventually make a big difference in your life.

December 28

Don't Go Down

So I sent messengers to them with this reply: "I am carrying on a great project and cannot go down. Why should the work stop while I leave it and go down to you?"

NEHEMIAH 6:3

Nehemiah and his men had begun the formidable task of rebuilding the walls of Jerusalem that had been destroyed by the Babylonians. He faced great opposition and ridicule but was determined to finish the assignment that God had given him. When the walls were almost completed, his enemies schemed to harm him, doing all that they could to make him stop his work and come down from the wall to meet with them.

Nehemiah was so focused on what God had called him to do that he would not be sidetracked or tricked into coming down. "Why should the work stop while I leave it and come down to you?" he answered his scorners. Therein was his power of focus. He would not engage in petty debates or any activity that would take him away from the great task that he had undertaken. In the midst of extreme pressure and a great battle, he was still able to clear away all the clutter and focus on what mattered most.

In the same way, if we consider the work that God has given us to do—the single most important thing—then it is easier to have the courage to say no to any lesser thing. Often we are easily distracted because we have not decided to focus exclusively on the one thing that God has given us to do. When you make the main thing the main thing, then everything else fits in around that priority. When you have not made that decision, then you leave yourself open to becoming sidetracked and eventually getting off course. Before you know it, you have done many things but not the one thing that was assigned to you to complete.

Extraordinary results in the kingdom of God are rarely happenstance. They come from the daily choices we make and the actions we take. We must determine to stay singleminded and remain focused on the task. There are so many semi-completed projects in the kingdom of God—great works unfinished because people came down from their wall to lesser things.

As we near the end of another year, decide to look at every area of your life and determine whether you are "still on the wall." If not, then perhaps it is time to let go of the lesser thing and get back on your wall to complete the most important thing. It is never too late to go back and finish what God has asked you to do.

MOMENT OF REFLECTION

Do you consider the work that you are doing for the Lord
a greater work than anything else you could be doing?
Have you left the wall for any reason?

December 29

Back on Course

But Jonah ran away from the LORD and headed for Tarshish. He went down to Joppa, where he found a ship bound for that port. After paying the fare, he went aboard and sailed for Tarshish to flee from the LORD.

JONAH 1:3

How many times has God spoken to us through his Word and asked us to do something that we did not want to do? Perhaps he asked us to be the first one to apologize to our spouse even when the argument was not our fault, or to take a meal to a sick neighbor when we already had made other plans, or perhaps even to give away a pair of brand-new shoes before we had worn them once?

We seem to be able to readily obey God when it is convenient, or when we like the task or the person that God has asked us to help. But our human nature resists wanting to obey the Lord when we simply do not like the thing he has asked us to do or the people to whom he has sent us.

Meet Jonah.

God had sent him to Nineveh, but Jonah so disliked the people of that city that he literally went and paid the fare to sail on a ship going in the opposite direction. It's easy to judge Jonah for such blatant rebellion, but the truth is we often do exactly the same thing. God tells us to go one way and we choose another. God asks us to do one thing and we do the opposite. God asks us to say one thing and we say another, and on it goes. Before long we are traveling in the opposite direction to where God sent us and are thus totally out of the will of God for our lives.

Jonah had to pay the fare to get on the ship because there is always a price to pay for disobedience. If you want to run from the will of God, you will always find something or someone to help you go the other way. The devil will always make sure that a "ship" will be in port to take you as far away from the will of God as possible.

Never forget that the price of regret is always much higher than the price you pay to obey.

Jonah subsequently jeopardized the lives of the other sailors, because when we are doing what we should not be doing in places where we should not be our actions always impact others. Eventually Jonah found himself in the belly of a fish and it was in this place of confinement that he cried out to God. It is often in places of great frustration and containment, when we feel trapped and see no way out, that God does his greatest work in us and launches us into our purpose. He needs to bring us to a place where we finally stop running long enough to be still and to hear his voice again.

The good news is that the word of the Lord came to Jonah a second time. I love that about Jesus, that he always gives us another chance. No matter where you have been this year, you have a chance to get back on track as we start another. If you have been running away from the will of God, let this be the moment that you decide to stop running and come back to him. Today is a good day to get off the boat taking you the wrong way and get back on course with your destiny.

MOMENT OF REFLECTION

Is there any area of your life where you have been running from God?

December 30

The Harvest Is Plentiful Right Where You Are

The harvest is plentiful but the workers are few. Ask the Lord of the harvest, therefore, to send out workers into his harvest field.

MATTHEW 9:37–38

Many Christians spend too much time wondering what they have been called to do and waiting for God to drop their destiny out of the sky. While we sit around waiting for something to do, we are missing out on doing what is right before us. In today's Scripture Jesus does not lament a lack of Christians, a lack of need, a lack of projects, a lack of opportunities, a lack of commentators, or a lack of wannnabe superstars. He tells us that there is simply a lack of laborers.

The harvest is plentiful right where we are. People are waiting for us to go to them every single day, wherever "our world" is. The challenge is that most of us do not want to work. We do not want to be colaborers with God. We want to be heroes for God, celebrities for God, party coordinators for God, commentators for God, critics for God, experts for God ... but not laborers.

We can be used for God's great purpose in his harvest field today, wherever we are and in whatever season of life. To be used by God as a laborer, we need to be prepared to be anonymous. Sometimes the only thing holding us back from destiny is our need to feel important rather than actually being useful in the harvest field. Wherever there are people, there is a potential harvest. Somehow we expect destiny to feel differently than it does. We must remember our work is not about us or for us. We have the privilege every day of coworking with Christ in his harvest field. Let's determine to show up for work today.

MOMENT OF REFLECTION

Do you consider your everyday life as an opportunity to colabor with Christ?

December 31

Teach Us to Number Our Days

All the days ordained for me were written in your book.

PSALM 139:16

I am so thankful to be here today where I am: expectant, hopeful, and believing in God for the best year yet! This year is the only one of its kind, the only one just like this that we will have in all of time and eternity; therefore we must decide that we will not waste a single day. Our days are numbered; they are ordered by God; and we have a specific purpose we are called to embrace and move into.

Before we ever arrived on earth, God had a plan, a purpose and an assignment for our lives. The welfare of others is attached to our obedience and courage, for it will take all of us taking our place in the body of Christ for God's kingdom to be advanced on earth. The needs are great, but we must remember that the God we serve is *big* and that as we all take responsibility for our assignments (instead of comparing ourselves to others), then together we can fulfill his plans in the world.

The new year ahead has the potential to be the most impactful, fruitful, and best year on earth ever . . . but the choice is ours. Are we willing to trust God and step into our place in the body of Christ to take hold of all that God has created us for?

I am full of faith, hope, expectation, and anticipation. I believe that the greatest days for the church are before us and not behind us. I believe that God is for us and not against us, and that the year ahead is full of promise, purpose, and potential. Let's believe God like never before.

Remember . . . time is ticking away.

MOMENT OF REFLECTION

How are you approaching the year ahead?

99% OF HUMAN TRAFFICKING VICTIMS ARE NOT RESCUED... YET.

When confronted with the horrific statistics surrounding human trafficking, most people are quick to agree on the fact that someone should **do something.** The A21 Campaign was born when we decided to raise our hand and be the ones who would do something. The A21 Campaign was born when we decided to raise our hand and join the ranks of "someone." In 2007, with little knowledge and a lot of passion, we set out to make a difference. Today we are strategically positioned in Europe, North America, and Australia to abolish the injustice of human trafficking and rehabilitate victims.

The goal of A21 is fourfold:

1. Prevent people from being trafficked.
2. Protect those who have been trafficked, and provide support services.
3. Prosecute traffickers, and strengthen legal responses to trafficking.
4. Partner with law enforcement, service providers, and community members to provide a comprehensive front against trafficking.

BECAUSE... everyONE matters.

www.TheA21Campaign.org

Undaunted

Daring to Do What God Calls You to Do

Christine Caine

Christine Caine offers life-transforming insights about how not only to overcome the challenges, wrong turns, and often painful circumstances we all experience, but also to actually grow from those experiences and be equipped and empowered to help others. Using her own dramatic life story, Caine tells how she overcame abuse, abandonment, fears, and other challenges to go on a mission of adventure, fueled by faith and filled with love and courage. Her personal stories inspire readers to hear their name called, just as Christine heard her own — "You are beloved. You are the hope. You are chosen" — to go into a dark and troubled world, knowing each of us possess all it takes to bring hope, create change, and live completely for Christ. Part inspirational tale, part manifesto to stir readers to lives of adventure, *Undaunted* shows the way with spiritual wisdom and insight.

ALSO AVAILABLE

Undaunted Participant's Guide with DVD

This compelling five-session video-based Bible study offers life-transforming insights about how not only to overcome the challenges and often painful circumstances we all experience, but to actually grow from those experiences and be equipped and empowered to help others. So what are you waiting for? Be THE LOVE. Be THE HOPE. Be THE CHANGE that this world needs.

Available in stores and online!